APA Style®
& Citations

by Joe Giampalmi, EdD

for
dummies®
A Wiley Brand

APA Style® & Citations For Dummies®

Published by: **John Wiley & Sons, Inc.**, 111 River Street, Hoboken, NJ 07030-5774, www.wiley.com

Copyright © 2021 by John Wiley & Sons, Inc., Hoboken, New Jersey

Published simultaneously in Canada

For general information on our other products and services, please contact our Customer Care Department within the U.S. at 877-762-2974, outside the U.S. at 317-572-3993, or fax 317-572-4002. For technical support, please visit https://hub.wiley.com/community/support/dummies.

Wiley publishes in a variety of print and electronic formats and by print-on-demand. Some material included with standard print versions of this book may not be included in e-books or in print-on-demand. If this book refers to media such as a CD or DVD that is not included in the version you purchased, you may download this material at http://booksupport.wiley.com. For more information about Wiley products, visit www.wiley.com.

Library of Congress Control Number: 2021935723

ISBN: 978-1-119-71644-0

ISBN: 978-1-119-71646-4 (ebk); ISBN: 978-1-119-71645-7 (ebk)

Manufactured in the United States of America

SKY10026162_040721

Contents at a Glance

Table of Contents

Introduction

I f you're a college student reading this book, you face the stresses of papers, readings, classes, commitments, and exhaustion — in addition to tuition, student loans, and transportation. Keep remembering that your college days are the best days of your life.

Writing assignments are the stress du jour for many of you. Add APA citing and formatting and it's like starting the day with a flat tire and dead battery. Being the resourceful and intelligent person you are, you bought *APA Style & Citations For Dummies* to help yourself and your grade. Good decision.

You're holding the solution to reducing a current stress and improving your research writing and citing sources — in addition to eliminating another potential stress, inadvertent plagiarism. Sorry I can't help you with other stresses, that's other *For Dummies* books, but I can help you charge your brain with APA and college writing skills.

If you're a high school student reading this book, congratulations on the initiative and good judgment. You're taking a major step toward developing your APA style and citation skills and preparing yourself for college writing and research.

About This Book

APA Style & Citations For Dummies emerged from the need of college and high school students to interpret the APA manual. This *For Dummies* book isn't a textbook or workbook. It's a college-level (and high school) adaptation of the *Publication Manual of the American Psychological Association, Seventh Edition*. (Note the adjective "publication" in the title.) The APA publication manual is written primarily for professional scholars fulfilling requirements for advanced degrees and publishing their research in scholarly journals.

Only about 25 percent of the seventh edition offers direct guidance aligning APA with citing and referencing in traditional undergraduate research projects. This book offers 100 percent direct guidance for APA academic style writing and citing for most common undergraduate research projects.

I wrote this book based on my decades' experience teaching APA at the high school and college levels and teaching and grading thousands of research projects. This book provides you APA fundamentals for academic writing, citing, referencing, and formatting. It provides strategies for

>> Bias-free writing

>> Revising

>> Citations and references

>> Front and back required and optional sections

>> Title page and page layout elements

>> Source engagement

>> Summaries, paraphrases, and quotations

The APA manual is written in a formal and scholarly tone, appropriate for its content and professional scholars respectfully obsessed with their research. This book is written for the *For Dummies* audience, professional scholars-in-training who enjoy a road-trip more than a research project.

This book, like your laptop manual, wasn't designed to be read cover to cover. Here's a quick-start menu to help you locate topics you're looking for:

>> Plagiarism (Chapter 4)

>> Citations and references (Chapters 10–12)

>> Formatting (Chapter 14)

>> Writing style (Chapter 5)

>> Revising strategies (Chapter 8)

>> Grammar and conventions (Chapters 6 and 7)

>> APA and essays (Chapter 15)

>> APA and response papers (Chapter 15)

>> APA and reviews of literature (Chapter 16)

>> APA and reports (Chapter 17)

Note: This book focuses on explaining the *Publication Manual of the American Psychological Association, Seventh Edition* — in the *For Dummies* brand style. The *For Dummies* brand uses Chicago Manual of Style (like most book publishing does) and its own styles, so you may notice some formatting and such that doesn't look like APA. Just a heads-up that the text is consistent with the *For Dummies* brand except when it's necessary to illustrate a point, and then I make sure the text illustrates APA formatting and style.

Specifically, you'll notice formatting and style differences with these types of things:

>> End punctuation with bulleted lists

>> The use of contractions

>> Font variations

>> Book style page formatting

So basically when writing your research papers and essays, do as I say, not as *For Dummies* does.

Foolish Assumptions

I assume you share similar interests with college students I taught for decades. When I wrote this book, I made the following assumptions about you, my dear reader:

>> Your life is in your phone, which is more important to you than your keys.

>> You appreciate your parents and family for their support of your academic goals.

>> You have an active life, but next to your family, academics are your priority.

>> Your interests include music, food, friends, road trips, college activities — and some of you even listen to Frank Sinatra.

>> You prefer not to talk too much waiting for a class to begin; you'd rather text and post on social media.

In other words, you're busy, but you find a way to achieve academic excellence.

Icons Used in This Book

The APA publication manual includes the organization and searchability of a smartphone, with every topic tabbed and numbered to two decimal places. It's impressive construction. *APA Style & Citations For Dummies* — not as impressive, but half the cost — offers you four icons to help you explore points of interest:

TIP

When information needs highlighting, such as Chapter 5's "reading from the perspective of the writer," I identify it with this icon.

WARNING

Warning icons, like academic progress notices, indicate caution such as Chapter 8's warning that "writers sometimes experience false starts."

TECHNICAL STUFF

Technical stuff signifies a brief digression in the flow of information such as Chapter 7's "unconventional spellings of brand names." This information is interesting, but not essential to you understanding what's important.

REMEMBER

Remember icons highlight points of information such as Chapter 15's reminder that "your professor's assignment guidelines supersede APA's guidelines and guidelines I offer you in this book."

Where to Go from Here

This book represents a starting point for verifying APA professor preferences. APA offers the standard for academic style writing, citing, and formatting, which are detailed for you here. But APA doesn't award your grade, and it recognizes that departments' and professors' guidelines replace APA requirements.

Many professors, for example, require variations of APA's title page, appendices, annotated bibliographies, and page number requirements with citations. To help you identify specific professor variations, chapters list questions to ask your professor. Similar resources include visiting your professor during office hours and visiting your writing center.

Feel free to start with Part 1 to get an overview to the APA or peruse the Table of Contents and Index to find a topic to pique your interest. You can then flip to that chapter and read more about what you want to discover.

For additional information related to adjusting to college life and college essay writing, check out the Cheat Sheet at www.dummies.com. Just search for "APA Style & Citations Cheat Sheet" to reference whenever you need.

1

Conforming to Standards: APA and the Academic Environment

Discover the storied history of the American Psychological Association (APA) that shaped today's guidelines for academic writing, research, and documentation in almost every academic field — and resulted in APA becoming the leader among its peers.

Examine grade-influencing differences between APA's sixth and seventh editions that affect title page design, page layout, citations, and references.

View side-by-side comparison charts of APA and MLA that reveal subtle game-changing differences for students transitioning documentation styles.

Apply lessons from adversity that will help you master APA, improve your writing, and succeed in college.

Read APA and college-adapting advice for nonnative English-speaking students confronted with cultural differences and language-barrier challenges.

Avoid habits highly conducive to plagiarism such as super citations, citation procrastination, and conditional common knowledge — and read a professor's perspective on plagiarism.

Motivate yourself by visualizing your college graduation day protocol: faculty procession, academic regalia, tassel toss, and "Pomp and Circumstance."

» Positioning APA among leaders

» Crossing the curriculum with APA

» Studying English and APA as an add-on language

Chapter **1**

Capitalizing on Consistency: APA and the Academic Classroom

The hours you commit to studying APA style and citations, working on research and writing, and completing your required readings moves you days closer to achieving your academic goal of earning your college degree.

Congratulations on the academic success you achieved to date and your hard work that positions you toward earning your college degree in the near future. Your degree will change your life and your family's future, especially if you're a first-generation college graduate. Your school success has been punctuated with accomplishments and milestones such as the following:

>> Navigating your first day of school without your parents

>> Reciting the alphabet

>> Learning to read and write

>> Meeting your first forever best friend

>> Experiencing your first love and first heartbreak

You also survived fractions and decimals, school lockers, middle school hallways, social media embarrassment, and getting lost your first day of college classes. Some of you may even have attended the wrong class on the first day of college, but you survived the obstacles.

Today you face another challenge on your educational expedition: studying and implementing a documentation style that credits, formats, and organizes writing projects consistent with standards in your field of study. You (more likely your professor) chose the *American Psychological Association* (APA) style and citation guide and not *Modern Language Association* (MLA) or *Chicago Manual of Style* (CMoS) because you're studying a social science subject such as sociology, political science, anthropology, linguistics, education, business, or communications.

Although MLA and CMoS also offer a high-quality documentation style, APA continues to grow as the documentation style of choice among academic institutions today.

Familiarizing yourself with APA and any documentation style, less challenging than navigating middle school hallways, can cause you some frustration but will eventually hardwire your brain for user-friendly access to standardize, organize, and document your academic papers. And mastering APA will make you feel as proud as surviving AP English.

Consider this chapter your jumping-off point to the APA. Here I explain a brief history of APA, the importance of documentation, and APA's position among other documentation styles. I also offer advice for non-native language students who face the challenge of APA along with the most challenging skill for the brain — writing in a second language.

Understanding APA and Academic Standards

APA, the world's largest association of psychologists, establishes standards for scholarly writing in most of the social and behavioral sciences for academic writing style, citing sources, and formatting documents. More than a hundred years ago, APA established organizational consistency guidelines for professional scholars, undergraduates, and high school students who created papers for scholarly publication and classroom submission. APA's style and citation guidelines set a standard for writing and reading academic documents as well as helping manage volumes of scholarship for academic writers and readers.

TECHNICAL STUFF

A documentation style, such as APA and MLA, standardizes crediting works of others, citing sources, listing references, and organizing documents from the title page to appendices. A consistent format guides readers through text with visual consistency, logical flow of headings, and systematic organization to retrieve sources on demand. Standardization also reduces bias when sources are presented. Documentation standards are as important as punctuation standards.

Your professor and university have competitive choices for a style and citation guide. They chose the publication manual (*Publication Manual of the American Phycological Association, Seventh Edition*) that sold millions of copies worldwide in multiple languages. APA's popularity continues to grow across academic disciplines and universities. In addition to APA's growth, it's the only documentation style with its own *For Dummies* version. What more could you ask for?

The following sections focus on the role of the APA supporting research in the social sciences and beyond. An early internal conflict within the APA resulted in publishing its first style guide. Students today share responsibility to honor those academic standards that were established over a century ago.

THE ORIGIN AND PURPOSE OF APA

The American Psychological Association (APA) began with a few dozen psychologists who organized around 1900 for the purpose of promoting scholarship and standards among growing numbers of academicians in the social sciences. Like many groups of academicians passionate about their beliefs, pioneering APA members experienced an intellectual dichotomy between academic diversification and academic standardization. Some members believed APA should expand academic interests into other fields of scholarship beyond the social sciences. Other members believed APA lacked the intellectual maturity to expand and should first develop standards for their specialized interests at the time.

Proponents of standardization emerged, as well as an official seven-page writing and style guide. The purpose of the early style guide was to promote professionalism and help readers manage growing libraries of research materials.

Looking back from today's perspective, both groups were right. APA expanded academically far beyond the social sciences, and its standards for academic writing, scholarly publishing, and citing sources ranks at the top of the industry.

Standardizing how you handle topics

The APA establishes standards that provide structure and meaning to a research document. Standards identify guidelines that are important and how to achieve them. Lack of standards is like a marching band without marching orders.

APA publishes standards for topics such as

>> **Academic writing style:** Active, direct, and concise writing that communicates clearly and succinctly

>> **Grammar, mechanics, and conventions:** Writing guideposts that help readers smoothly navigate from page to page

>> **Bias-free language:** Language that respects diverse populations

>> **Citations and references:** Conventions of scholarship that credit works of others and expedite searching their sources

>> **Document organization and formatting:** Standards for organizing title pages, text pages, references, and documents

Respecting the academic environment

APA's respect of scholarship aligns with the academic sanctity of the college classroom. The classroom environment respects scholarship, values sharing of ideas, and welcomes debate based on evidence. APA's standards of scholarship seamlessly blend with classroom expectations, like sunshine blends with a warm day at the beach.

Learning resembles a participation sport. Your obligation as a student includes dedication to new ideas, commitment to preparing for classes, and an open mind to new learning. Your participation includes attending every class — and mastering APA guidelines.

A recent study showed three habits common to students who achieved success in college and graduated, which the following sections identify in greater detail:

Attending class

During my decades of college teaching, I can't recall a student who attended every class in a course and earned less than an A for the course. Those students didn't earn the A because they perfected attendance, but because they perfected learning habits. Regular class attendance creates a learning rhythm of understanding course content and class organization.

When you attend class, you experience regular exposure to APA content such as citing, referencing, formatting, and engaging with sources. You regularly see models of other students' assignments and hear professors' comments on work and other students' questions. In addition to content experiences, you're regularly reminded of deadlines, helpful resources, and adjustments to assignments.

REMEMBER

You have immediate access to ask questions before class, during class, and after class. You actively participate in class and absorb instruction that you paid tuition for. Daily class activity is as important as daily physical activity.

Completing assignments

A body of research correlates the quality of your first college writing assignment with graduating from college. You read that correctly. You're a risk not to graduate if you neglect or fail to submit your first college writing assignment.

Your assignments, mostly writing, show what you learned. They demonstrate your knowledge of content and your knowledge of APA writing, citing, and formatting. College writing assignments can't be successful if you begin them a day or two before deadline, similar to habits of some high school students. Frequently, a college writing assignment is longer than essays written by some high school students.

TIP

To help you complete your assignments, keep the following tips in mind:

» **Begin assignments early.** Check out Chapter 5.

» **Follow APA strategies.** Chapter 5 offers some simple strategies.

» **Utilize resources available to help you, such as professors' office hours and your university writing center.** Refer to Chapter 20 for more details.

» **Read extensive background on topics you're writing about.** Chapters 9 and 18 discuss this topic in greater detail.

Making friends

Don't underestimate the importance of socializing in college, which can sometimes take two or three semesters to achieve a level of comfort. Feeling uncomfortable the first semester or two isn't unusual. Give it time. Get involved in college activities, whether you're a resident or commuter.

Colleges recognize the importance of incoming students assimilating into both the college discourse community and social community. Colleges offer academic, social, and athletic events. Take the initiative to introduce yourself to people. Talk with other students in your classes. Make eye contact as you walk around campus. Some of the people you meet in college will be your lifelong friends. Nerds are popular in college, both academic and social nerds.

APA AND OTHER STYLE GUIDES

Early in my college teaching career, my university required teaching MLA for writing courses and teaching APA for business courses. Later in my career, APA became the standard throughout the university. APA continues to trend throughout universities as the five-star writing and citation guide.

Here's a look at three major documentation styles:

- **APA:** APA expanded from its initial use as the style and citation guide primarily for psychology and now extends as the standard for sociology, anthropology, political science, geography, history, economics, business, education, communication, nursing, science, and other fields.

- **MLA:** MLA, founded in the late 1800s as an advocacy organization for scholars in the study of literature and modern languages, publishes its *MLA Style Manual* for students and professional scholars in the fields of language and literature. The manual sells millions of copies and published its ninth edition in 2021. Similar to APA, MLA survived philosophical disagreements.

- **CMoS:** The Chicago Manual of Style (CMoS), first published in the early 1900s, offers style and citation guidelines for students, teachers, and librarians. Chicago recently published its 17th edition and is commonly used in publishing. CMoS lacks the extensive academic use of APA and MLA. This *For Dummies* book uses CMoS.

Other specialized style guides and their primary content area include the following:

- **Harvard:** Economics

- **Vancouver** and **AMA (American Medical Association):** Medicine

- **OSCOLA:** Law

- **IEEE (Institute of Electrical and Electronic Engineers):** Technical studies and electrical engineering

- **ACS (American Chemical Society):** Chemistry

Comparing APA and MLA

Unlike many of your professors who generally have a choice of documentation styles they teach, you're frequently required to alternate documentation styles. You may also have the misfortune to use two different styles in two different courses. APA and MLA have enough similarities that they're easily confused. (See the nearby sidebar for more about MLA.)

APA offers standards for organizing and developing sections of your paper's beginning, middle, and ending. It recommends procedures for designing the title page, numbering pages, setting margins, and positioning headings and subheadings. APA prioritizes formatting for crediting and citing sources.

Not surprisingly, many professors are possessive of the content they teach, thinking they understand their specialty better than many other experts, sometimes referred to as *discipline envy*.

Furthermore, a content rivalry exists between APA and MLA. It's not exactly Buckeyes versus Wolverines or Beatles versus Stones, but it's strong enough that mixing styles of formatting isn't healthy for your grade. Table 1-1 looks at the differences between the two most popular documentation styles for students and chapter numbers where you can read more about these topics in this book.

TABLE 1-1 **Comparing APA and ML**

Formatting	APA	MLA
Citations One author (Chapter 10)	(Lee, 2020, p. 84)	(Lee 84)
Citations Two authors (Chapter 10)	(Lee & Tyler, 2020, p. 47)	(Lee and Tyler 47)
Citations Three-plus authors (Chapter 10)	(Lee et al., 2020, p. 56)	(Lee et al. 56)
Headings and subheadings (Chapter 14)	Five-levels of subheadings	None

(continued)

TABLE 1-1 *(continued)*

Formatting	APA	MLA
Title page (Chapter 14)	Requires formatting	None
Reference page title (Chapter 12)	References	Works Cited
Source titles punctuation (Chapter 7)	Sentence case	Title case
Running head (Chapter 14)	None for students	Last name and page number
Block quotations (Chapter 10)	40 words or longer are blocked	Block 5-plus lines of prose Block 4-plus lines of verse
Punctuation following URL or DOI (Chapter 12	No period follows a URL or DOI in references	A period follows a sentence-ending URL or DOI

Additional variations between APA and MLA are as subtle as the ones in Table 1-2:

TABLE 1-2   **Subtle Variations between APA and MLA**

Style	APA	MLA
Page (Chapter 12)	Okay to abbreviate as p.	Doesn't reference.
And	Okay to use &.	Use and.
URL/DOI (Chapter 12)	Don't insert a period after.	Use a period after.
Reference titles (Chapter 7)	Use sentence case.	Use title case.
List of resources (Chapter 12)	Title as References.	Title as Work Cited.

In my decades of teaching APA, the following patterns of APA errors appeared regularly:

>> Neglecting a *hanging indentation* (first line flush left, all following lines indented five spaces) on the first line of reference items

>> Underlining the title on the title page

>> Incorrectly positioning the period before sentence-ending parenthesis rather than after parenthesis

>> Alphabetizing reference items by criteria other than the author's last name

>> Not coordinating citations and references, which requires all citations to appear in references and all reference items to appear in citations

>> Not referencing figures and tables in text

>> Neglecting to include date in citation

The inconsistencies of APA and MLA formatting styles are evidenced by the limited consistencies of both. Here are three significant formatting similarities of both styles:

>> Prefer 12-point Times New Roman font (see Chapter 14).

>> Set one-inch margins of four sides (see Chapter 14).

>> Double-space lines of text (see Chapter 14).

Identifying Your Role in Academic Process

Early in your academic career, education was a partnership between you, your family, and your teacher. Your family provided guidance that resulted in your academic independence, enabling you to accept primary academic responsibility today. And as you discover in Chapter 9, many successful people educate themselves exclusively by reading. I emphasize the importance of reading throughout this book. You become educated by reading, such as learning about APA. In addition to reading, you educate yourself by committing to your schoolwork and satisfying curiosity.

To educate yourself in the academic environment, add two ingredients: commitment and curiosity. Your role as a college student is to bring your best effort, your A-game to every class, every assignment, every semester. That level of commitment requires work and sacrifice. College degrees are earned, not awarded. In fact, only about one-third of American adults have earned a college degree. Earning your degree requires sacrificing play time, social time, and social media time — and using that time for reading, writing, researching, and thinking. As a committed college student, you frequently need to say: "Sorry I can't go. I have schoolwork to do."

Becoming educated requires thinking and satisfying curiosity with topics you're presented in the classroom. Your brain is wired with a natural curiosity to discover, a practice you began when you learned to crawl. That early curiosity was focused on objects, such as staring at your foot and wondering how it got there.

Stepping forward, your curiosity today is focused on ideas. For example, if you experienced your first view of the Grand Canyon over the South Rim, you wondered how such an expansive gash in the earth got there. When you started to talk, you had more questions than answers. Now as a college student, those answers result in more questions. The more you read and experience classes, the more you question. The more you write, the more you discover. When you write, question, and theorize, you're thinking critically and becoming educated.

The role of APA in your life as a scholar is to provide stability and consistency as you commit to academics and satisfy curiosities. APA helps you navigate the language of scholarship as you write and read. APA is your GAS, your Guidance Activation System, that navigates you through the world of scholarship and provides you opportunities to be your best you.

Your role in the academic process includes continuing to develop your APA skills throughout high school and your college experiences. Gradually increase the complexity of your research reading so that you may apply complex sources to your research writing.

APA and high school classrooms

Your first introduction to APA in high school validates why school subjects are called disciplines. An early academic lesson (and life lesson) is that before you become a rule maker, your survival depends on being a rule follower. APA is the rule-maker, and you are the rule follower. Mastering APA requires academic discipline.

If you had the good fortune of being taught by a high school teacher obsessed with teaching you the details of APA, or MLA or CMoS, treasure them and express your appreciation to them for their passion towards academic protocol. That teacher helped inspire you to buy this book and learn additional strategies about APA.

A prerequisite for writing APA research papers requires completing the following:

>> **Write fluent sentences.** Master writing clear concise messages that don't distract the reader with compromised sentence structure, incorrect grammar, or misused language conventions.

>> **Integrate sources:** Read to develop ideas to incorporate into your writing. College writing requires integrating college ideas into your writing — called *source engagement* (Chapter 11). College audiences demand more than your unsubstantiated opinion, they want opinions of experts and how your opinion integrates with experts' opinions.

>> **Document with APA guidelines:** Academic audiences expect you to document your sources consistent with standards in your field of study, APA.

APA and college courses

APA is the common denominator of writing in most college courses — similar to chocolate being the common denominator of most desserts. If APA is the standard documentation style throughout your university, you'll master it easier because you'll be practicing it more frequently. Until you experience that regular practice, applying APA will test your patience. It will be like trying to benefit from exercising by going to the gym once a week. Perfect practice produces perfect performance.

Your success and your degree require commitment and curiosity. Earn your degree one assignment at a time, one class at a time, one course at a time, and one semester at a time. And you already demonstrated your initiative and commitment by buying this book.

TECHNICAL STUFF

Critical thinking in college includes establishing relationships between ideas studied in different courses. For example, hypothesize answers to course-related questions such as

>> What is similar about revising writing in a composition course and continental drift in a geography course?

>> What is similar about textures in art and scales in music?

>> What is similar about the scientific method in chemistry and quadratic equations in physics?

APA strategies help you achieve academic success as you fulfill writing course requirements — and accumulate credits — throughout your college experience.

APA and comp courses

Your most challenging academic commitment following high school will be your first-year writing courses, usually titled College Composition I (CCI) and Composition II (CCII), essay writing courses that require research. An unfortunate statistic is first-year writing courses result in as many as 30 percent of freshmen dropping out of college. In addition to learning college writing, you'll also be learning APA standards with that writing.

Although 30 percent of first year college students fail first-year writing courses and drop out of college, 70 percent succeed in those courses and go on to graduate. Let me help you become one of the 7 out of 10 first-year students who graduates from college.

Yes, college essay writing with APA documentation is a difficult course, and you'll be additionally enrolled in three or four other courses that also require writing. Welcome to the world of college where four years of hard work can change your life and the lives of your children and family.

Successful essay writing requires essay writing skills (refer to Chapter 15), and APA style, documentation, and formatting skills (check out Chapters 10 through 14). Successful research writing, CCII that usually follows CCI, requires intense research and more complex documentation. APA use in essay writing, your first college writing course, lacks the intensity of APA in CCII.

REMEMBER

CCI is one of your first and most challenging college courses, especially if you weren't an A–B essay writer in high school and especially if you aren't an avid book reader. Success in your first-year composition course requires following these three points for successful college writing:

>> **Start writing assignments the day they're assigned to you in class.**
Analyze the assignment and read extensive background material on the topic. Apply APA strategies as you read:

- Complete APA reference elements as you read each source (see Chapter 12).

- Identify source content (with page numbers) that you could use as summaries, paraphrases, and quotations.

- As you commit time and thought to drafting your essay, complete APA citations and references in your draft.

During my decades teaching first year writing students, I frequently tracked strategies of students who wrote model essays. They began assignments early, read extensive background material before drafting, and committed to revising (refer to Chapter 8).

>> **Commit to recurring feedback and revising.** Source engagement (see Chapter 11) can significantly influence your grade.

>> **Allocate time to review APA documentation with your professor (during office hours), a peer, and your university writing center.** Refer to Chapter 20 for more details.

APA and content courses

APA style and documentation that you learned in your composition and research courses can make you an expert-level student in your content courses. And if you earned Bs in your essays in composition courses, you should earn As in your writing assignments in content courses.

Here's why. Most professors in content areas lack experience teaching writing like your writing professors. Consequently, their expectations for writing assignments are less than their expectations for content in their courses. Advantage you.

Stick to this three-step plan for writing APA essays in your content courses to earn a letter-grade higher than essays in your composition courses:

1. **Nail APA guidelines such as title page, page layout (see Chapter 14), citations (refer to Chapter 10), and references (check out Chapter 12).**

2. **Reference four or five sources to support your thesis.**

   Engage with those sources as I discuss in Chapter 11.

3. **Connect support of your thesis with class lectures, best-selling books, current events, and content in other courses.**

As a reading tool (refer to Chapter 9), APA helps you identify the credibility behind ideas, the supporting details validated by scholars in the field. APA provides the skills to further explore citations and references. APA also provides the writing tools to stand out among your peers, tools such as source engagement and critical analysis like I discuss in Chapter 11.

Finally, use write-to-learn strategies to learn content and develop your writing. Chapter 9 includes explanations and examples. It's like a two-for-one sale: You learn content and you develop your writing.

APA and online courses

You may have discovered from the pandemic that remote learning lacks the excitement (your friends) of classroom learning. And some of you discovered the convenience of remote learning and that it matched your learning style. More importantly, colleges discovered that online courses are an inexpensive and convenient platform to deliver instruction. Advantage university. You can expect online course offerings to grow.

If your student experience includes an online writing course with APA documentation, you have taken the first step toward success by buying this book. You face two challenges taking an APA online writing course and learning college writing. You miss

>> The face-to-face support of a class

>> The face-to-face support of a classroom instructor

Parts 2 and 3 help you with both challenges.

TIP

Here are a few tips for succeeding in online courses:

>> **Maintain regular email and platform contact with your professor.** The easiest plan for an unsuccessful online experience is going MIA (missing in action).

>> **Use online office hours to answer your APA questions.** As you complete your citing and formatting, identify your top two to three questions to email your professor during online office hours.

>> **If you're unsure about APA documentation, plan to have your documentation reviewed by your writing center or a trusted peer.** As you work on your research, record APA issues to review with your writing center and a trusted peer.

>> **Regularly utilize class tools available through your learning platform.** This strategy not only provides you with course learning tools but also identifies your online presence for professors who use tracking tools to monitor students' online participation. Focus on utilizing class handouts that contain models of APA requirements that you find challenging, such as citations and references.

>> **Don't fall behind with assignments.** Because professors' recording of assignments requires more time for online courses, missing assignments may not be revealed until final grades. When life priorities interfere with completing an assignment, communicate with your professor well before the assignment due dates. Professors usually prefer visiting during office hours rather than emailing or phoning.

Utilize these strategies for improving your writing and online documentation in online courses. Here are some suggestions and their locations:

>> The previous section provides background for succeeding in a writing course; almost all information is applicable to online courses.

>> Chapter 5 strategies for APA style adapt to online writing assignments, including research papers. I explain essays and response papers in Chapter 15, review of literature in Chapter 16, and report writing in Chapter 17.

>> Chapters 6 and 7 explain APA's focus on parts of speech and conventions that support writing.

>> Chapter 8 familiarizes you with a three-level approach for revising your writing. Don't underestimate the importance of revising your college writing.

Confronting Cultural Differences — APA and Nonnative English Students

Many college students sacrifice to educate themselves. Students who work full time to support a family while pursuing a degree attend American colleges and deserve admiration from the academic community. One million nonnative English-speaking students travel to the United States to educate themselves at one of the world's best systems of higher education.

Throughout my college teaching career, I taught essay writing and business writing to students who were learning English as an additional language. Both courses required APA citations and formatting. The commitment of students in both courses enriched my life by seeing their relentless drive to learning. I recall, for example, a student from Southeast Europe who wrote A-grade essays by checking spelling of almost every word with a tattered dictionary she carried with her until she graduated. English was her fourth language, and she studied business pursuing a career in international business.

Colleges that accept you want you to graduate and offer you the support you need to succeed. Your challenge includes finding that help. What follows are some practices to get you started.

Seeking a professor who supports language learning

If you as an international student aren't offered scheduling priority to enroll you into a course that supports learning an additional language, ask your advisor to schedule you with a professor experienced teaching this specialty. If you can't identify such a professor, ask for recommendations from an upper-level peer who is also a second language learner. Although some professors specialize teaching second language learners, many professors are experienced with strategies that support second language learners.

REMEMBER

To help you identify these professors, here are examples of teaching strategies conducive to learning styles that meet your needs:

>> Guided reading strategies that include providing a reading purpose prior to reading assignments

>> Nonlecture teaching styles such as hands-on and active-learning classes

>> Numerous handouts

>> Team assignments

>> Student-centered rather than content-centered

If this is your first experience in a course learning to write English (with the added challenge of APA documenting and formatting), be patient with yourself. You'll succeed as long as you continue trying. You've overcome greater challenges to be where you are. You're learning to write a difficult language that many native speakers struggle with. Don't be surprised if you need to take the course a second time to succeed, not a setback but opportunity to additionally improve your English proficiency.

TECHNICAL
STUFF

The brain possesses a property called *neuroplasticity*, the ability to rewire itself and adapt to new learning experiences. Research shows that one of the brain's most challenging adaptations is learning a new language and adapting to a new culture, which requires about a generation to learn. You ensure failure only when you stop trying.

Understanding that English isn't easy

English is a difficult language to learn because its foundation is a combination of languages (including Greek, Latin, German, French, Spanish, Japanese, Russian, and Italian) with a combination of rules. Difficulties learning English include the following:

>> Inconsistent spelling rules

>> Pronoun agreement variations

>> Inconsistent plural formations with numerous irregular forms

>> Numerous irregular verbs

>> More prepositions than other languages

>> Word positioning sequences inconsistent with other languages

>> Language convention rules inconsistent with other languages

>> Nonverbal communication differing from other languages

Additional challenges of learning English include

>> **Illogical academic vocabulary:** GPA, priority registration, major and minor

>> **Eye contact:** Offensive in some cultures, expected with English

TIP

» **Addressing professors:** Informal in some cultures, formalities expected with English culture

To develop language skills addressing professors, role play language exchange with a peer. You can also role play questions you'd ask in class and offer comments on class topics. Professors in most Western cultures expect to be addressed formally in speaking and email. Use formal language and tone, like you're addressing an older well-respected family member. Also, look professors in the eye when you speak, an expectation of Western culture.

» **Inconsistent writing structure:** Beginning, middle, and end in English inconsistent with other cultures that require writing support to precede main ideas.

Making the transition seamlessly

If you're learning English and APA as a second (or third) language, here are some strategies to help you make the transition:

» **Read aloud and record examples of APA documented literature.** Include reading aloud punctuation for citations and sources in reference lists.

» **Make a recording of APA-related words and phrases that challenge you.** Include spelling and meaning, words such as DOI (digital object identifier), source engagement, crediting sources, plagiarism, attribution, format, bias-free, in-text, and signal phrase.

» **Make a recording of writing-related words and phrases**. Include prewriting, peer-feedback, approach, audience, purpose, and tone.

» **Meet with a tutor or visit your writing center.** Set the meeting for the exclusive purpose of reviewing APA in your paper.

» **Read about and talk with peers about plagiarism, especially if your native culture accepts referencing sources without crediting them.** See Chapter 4 for more information on plagiarism and add-on language students.

» **Write (in English) describing your use of APA in your writing and include a list of questions about APA use.** Writing about APA in English will help you learn English and APA. Write with vocabulary common to APA.

» **Limit your research.** Focus on basic sources such as books and scholarly journal articles that you can duplicate citation formats and reference element formats.

» **Over-document with citations.** Eliminate unnecessary citations with your tutor's recommendation.

ADVOCATING FOR YOURSELF

As a college student, regardless of your cultural background, your academic and social survival depends on advocating for yourself, accepting responsibility that your happiness and adjustment to academics and college life depends on how well you attend to your own needs. For example, academically, you accept responsibility by securing your needs for classes: advisors, tutors, peer reviewers, and APA reviewer. You also accept responsibility for paying your tuition and registering for classes. If you need to shop off campus, you coordinate transportation. Be your own best friend, recognize differences between needs and wants, and figure things out.

TIP

Meet with your professors as soon as you can after the first class. Immediately following the first class is usually a good time. Introduce yourself and explain that you're learning English as a second (third, fourth, or fifth) language and that you've been successful in past courses with the help of a tutor and support the university offers. Ask them if they can recommend additional resources to help with the course. Also ask if you may record classes to help you with notetaking.

Chapter **2**

Updating and Debugging: APA Seventh Edition

Since its inception in Philadelphia in 1892, a little more than a hundred years after the signing of the Declaration of Independence, APA has passed the test of time and established itself as the sultan of citation. Its leadership envisioned the importance of timely updates and the reinforcing of its position as a guide for scholarly writing and reading. The first APA 7-page writer's guide, published in 1929, evolved into the 427-page seventh edition, which was released in October 2019.

The seventh edition expands on the theme of inclusivity with continued emphasis on bias-free language and technological accommodations. It also represents a coming of age for undergraduate nonprofessional scholars (and high school students) with an introduction to the student title page and expanded advice on a half-dozen essays, reaction papers, précis, and an annotated bibliography — in addition to the traditional research paper.

In this chapter, I trace the transition from the sixth edition to the seventh, explain a major language innovation ensuring gender-neutral usage, and review clarification and standardization of citations and reference entries.

The traditional focus of APA guidelines has been on publication preparation for scholarly articles written by professional scholars. An increasing APA guideline focus in the past two editions has been on student papers. This chapter also offers encouragement and a plan for college students' publishing.

Transitioning from the Sixth: APA for Today

A wise scholar once asked, "How do you know how to get there if you don't know where you came from?" APA arrived at the sixth edition (the second sixth edition) following a detour resulting from the first sixth edition containing misprint errors in examples. A segment of the scholarly community expressed its disapproval in an unscholarly manner.

Citation and documentation represent a complex process. Describing that process in a publication manual requires the skill of a brain surgeon. The sixth edition was followed with guidelines that simplified and standardized citations and references, the most complex features of documentation style. The citation and documentation process is complex and the standards high. The expectation is perfection, although near-perfection is not failure.

The APA manual was originally created as a literacy manual to improve the writing of scholarly documents in the social and behavioral sciences. It developed into a writing manual for professional publication and for assignments submitted in the classroom. The primary audience has been professional scholars writing for advanced degrees and scholarly publication.

The seventh edition encompasses an approximate 33 percent increase in content from the sixth edition. Notable differences in the seventh edition include flexible pronoun agreement, font accommodations, spacing following a period, and a title page for students. Table 2-1 offers a brief comparison of the two editions.

TABLE 2-1 **Differences between the Sixth and Seventh Editions**

Topic	Sixth Edition	Seventh Edition
Manual size	8 Chapters	12 Chapters
Font flexibility	Times New Roman 12	Times New Roman 12, Calibri 11, Arial 11, Lucida Sans Unicode 10, or Georgia 11
Title page	One format for both student and professional papers	Individual formats for students and professionals
Running head	Student and professional papers	None for student papers
Major section headings	Centered and not bolded	Centered and bolded
Pronoun agreement	Singular: he, she, his, her Plural: they, their	Singular and plural: they, their

Topic	Sixth Edition	Seventh Edition
Period spacing	Two spaces after a period	One space after a period
Publisher location	Include with books in reference list	Exclude with books in reference list
Linguistic examples	Italicized	Marked with quotations

Focusing on the Title Page and Page Organization

Education moves at the speed of a cruise ship in low gear. After almost a hundred years and a pandemic, APA's seventh edition provided an exclusive title page for student papers, notable recognition for the junior scholar population. APA also updated and expanded guidelines for page organization.

For professional papers and student papers, the *byline* (your name as the author and university affiliation) has been updated to align with publishing standards. This means that how your name and affiliation appear on your paper resembles how they'll appear in a publication. With this alignment change for student papers, APA recognizes that high school and college students, like you, publish their work. The section, "Student Publishing: Your Goal As a Serious Writer," later in this chapter offers recommendations for students to publish their work.

The new student title page resembles the professional page, but the running head has been deleted. APA also clarified other requirements of the student title page:

REMEMBER

- >> Title bolded and centered in the upper half of the page
- >> Student's name (or names of team members) centered, two line-spaces below the title

   Team names are positioned with the primary writer listed first.

- >> Department name and university affiliation double spaced and centered below the student's name
- >> Course name and number double spaced and centered below the affiliation
- >> Professor's name
- >> Due date of assignment
- >> Page numbering in the upper-right corner

You can find detailed information on title pages in Chapter 14, including a template to use for your title pages.

Your professor's preferences supersede APA guidelines for the title page and all other requirements. APA provides recommendations, not mandates. Your professor mandates.

The seventh edition also clarifies and expands page organization features that improve the reading experience. The following sections offer a look at APA clarifications and updates for page organization.

Running heads

Running heads aren't required on the title page or any other page throughout the student paper. Running heads were needed when hard copies of assignments were required, and stray pages needed to be identified. Electronic submissions mostly eliminated the need for running heads.

Period spacing

APA changed spacing that follows a period from two spaces to one space. The change to one space also follows a colon, exclamation point, and question mark. See Chapter 7 for additional information and examples. The change was encouraged by electronic publishing to improve page aesthetics and save space(s). Pun intended.

Levels of headings

Use title case (see Chapter 14) for heading levels 3, 4, and 5. Align level 3 headings flush left. Indent level 4 and 5 headings. You can find examples of five levels of headings in Chapter 14. These levels of headings apply to your daily academic writing and add consistency and readability to your writing, in addition to enhancing its professional presentation.

Font options

Font options were increased to accommodate reading needs of special populations. These are now the font choices:

>> Times New Roman 12

>> Calibri 11

>> Arial 11

>> Lucida Sans Unicode 10

>> Georgia 11

If you choose a font other than Times New Roman 12, check with your professor.

DOI and URL Formatting

DOI (Digital Object Identifier) and URL line breaks shouldn't be inserted manually. Breaks inserted automatically by your word-processing app are acceptable. See Chapter 12 for detailed information on DOIs.

Paper length

The seventh edition recommends determining paper length by word count rather than by page count. Word count includes all words in the body of the paper and all optional sections.

TIP

Activate the word count feature under Tools in Microsoft Word.

Bold section headings

APA clarifies that major and optional section headings (abstract, table of contents, reference, appendices, and so forth) are centered and bolded at the top of a new page. Formatting requires a hard page break preceding a new page.

Writing improvement plan

The new edition includes strategies for improving your writing. You can find comprehensive writing- and reading-improvement strategies in Chapter 9.

Page order

APA updated guidelines for order of pages. Required parts include the title page, body of text, and references.

REMEMBER

The preceding order of pages represents APA's basic organization of a piece of writing. APA also provides a list of optional sections (See Chapter 14) to improve organization of your writing.

The sequence of optional parts (with details that I explain in Chapter 13), combined with required parts, looks like the following:

>> Title page

>> Abstract (or executive summary)

>> Table of contents

>> Body of text

>> References

>> Tables and figures

>> Appendixes

REMEMBER

Page and organization guidelines complement APA's basic formatting for a page of text that includes the following:

>> Use 8.5 x 11-inch white paper.

>> Use 1-inch margins on all four sides.

>> Align text flush left.

>> Indent five spaces for new paragraphs.

>> Use double-spacing for the lines of text.

>> Use 12-point Times New Roman as the preferred font.

>> Position page numbers in the upper-right corner, and include the number on the title page.

TECHNICAL STUFF

With hard copies of assignments becoming obsolete, guidelines for paper color are becoming antiquated. To ensure formatting of other page elements, email assignments to yourself before submitting them to ensure no loss of formatting. A common formatting error is lack of hard page breaks before a major heading that begins on a new page.

Eyeing the Changes with Citations and References

Citations and references represent the heart and lungs of the documentation system. The heart functions well with APA's standardized citation system, the most user-friendly system among documentation styles. The lungs, the reference system, will frustrate you. Mastery of references requires a committed effort, a common requirement among college students. The good news is the changes concerning citations in the seventh edition are easy to implement.

The simplicity of APA's citation style (see Chapter 10) includes the author and date listed in parentheses at the end of the sentence that includes the citation. If the author is attributed in the sentence (refer to Chapter 10), include only the date in parentheses. If the cited reference contains a quotation, include page numbers. Page numbers aren't required for paraphrase and summary, but many professors prefer to see page numbers referencing all extracted information. Page numbers for quotations, paraphrase, and summary offer insurance protection against plagiarism (refer to Chapter 4 for more about plagiarism). You'll impress your professor with page numbers added to citations for paraphrases and summaries (in addition to their being required for quotations).

The seventh edition contains one significant citation update for citing three or more authors: Name the first author and include the abbreviation "et al." in every citation, as in this example: (Conwell et al., 2020). Be sure to follow the abbreviation with a comma, and position the period outside the parentheses. The purpose of the abbreviation is to streamline a citation by eliminating a list of names in the citation. All author names (up to 20) are listed as references.

Reference elements (including seventh edition clarifications) cause most students' formatting errors. Fortunately for you, most professors of undergraduates aren't obsessed with reference perfection, but they expect mastery of reference formatting basics (detailed in Chapter 12) such as the following:

>> Hanging indentations

>> Alphabetizing by last name of the first author listed

>> "References" bolded and centered at the top of a new page immediately following the text body, and not "Reference List," "Bibliography," or "Works Cited"

>> Mastery of basic sources such as books, reference works, websites, and popular journals

Seventh edition updates and clarifications highlighted for references include the following:

>> **References standardized:** Journal article references always include the issue number. See Chapter 12 for details and examples.

>> **Annotated bibliography:** The seventh edition offers a model of an annotated bibliography, a common requirement for research papers (see Chapter 12). Avoid incorrectly typing "Annotated References."

>> **Oral traditions:** Oral traditions and knowledge of Indigenous peoples are listed as a new reference category.

>> **Multiple citation authors:** Three or more authors in a citation are listed as the name of the first author and the abbreviation "et al." Examples are included in Chapter 10.

Citations list only one author and the abbreviation "et al." (meaning "and others"). References list up to 20 authors.

>> **Multiple reference authors:** Include up to 20 authors in references. (See Chapter 12.)

>> **Paraphrasing:** APA clarified paraphrasing without overciting. (See Chapter 11.)

>> **DOIs and URLs:** Use a DOI in references when available. Avoid the phrase "Retrieved from" in almost all situations. The label "DOI" is no longer necessary.

>> **Media categorization:** Direct quotations from audiovisual materials require a time stamp in place of a page number, identifying the beginning of the quotation (for example, 1:23).

Addressing Bias-Free Writing Style and Updated Mechanics

Disrespect begins with words. The nickname of a National Football League's team changed in 2020 because the original name was offensive to a specific population of people. Offensive language offends people.

APA has advocated for bias-free language that affects not only the academic world, but also the publishing world and speakers of the English language. With the goal of including all groups of people, APA continues to develop model guidelines that affect people's writing and speaking. Recognize the importance of bias-free language in your writing and everyday language.

New seventh edition guidelines promoting bias-free language include examples that encourage respectful and inclusive language for references to age, gender and gender identity, disability, sexual orientation, race, and ethnicity.

In addition, APA stopped a cruise ship on a dime by championing the use of "they" as a singular pronoun when gender is unidentified or irrelevant. This change represents the reversal of a pronoun agreement rule that existed for generations. The change shows that respect for people supersedes respect for rules. See Chapter 6 for additional information and examples.

Additional updates and clarifications to writing style and mechanics include the following:

>> **Spelling:** APA recommends that spelling conform to Merriam-Webster.com. Preferred spellings include *email*, *webpage*, and *internet*.

>> **Numbers:** Preferences for numbering were updated. For example, numbers are now accepted in an abstract. See Chapter 7 for details and examples.

>> **Examples:** Quotation marks are used to identify words used as linguistic examples, replacing italics.

>> **Lists:** Itemized lists are now acceptable as bullets, numbers, or letters. See Chapter 14 for guidelines and examples.

>> **Proper nouns:** Use of proper nouns has been expanded to include selected name titles, diseases, and disorders. See Chapter 7 for guidelines and examples.

>> **Abbreviations:** The new addition has updated guidelines for using abbreviations in parentheses. Details and examples are included in Chapter 7.

>> **Linguistic examples:** Quotation marks replace italics for identifying linguistics examples (for example: My favorite word without a vowel is "nth.").

Approaching APA Updates: Mindset

By this point in your life, you've learned that living requires adjustments. For example, if your university changes a graduation requirement, you make the adjustment; you find a way. APA's seventh addition updates and clarifications require you to adjust. If you used APA in high school, you may have used the sixth edition, but seventh edition changes apply to you. Clarify with your professor that APA's seventh edition, released in pre-pandemic October 2019, is required.

REMEMBER

If APA is your first style guide, no previous edition adjustments are required. If the seventh edition is your first love affair with a documentation style, it's like the old custom of an arranged marriage; you have no choice. But your chances of being successful with APA are greater than those shown by research on the success of arranged marriages. APA's formatting is as intuitive as navigating your cell phone. As you use your phone, you become more adept at finding features, even those that you only use occasionally. You'll find that adjusting to APA is similar to adjusting to new technology.

Learning a documentation style requires perfecting citations and references. APA citations, 99 percent standardized, require that you list the author and date. The few citation exceptions include "personal communication," such as citing class lectures and experts' communications (see Chapter 10). APA requires that you cite all source information and coordinating citations in references. I describe information that doesn't require citing ("common knowledge") in Chapter 10.

As you research your sources, you should study citations and references — including non-APA styles. Using citations is like saying "thank you" to the author who provides you with the source. If you've learned to say "thank you," you can learn to cite sources. Every researcher that you reference in your writing deserves (and requires) a "thank you."

Correctly listing your research sources in the reference section will frustrate you, but you can learn how to do it. Remember how you learned the intricacies of your phone, software updates, or a new video game? With practice and patience, you can learn formatting references. You can learn anything that you're determined to learn. You only fail when you stop trying. Assume the mindset that you can and will learn how to reference formatting, and then help your peers learn it.

To learn how to use APA references, initially prefer sources requiring less complex formatting such as books and websites with DOIs. (Review elements of a source in Chapter 10.) Begin by researching books, reference works, websites, and popular journals.

When you reference, create a to-do checklist using the headings in bold format that I discuss in the section, "Eyeing the Changes with Citations and References," earlier in this chapter. Similarly, create a to-do checklist from reference guidelines in Chapter 12. You have been successful academically because you can read and follow directions. If you as a college student can cook and follow recipe directions, you can learn APA. If you can't cook and you eat at fast food restaurants, study this book while you are eating. Hang out all day and study APA.

If you time-manage your research papers, you have the advantage of a safety net to review your citations and reference sources. Schedule conferences with your professor and your writing center to review your documentation. Crawl before you walk, and take small steps before you take large steps; create your to-do checklists for updates and basic formatting, and APA will automatically update on your mind's hard drive. You can do what you commit to do and what you're determined to do.

Student Publishing: Your Goal As a Serious Writer

The day I finished my last college course before graduation, I walked out of Wolfgram Memorial Library on the campus of Widener University (Chester, Pennsylvania), pumped my right fist into the air, and said aloud, "I'm going to write a book." The first book, 15 years after graduation, was followed by a second book, third book, and this book — with more to follow. Between books, I wrote a twice-monthly newspaper column for 34 years, never missing a deadline. I graduated from college determined to write (with a day job).

"If you can dream it, you can do it," said Walt Disney. We can all dream, but we don't all "do." If you dream with a plan, you increase your chances of achieving that plan. Research shows that you increase your chances of reaching goals if you write them on a piece of paper and carry them with you.

Writing chose me to publish, and if you have the inspiration, you can commit the perspiration. Seeing your writing published is like celebrating your 21st birthday, again, and again, and again. If writing doesn't motivate you, discover another dream and pursue it. Your dream ends only when you stop pursuing it. But dream responsibly.

The APA manual provides guidelines for professional scholars to publish their scholarly works (see the nearby sidebar for more information). A number of high school and college students also published their writing while earning their degrees; they also continue to dream.

Propose an article (that you have thought about) on a topic you have experienced, or talk and read about regularly: a hobby, travel, music, sports, gaming, and so forth. Also consider topics relevant to college life: budgeting, time management, career planning, finance, socializing, volunteering, test taking, and so forth. Tell the editor you can deliver a 700-word article in four days.

You can find the basics of writing skills throughout this book: audience, purpose, focus, tone, transitions, and so forth. But your college audience expects more than the information-centered writing you submit to your professors. Your college audience also wants to be entertained and surprised, skills you can search online for "how writers entertain and surprise." After you celebrate your first publication, ask if you can write a regular column for the remainder of the semester.

Chapter 9 surveys opportunities to publish online. If you're serious about writing, which complements any career, write regularly and be persistent in publishing your writing. Published writers relentlessly pursue their writing goals. Your library has a copy of *Writer's Market*, a resource listing hundreds of writing markets, magazines, and publishers who buy articles and other content. You have limitless opportunities to publish your writing. And you have no limits on how often you can celebrate your 21st birthday.

ASKING QUESTIONS BEFORE YOU START WRITING

To clarify your understanding of seventh edition upgrades and your professor's preferences, ask your professor the following questions related to APA's seventh edition:

- What edition of APA are you requiring?

- Which APA edition samples are you providing for class? For example, do samples have seventh edition updated requirements such as lack of running heads on the title page, use of singular "they," and current formatting requirements for the annotated bibliography?

- Do you recommend any resources for learning APA and the seventh edition?

Chapter **3**

Understanding Expectations: APA and Discourse Communities

"Y ou have to work your butt off to earn a B," complained a former student on one of my course evaluations, while expecting an A. Did the student expect to earn a B without working hard? When teachers expect more, students achieve more. Earning an A requires more work than earning a B.

When your professors establish high expectations and provide the tools to achieve them, thank them rather than complain about them. My fear as a professor is that I'll expect too little from my students, and they'll achieve it.

College expectations require higher effort than high school expectations. That's why it's called higher education. The demands of high expectations justify the value of the college degree and may explain why only approximately one-third of American adults have earned a college degree.

THE HISTORY OF HIGHER EDUCATION EXCELLENCE

In 1636, Harvard was established as the first research university in the United States. It was soon followed by seven other private research universities in the Northeast: Princeton, Columbia, Yale, Pennsylvania, Dartmouth, Brown, and Cornell. Known as The Ancient Eight and eventually Ivy League schools, they represent academic excellence and rank among the most prestigious universities in the world.

College success also depends on understanding the language of each academic discipline, referred to as the *discourse*. Familiarizing yourself with APA, another discourse, also requires getting to know the language of the learning community. Not studying a discourse language is like travelling in a foreign country alone and not speaking the language. Studying the language, the discourse, is like living at home and speaking the native language.

In this chapter, I identify academic expectations of college classes, explain the advantages of failure, and explore the importance of discourse communities in the academic setting. It's time to shift your brain into academic mode and satisfy some of your curiosity.

More than likely, you're a first-year college student required to write a paper using APA style and citations. You're encountering the academic expectations that I describe in the following sections. If you're a high school student, this information will give you a preview of the college expectations in your future.

Understanding Academic Expectations in College

Your high school teachers told you what to expect in college compared with high school: more papers to write, more books to read, longer study hours to prepare for more challenging tests, and shorter semesters to complete everything. As you've learned in your short time in college, your high school teachers were wrong — college expectations are much more challenging than what they described.

As an entry-level college student, you're adjusting to college life and the academic rigor and expectations of the college classroom. Your first-year writing courses that include APA style and citations represent prerequisite skills that prepare you for your sophomore year and beyond.

Your college success depends on understanding your academic goals (your wants) and your professors' expectations (your needs), which differ from your high school teachers' expectations. The next two sections offer a closer examination of those wants and needs.

Figuring out what you want to achieve in college

Looking at the big picture, your degree is just one of your college goals. Expectations of your college experience also include the following:

>> Discovering your passion for a major field of interest

>> Completing field experiences in your area of study

>> Building a network of professional resources

>> Earning an entry-level career opportunity

You achieved expert status as a high school student. As a senior you capitalized on the sympathies of teachers, earned almost all A's, manipulated excused class absences, and justified early dismissals. Your last few months of high school lacked much academic rigor because you had earned your college acceptance. That part of your academic life is over and carries as much value in college as a permanent high school hall pass. You'll never again sit in an assigned classroom seat.

In high school, most of your learning took place during classes. In college, your most extensive learning takes place outside of classes. Your college professors expect higher levels of reading, writing, thinking, and responding in class.

Your professors aren't impressed with your academic awards, student-of-the-month recognitions, endless list of activities, or even your high school grades. They're focused on "Show me the knowledge." Table 3-1 shows the differences between your high school teachers and your college professors.

TABLE 3-1 **Differentiating between High School Teachers and College Professors**

High School Teachers	College Professors
Almost always available	Available during office hours
More approachable	Less approachable
Offer daily verbal reminders	List reminders once in syllabus
Hold students minimally accountable for outside readings	Hold students fully accountability for outside readings
Accept responsibility for cultivating student-teacher relationship	Expect students to accept responsibility for cultivating student-teacher relationship
Offer extra credit for poor or late assignments	Offer no extra credit; accept assignment only on due date

College life abounds with exaggerated stories and unproven beliefs. Here are a few myths and realities about college life.

Myth: First-year students gain an average of 15 pounds.

Reality: Research showed that one-fourth of freshmen lose weight and that only 10 percent gain 15 pounds or more. Another study showed that students' body mass index (BMI) remains constant from freshman year to graduation.

Myth: Liberal arts degrees lack value in the workplace.

Reality: A recent study of business executives endorsed the value of a well-rounded education in the arts. More than 90 percent of executives described liberal arts graduates as "very well qualified" for career opportunities.

Myth: Most college students earn their degrees in four years.

Reality: More than half of college students earn their degrees in five or six years.

Myth: College students don't get homesick because they're having too much fun.

Reality: Homesickness is part of college's normal adjustment. You lived at home for many more years than you will have lived at college. Being homesick occurs during alone time, but you will adjust as you get involved in college life. You'll learn to enjoy college life, while you continue to appreciate the value of your homelife.

Fulfilling your professors' expectations: Your needs

Your high school teachers specialize in their subject matter and generalize in supporting you as an adult-in-training. Your brain, especially the emotional-responsibility part, requires at least another year or two to fully develop. For example, you may have committed the ultimate high school crime of academic students like you — cutting a day of school. But because you lack the skills of a frequent offender, you probably got caught.

Your college professors specialize in content with the expectation that you appreciate learning. They grade you on test performance of content — no personality points. To fulfill professors' expectations, achieve your academic goals, and meet the demands of academic life, you're expected to achieve the following:

Engage in class

The following tips can help you be an engaging student:

>> Attend every class. You don't grow up until you show up.

>> Arrive a few minutes early and sit near the front, ready to learn and prepared with readings and assignments completed.

>> Dress academically and listen attentively.

>> Contribute to class discussions and ask timely questions.

>> Make class meaningful by refining notes within 24 hours and connecting ideas to previous content, course readings, and other courses.

Rely on yourself

Part of growing up and adjusting to college includes relying on yourself to figure things out. Do the following to be more self-reliant:

>> Ask questions. Faculty and staff choose their careers to help people like you. They are accustomed to seeing new students looking confused.

>> Make time to explore your campus to discover what's available.

>> Familiarize yourself with your school's web page and learning platform. Your school also has a technology center willing to help you with computer problems.

>> Prepare yourself to be a resource for other students.

>> Rely on self-motivation in the following ways:

- Post signs in your work area, reminding yourself of your short- and long-term goals.

- Post signs in your study area and write inspirational notes to yourself in your textbooks.

THE ART OF ASKING QUESTIONS

Your best source of course information comes from answers to questions you ask your professors — before, during, and after class, and during office hours. Ask your questions strategically and in a timely manner. Questions that can be answered quickly before and after class, and by email, include the following:

- "May I use your name for a reference?"
- "Is this an example of the type of artifact you suggest for the project?"
- "May I leave class a few minutes early for a job interview?"

During class, ask questions directly related to topics being discussed. If you consider prefacing a question with, "This is a little off topic, but. . .," don't ask the question at that time. Avoid prefacing questions with, "You're confusing me. . ." or "I'm confused. . ." Prefer language such as, "Could you clarify. . ." or "Could you further explain. . ." Also avoid asking questions such as, "Can you tell me everything that's due and when it's due?" You have the syllabus to answer that question, but you can also talk with the people at your academic success center about understanding syllabi.

For questions related to your grade, reviewing a paragraph or a project, and a questionable citation, visit your professor during office hours. And if you're questioning a grade, which you have the right to do, your tone says more than your words.

Finally, avoid asking logistical questions answered in the syllabus such as, "What time are office hours?" or "What's your email address?" You're telling your professor you haven't read the syllabus.

>> Absorb the academic energy of campus life that surrounds you — the mass of students migrating between classes to new learning opportunities, impromptu groups discussing classes, students in the dining hall studying while eating, and students reading in creative spaces. Immerse yourself in that community.

Study the syllabus

Your syllabus represents an almost legal document that binds you and your professor to completing course requirements. It lists all important course topics such as required books and materials, assignments and due dates, grading procedure, and office hours. It contains links to university policies regarding attendance, plagiarism, and class conduct, as well as to support resources. It contains your professor's contact information, such as email, telephone, and office location.

Use the syllabus to identify the exact spelling of your professor's name and the official course name and number. If the syllabus information requires updating, your professor will usually send you written notification.

If you don't understand syllabus language, which is a unique writing genre, visit your academic success center and the staff will review your syllabus with you.

Utilize class resources

Don't underestimate the resources that are immediately available to you: the syllabus (see the previous section), your professor, your learning platform, your own resourcefulness, and your classmates.

The following tips explain how you can use these resources to your advantage:

>> Refer to class examples and models whenever your professor provides them. They show your professor's expectations and represent A-work; otherwise, your professor wouldn't model them.

>> Search learning platforms for handouts your professor may not have identified in class.

>> Discuss ideas with your classmates. Ask them for their perspectives on class content.

Utilize office hours

Meeting with professors during office hours is as popular with college students as losing room keys is among first-year students. Professors choose their career to educate students, not to accumulate wealth. They're required to allocate approximately two walk-in office hours weekly for student availability. Use the opportunity. Walk in, introduce yourself, and ask your question. Your visit reinforces your commitment to your academics and your initiative to learn.

Utilize university resources

You're surrounded with resources to help you navigate requirements; these support services are included with your tuition. Resources are linked on your school's webpage, and many are included on your syllabus.

Most campuses provide services such as a writing center, academic success center, student tutoring services, advising center, campus safety facility, health and wellness center, psychological services, and fitness center.

If you have a support need as a college student, most campuses have a service to help you, or they can direct you to the help you need.

Cultivate relationships

At the college level, you accept responsibility for cultivating relationships with faculty, staff, and peers. Your professors teach about 80 students and meet with them about twice a week. You're taking classes with four or five professors. The math requires you to take the initiative.

Your professors learn your academic identity when you respond in class with perceptive comments, submit exceptional assignments, and ask thoughtful questions. Unfortunately, they'll also learn your identity when you fall short of expectations, miss class, or neglect assignments. When professors call you by name in class, you know you created an impression.

TIP

Cultivate relationships on campus by smiling and being prepared to offer a friendly "Hi." When in a group of students, initiate conversation with a "Hi, where're you from?" Researchers have identified "Where're you from?" as the best conversation starter because everyone is from somewhere.

Communicate

Communicate course issues with your professors before you miss a class or assignment. Email them when you'll miss class, arrive late, miss an assignment deadline, or experience a family emergency. Your email shows your concern for missing class. Don't ask if you missed anything and if class included anything important.

TIP

Partner with another student to take notes when either of you misses class.

When life circumstances result in you missing a deadline, communicate with your professor as soon as possible prior to the deadline. As much as professors like to say, "No late assignments are accepted," they're human and bend rules based on student circumstances.

Exercise

If you're self-motivated to work out, you understand the benefits of exercise and recognize the advantages of having fitness facilities on campus. College students need exercise to reduce stress and stimulate brain cells. Exercise also boosts energy and reduces health risks.

TIP

If you're not the gym-type, walking can achieve similar benefits. Walk regularly for about an hour at a pace of 15 to 20 minutes per mile.

REMEMBER

If you're beginning a new exercise program, check with your healthcare provider.

Examining APA Expectations

APA standards parallel expectations of the academic community requiring students to produce accurate and successful writing, citing, and formatting. College and high school students are expected to demonstrate proficiencies in standardizing research and learning the language of research and academic writing. Like other standards in higher education, learning APA requires commitment.

The complexity of APA requirements increases from high school through graduate school. Some high schools offer mini-courses dedicated to teaching APA. Like studying many languages, you study APA with immersion and regular practice. Many institutions recognize the challenge of learning a citation style and require that all their members follow one dedicated documentation style.

APA's expectations for documenting and formatting include the following:

>> Crediting research sources integrated into writing assignments and avoiding plagiarism

>> Establishing academic credibility with accurate citations and references

>> Providing information for readers to retrieve cited sources

>> Writing bias-free language that respects all populations

>> Following formatting guidelines that establish consistency for pages, heading levels, and section headings

Expectations also include the initiative to follow up questions on APA with your professor, writing center, and the *Publication Manual of the American Psychological Association, Seventh Edition*, in addition to this book.

Overcoming Adversity

You can turn failure into success by how you choose to respond to it. For example, if you fail a major test, you can accept it and do nothing — or you can talk with your professor, visit your school's academic success center, and gather information to develop an improvement plan. Unfortunately, students are also motivated by an adult in authority (such as a professor, parent, high school teacher, or advisor) who tells them they can't do something.

REMEMBER

You have overcome adversity to reach your present college academic level, and you'll continue to face adversity when learning APA. Use your failures as motivation toward success. Like most college students, you can accomplish much more than you think you are capable of.

Consider these names: J. K. Rowling, Steve Jobs, Bill Gates, Albert Einstein, Charles Darwin, Stephen King, Henry Ford, Thomas Edison, and Abraham Lincoln. Are they names of people who achieved innumerable successes? Yes, but they're also names of people who experienced innumerable failures.

Abraham Lincoln, for example, lost eight elections for public office, including two races for the U.S. Senate. He also experienced personal tragedies such as his mother dying when he was nine, poverty and bankruptcy, debilitating health issues, rejection from law school, and his fiancée dying.

J. K. Rowling's "Harry Potter" pitch was rejected by dozens of publishers, and Einstein was rejected for at least two teaching positions. Henry Ford failed to attract investors after failing in business several times, after which he said, "Apprentice yourself for failure." But all these icons credit their failures with producing their successes.

Research says that if you don't occasionally fail, you aren't trying hard enough and not challenging yourself enough. You most likely experienced failures before college, you'll also experience failures after college, and you don't receive an exemption from failure during college. College will challenge you physically, emotionally, socially, and academically. You'll experience failure with tests, courses, and also people.

But Lincoln, Ford, Einstein, Rowling, and the others named here learned from their failures and used them as motivation to succeed. They learned that failures often precede success and teach life lessons such as these:

>> Re-evaluating and revising your approach

>> Renewing your determination to succeed

>> Problem-solving from a different perspective

>> Increasing your determination to discover a solution

>> Learning what doesn't work

A major difference between overachievers and underachievers is that overachievers learn from their failures while underachievers don't. Recent research showed a high correlation between learning from your failures and transforming failures into successes. Other research showed that overachievers who produced masterpieces also produced a large number of poor-quality works. In other words, Edison produced boxcars of light bulbs that never saw daylight.

Identifying Discourse Communities You'll Encounter in College

Many college campuses include quiet buildings planted among open spaces. Within those buildings, voices speak *discourse*, the language of academia. Two cool-sounding words you'll hear your first few days on campus are pedagogy and discourse:

>> **Pedagogy:** You'll find it in every classroom. *Pedagogy* is the bubble that surrounds your classroom life, strategies identifying how you're taught, such as the following:

- Reading-centered instruction

- Team-oriented projects

- Lecture-style delivery

- Writing-centered assignments

- Discussion-centered instruction

Pedagogies, or teaching strategies, include learning theories such as Swiss psychologist Jean Piaget's (1896–1980) Theory of Cognitive Development and American educational psychologist Benjamin Bloom's (1913–1999) Domains of Learning.

>> **Discourse:** You'll find it inside and outside the pedagogical bubble. Discourse is the language of scholarship and of academic communities.

When you entered college, you became part of a discourse community, a member of an academic group of people who share discourse such as the following:

- Goals and purposes

- Beliefs, assumptions, values, and debatable issues

- Specific language used for speaking and writing

  Discourse vocabulary, referred to by linguists as *lexis*, identifies words and phrases shared by the community.

- Organized platforms for communicating, such as text, email, and podcasts

Discourse is used as a noun and a verb. As a noun, discourse signifies a collection or exchange of ideas: "The Writing Arts Department exchanges regular discourse with the Communication Studies Department." As a verb, discourse means to talk or converse: "The two departments continued to discourse throughout the semester." The plural of *discourse* (noun) is also *discourse* and occasionally *discourses*.

Use the words *pedagogy* and *discourse* with your family and friends. Tell them you learned that each discourse community has its unique pedagogical approaches. They'll think you're learning new concepts in college.

Each new discourse community adds to your academic experience — from your first-year orientation, through your college courses and APA application, and finally your college graduation.

College communities

As a member of the college community, you share the value of a college education, the commitment required to achieve it, the importance of earning good grades fairly and honestly, and the ability of your university to offer viable educational opportunities. You have learned the vernacular of campus life, vocabulary such as *bursar*, *registration*, *core courses*, *drop-add period*, *syllabus*, and *prerequisites*.

College is an intricate collection of discourse communities, various-sized groups of intellectuals who share common academic interests. For example, a discourse community of writing professors communicate with language such as *rhetoric, composition, engagement, tone, audience, voice,* and *conventions*. Issues debated by the discourse community include the following:

» Is the quality of college writing declining?

» Is gender bias decreasing in college writing?

>> Are new technologies affecting writing?

The writing discourse community believes in assumptions such as effective writing results from the following practices:

>> Recurring use of feedback and revising

>> Development of multiple drafts

>> Language shaped from audience and purpose

>> References from required readings

As you navigate your first few semesters, you'll become aware of dozens of discourse communities such as the following:

>> Athletics

>> Emergency services

>> New student orientation

>> Performing arts

>> Radio and television

>> Student life

>> Wellness

When you began research and referred to this book, you became part of the academic research community. And when you enter the workplace, you'll become part of another discourse community.

TECHNICAL STUFF

The language of discourse frequently exceeds the meaning of generic vocabulary. For example, the common understanding of *audience* is as a group of people who attend a public event such as a movie or play. But as vocabulary within the context of a discourse community and writing classroom, *audience* assumes the meaning of readers addressed by the writer who have specific needs for information that provides context for understanding the writing. The discourse meaning distinguishes itself from the meaning of the audience who attend a public event.

TIP

Each time you begin a new course, take notes using vocabulary that is common to the discipline. For example, language common to chemistry includes *absolute zero*, *critical mass*, *delocalization*, and *mass*.

Table 3-2 shows some discourse communities that are common to college campuses, and examples of their specific language.

TABLE 3-2 **College Discourses and Relevant Language**

Discourse Community	Specific Language
College admissions	coalition application, articulation agreement, and early action
Academic advising	developmental advising, student-centric tools, and developmental academic advisor
Health and fitness	suppressed energies, circuit, cross training, and dynamic warm-up

A number of discourse communities are included under the umbrella of education. They include the following:

>> Pre-K education

>> Elementary school education

>> Middle school education

>> Special education

>> Physical education

>> Driver education

>> Career education

>> Technical education

Discourse communities beyond education include the workplace, mass media transportation, public health, government, finance, communication, and supply chains.

Course communities

Each course you're enrolled in represents a distinct discourse community with its own unique beliefs and language. Your classroom success depends on understanding the discourses (assumptions, values, issues, and language) of each academic discipline. For example, the discourse of your math class may include the following:

- » Presenting problems and explaining the process

- » Using math terminology such as *variable, coefficient,* and *constant*

- » Verbalizing steps while solving problems

APA community

APA plays a double role as a style and citation standard and is representative in the discourse community. APA as a discourse community believes in the value of writing in an academic style, recognizing authors of referenced materials, and documenting sources in a standardized format. APA believes its standards promote the highest level of scholarship for professionals in the field, college undergraduates, and high school students.

APA's manual endorses assumptions such as the following:

- » Formatting requirements differ for professional scholars and undergraduates.

- » Language conventions have unique applications for citations and references.

- » APA's publication manual requires revision at appropriate intervals.

- » Bias-free language represents the highest priority of APA.

Vocabulary common to the APA discourse community includes *contract cheating, creative commons, Digital Object Identifiers* (DOIs), *deficit-based language, eLocator, self-plagiarism*, and the singular *they*.

Graduation community

A college-graduation discourse community interests college students like you by addressing graduation issues such as choice of program speaker, weather contingencies, and accommodations for accessibility. It also addresses topics such as credit requirements, institutional obstacles, three-year programs, and dual-degree programs.

Values shared by a graduation discourse community include the following:

- » College degrees require equal accessibility for all populations.

- » Graduate support programs increase graduation rates.

» Institutional obstacles contribute to extending degree time frames.

» A college degree improves financial stability of graduates, their families, and their communities.

Shared vocabulary of the graduation community includes the following:

» **Graduand:** Student about to graduate

» **Macebearer:** Faculty member who leads the academic procession, usually the longest-tenured faculty member

» **Regalia:** Elaborate dress worn by commencement participants

» **Hood:** A piece of clothing worn over the head and on the back of a robe, in a color symbolic of one's field of study (music, pink; business, beige; political science, dark blue; communication and journalism, crimson; education, pale blue; history, white; engineering, orange; sciences, yellow; and psychology, gold)

» **Robe or gown:** Dating to the 12th century, when professors were members of clergy and wore similar garb, with sleeve shapes symbolic of degrees (bachelor's sleeves pointed, master's oblong, and doctor's bell-shaped)

» **Mortarboard:** Traditional graduation cap symbolic of a mason's mixing board and frequently decorated with a student message

» **Biretta:** Worn in the 15th century and symbolic of superiority and intelligence; a faculty alternative to the mortarboard

» **Tassel:** Representative of student academic experience, with the turning symbolic of new educational status

» **Commencement:** Graduation ceremony symbolic of a new beginning

» **"Pomp and Circumstance":** Traditional graduation march written by Edward Elgar and first performed for the coronation of Edward VII

TIP

Motivate yourself with your anticipated graduation date by carrying a copy of the date with you, posting it in your study area, writing it on the inside cover of your book, and writing it in your class notes. Use the date as a reminder of your short-term goal and as a reason why you study. You can also remind younger siblings and younger family members of their anticipated graduation dates. About 13 percent of adults with bachelor's degrees earn a master's degree. But don't get ahead of yourself.

VISUALIZE YOUR COLLEGE GRADUATION CEREMONY

The first day of my college freshmen classes every September, I end class early and walk my students on a "field trip" to the location of their college graduation ceremony. I describe the setting as I witnessed it as a faculty member on stage the previous May. I describe the crowd of thousands of family members and friends surrounding the campus green and encircling almost three thousand graduates seated in endless rows of brown chairs. I identify graduates' seating locations by hoods signifying colors of their degrees.

The approximate 60-minute ceremony begins with "Pomp and Circumstance," and then the graduation procession, which is led by the macebearer followed by the administration, faculty, and staff dressed in full academic regalia and wearing colors representative of their universities and degrees.

When participants are seated on stage, the ceremony begins with the university president awarding honorary degrees. Following a few brief speeches, the president awards degrees with language such as, "By the power vested in me by the state, I hereby proclaim that the candidates in front of me have fulfilled the requirements for degrees in their field and declare them graduates." The class president then leads the traditional tassel turning from right to left.

The serenity of the ceremony represents the effort behind the degrees that were earned with years of study, sweat, sacrifice, and sometimes tears.

The brief ceremony is followed by the exit procession and a final playing of "Pomp and Circumstance." Your family and friends await you for warm hugs and congratulations. Hugs include more intensity if you're a first-generation college graduate. You have opportunities for photos of you wearing your cap and gown on campus. Be sure to include photos with younger siblings and younger family members. You're a role model for them to also earn their college degrees.

Because of the increasing size of many universities today, they also conduct a brief afternoon ceremony where you walk on stage when your name is called, receive your actual degree, and have a photo taken. You'll hear your family cheer for you when your name is called. Your graduation day represents one of the most memorable days in your life.

» **Pledging against plagiarism**

» **Fulfilling responsibilities**

» **Colliding cultures**

Chapter **4**

Protecting Scholarship: Plagiarism

enjoy science and don't usually miss an opportunity to attend a science lecture on campus. I recently attended a lecture about landmark scientific discoveries and heard stories about scientific achievements such as the following:

» Invention of the light bulb, and America's greatest inventor

» Development of more than 300 uses of the peanut

» Creation of the assembly line and the Model T

» A Nobel Prize in physics and chemistry

The scientists credited with these discoveries represented legends in their field: Toni Grogan, Jason Culbert, Rex Miles, and Eric Huber. Don't recognize these legends? Without policies of academic integrity and plagiarism requiring attribution of sources, you may never have heard of the actual owners of the rights to these discoveries — Thomas Edison, George Washington Carver, Henry Ford, and Marie Curie.

When you think plagiarism, think of protecting Edison's intellectual ownership of the light bulb and other inventions. And if you write a book, remember that you're entitled to the intellectual properties associated with that book.

In this chapter, I explain your responsibilities of avoiding plagiarism and protecting intellectual ownership by not misrepresenting the works of others. I also explain academic integrity and cultural conflicts resulting from differences between Western and Eastern beliefs about intellectual properties.

Academic Integrity: Get Your Sheepskin

A banking system is based on the financial reserve behind the currency it circulates. A system of higher learning is based on the academic integrity behind the students it serves and the diplomas it awards. Academic integrity is built on the principle that degrees are earned honestly and fairly, not earned falsely and awarded indiscriminately.

As I discuss in the following sections, students, faculty, and administration share responsibility protecting scholarship by understanding academic integrity, defending threats of academic breeches, and responding to trending research in academic plagiarism.

Defining academic integrity

Academic integrity, the foundation of a university's beliefs, advocates for the elimination of academic dishonesty and ensures that degrees are earned honestly through the fair exchange of intellectual properties. University policies enforce the quest for knowledge, based on the principles of honesty, commitment, responsibility, fairness, and respect — obligations of all shareholders.

Students' contribution to academic integrity includes a commitment to learning and satisfying curiosity and honestly and fairly creating meaning from classroom content. Students commit to learn within the guardrails of academic honesty.

Students and faculty provide frontline protection against academic dishonesty by championing honest academic performance. Academic protection needs a voice on campus as an uncompromising value. Academic integrity results from respecting ideas of experts in research and ideas of others in the classroom, especially when those ideas are unpopular.

TECHNICAL STUFF

Faculty contributions include aligning academic policy with syllabi and assignments, proactively discouraging plagiarism throughout the course, and creating an interesting classroom environment and assignments that challenge students to perform at maximum intellectual levels. Faculty commitment includes utilizing plagiarism-detection software and other resources provided to them to monitor academic honesty.

All shareholders need to ensure that assignments show students' own thinking. Student expectations far exceed merely crediting sources to avoid plagiarism. They also include demonstrating thinking that aligns with the experts being credited.

Student violations of academic codes fracture the value of individual degrees and frequently result in life-altering consequences such as dismissal from school. Violations of academic codes, though fortunately infrequent, negatively affect all degree holders of a university. When you occasionally see news stories of systemic institutional dishonesty, you question the integrity of every degree holder from that university. Dishonesty is the enemy of teaching and learning.

Imagine an academic institution where fairness isn't enforced, assignments aren't students' own work, faculty don't enforce policy, and integrity isn't valued. You can imagine that degrees aren't valued in that kind of setting.

TECHNICAL STUFF

Diplomas in the Middle Ages were composed of sheepskin, literally the hide of sheep, because of their durability when academicians carried degrees with them. More recently, selling sheepskin diplomas was a thriving business of a New York retailer. Today, a few prestigious universities continue to award sheepskin; they aren't the diploma of choice among vegetarians.

Looking at the research

Current research on academic plagiarism shows a disturbing trend of increasing violations and acceptance of dishonesty among college and high school students. The research shows behaviors by college and high school students that threaten the value of a college degree and college education. The ripple effect could include employers devaluing the academic integrity of universities that neglect to defend their academic process.

Here's a look at what the research shows for the groups studied:

- ≫ More than half of high school students reported cheating on a test at least once in the past year, and a third reported cheating at least twice.
- ≫ A third of high school students reported plagiarizing on an assignment using an online source.
- ≫ A third of college students reported paraphrasing and summarizing without crediting a source.
- ≫ Almost half of students believed that their instructors sometimes intentionally avoided reporting plagiarism.

>> A small percentage of undergraduate students reported fabricating sources, buying a paper online, and paying someone to write a paper.

>> Two-thirds of college students said they cheated at least once every academic semester.

But the good news is that plagiarism decreased in classrooms where it was discussed prior to beginning assignments.

Plagiarism and Academic Dishonesty: You Know Better

You as a student know the problem of plagiarism better than I do as a professor. I know it from the violations level, and you know it from the application level. You and I both know that the academic climate today expects high-level performance at record-breaking speed. But while producing your best work, you and I want to ensure that it's your own work, that you're proud of it, and that you feel good about it — and your mother would be proud to post it on the refrigerator door.

Academic dishonesty today reveals many shades of gray. The following sections look at some of the major classifications.

Cheating

Overt cheating includes borrowing, buying, or downloading third-party papers. It includes practices such as using past course papers and materials the professor didn't authorize for general assignment use. Cheating also includes talking with someone who just took a test you're scheduled to take, as well as looking at an unauthorized past assignment. Cheating erodes the value of academic achievement and the value of academic degrees.

Self-plagiarism

Self-plagiarism includes referencing a paper you wrote for another assignment or another course. In some circumstances, referencing your own paper may be appropriate with the explicit approval of your professor. Even with professor approval, a self-written paper may result in plagiarism issues that you don't want to get involved with. Students may self-plagiarize as a shortcut to starting a new assignment.

A safer and better academic practice is to begin papers and projects with original ideas.

Patchwriting

An academically dishonest practice expedited by technology includes *patchwriting*, or changing a few key words within a pasted paragraph. Patchwriting refocuses the purpose of reading and writing and is easily detected by plagiarism-detection software. Paraphrasing and citing require less effort than patchwriting and are more effective — and honest.

Conflicts of interest

A subtle form of academic dishonesty includes referencing sources in which the author has a financial interest in the research results — for example, a researcher's findings showing the effectiveness of a product when the researcher has a financial interest in that product. APA requires authors to also disclose conflicts of interest in an author note on the title page (see Chapter 14). You as an undergraduate should reveal conflicts of interest, for example, in an essay promoting the value of team sports if you're an athlete.

Unauthorized collaboration

Professors usually clarify acceptable and unacceptable collaboration associated with assignments. *Unauthorized collaboration* includes working on an assignment with another person without the professor's approval such as collaborating with another student, another professor, or an expert in the field. Team assignments clearly permit collaboration among team members. Other types of assignment collaboration require clear authorization by the professor. Ask about collaboration at the start of the assignment.

Falsification

Forms of academic misrepresentation include fabricating survey results, falsifying research, creating fictitious references, and intentionally misspelling an author's name or source. Each example discredits the integrity of the author's work.

A PROFESSOR'S PERSPECTIVE ON PLAGIARISM

I trust my students, but I'm not naïve. I don't look forward to student plagiarism issues any more than students do, but I accept ethical and legal responsibilities to enforce university codes of academic integrity. The process of investigating plagiarism is time consuming for faculty, but necessary to enforce academic integrity. I don't want to teach at an institution that compromises academic honesty.

When I read and grade assignments, plagiarism is listed on my mental rubric. If I see an initial plagiarism concern as I read papers, such as an inadequate citation or a complete lack of citation, I read for additional plagiarism indicators such as lack of coordination between citations and reference items (see Chapter 10). If I determine an indication of patterns, I schedule a student conference to raise my concerns and listen to the student's explanation. I ask the student to bring research notes to the conference. I run the paper through sophisticated plagiarism-detection software that the university provides for faculty. I also select four consecutive words uncommon to the student's prior writing and run an online search.

If my concerns remain following the student conference, I meet with my department chair to discuss the issues and continue to follow university procedures for plagiarism. After meeting with the department chair, the issue either ends or my concerns are presented to the Provost office and eventually the university review board.

I accept my obligation to regularly redesign assignments and create assignments with unique approaches that discourage plagiarism. I also recognize my responsibility to discuss academic honesty with every assignment and clarify assignment practices that are authorized or unauthorized.

Plagiarism

Plagiarism includes misrepresenting works of others as your own, whether intended or unintended. Examples of dishonest academic practices include

>> Lack of citing a summary, paraphrase, or quotation

>> Misidentifying an author's name

>> Neglecting attribution of ideas

>> Neglecting quotation marks enclosing direct words

>> Misidentifying common knowledge (see Chapter 10)

>> Fabricating citations and references

The danger of plagiarism is that it stops the learning process and starts the detection-avoidance process. Student energy becomes focused on "looking like I'm smart, but not too smart." Students lose an opportunity to research, write, and cite. They also lose the skill of reading for the purpose of developing a thesis; they read for the purpose of identifying content they can plagiarize without getting caught.

On a larger scale, plagiarism contributes to the devaluation of a university and a degree. Imagine how worthless a degree and university can become when plagiarism becomes common practice.

Avoiding Plagiarism: Your Responsibilities

You've been warned about plagiarism since you submitted your first assignment that included a list of sources called a *bibliography*, a cool word for a young scholar. You were threatened with plagiarism penalties such as 20 years' hard labor, 40 days of bread and water, and forfeiture of your video-gaming system. You heeded the threats, and you're in college today where the penalties are harsher. Plagiarism can derail a career and stigmatize violators for a lifetime. A quick online search reveals a surprising list of plagiarists.

Intentional plagiarism, such as buying a paper or copying and pasting text, represents a breech of academic integrity and results in serious consequences, including revoking degrees after graduation and a transcript notation indicating that you committed plagiarism. *Unintentional plagiarism,* which is disciplined less seriously in some universities and more consequential in others, takes an emotional toll in all situations. Unintentional plagiarism can be avoided, and a good night's sleep assured, with responsible academic practices that include the following.

Manage your time wisely

Managing time wisely reduces stress, a contributor to plagiarism that pressures you to accomplish more in less time. Time management helps you avoid academic pressure caused by too many assignments due in too few days. Begin assignments early and progress regularly. Your university offers resources for helping you manage your time.

Advocate academic integrity

You're an intelligent academic person, probably assertive, and the significant adults in your life taught you right from wrong. You bought this book because you take pride in APA academic accuracy and also honesty. Become an activist for academic integrity. When appropriate, defend your belief with your peers. Read your school's academic honesty policy and ask your professors questions about acceptable practices for assignments. Be a source of accurate information for your peers. Do your part to prevent your university becoming a victim of degree deflation.

Identify assignment limitations

Responsible academic practices begin by studying the syllabus and the assignment. The syllabus provides general integrity parameters for assignments, answering questions such as these:

>> What are collaboration parameters for team assignments?

>> Are assignments individually or team structured?

>> Are specific research sources authorized or unauthorized?

>> Is collaboration with a peer or family member authorized?

>> Is collaboration with other professors authorized?

Detail your research

Generations ago, when high tech included pens that wrote on upward inclines, researching was organized on note cards that recorded source identification and cards that recorded source information in the form of summaries, paraphrase, and quotations. The principles for word processing research remain the same as for the card system. Each time you identify a source, record the elements needed to enter it in the reference list. As you identify information from each source, record it as a summary, paraphrase, or direct quotation, and record page numbers.

TIP

A strategy for successful paraphrasing includes turning aside after reading the selection and writing your paraphrase without looking at the selection. (See Chapter 11 for detailed information on paraphrasing.) Unintentional plagiarism frequently results from the careless transfer of documentation information from your notes to your writing.

Approach your documentation sequentially by following these steps:

1. **Identify a source.**
2. **Record reference elements.**
3. **Extract information (summary, paraphrase, or quotation).**
4. **Identify page numbers.**
5. **Integrate the idea into the text.**
6. **Create the citation and enter the source into a reference item.**

Practice responsible citing

Your best defense against plagiarism is responsible citing. APA follows a consistent format for citations: Record the author and date, separated by a comma (Aston, 2020). For quotations, APA requires page numbers (Aston, 2020, p. 245). Many professors require a page number for paraphrase and summaries, but APA doesn't require it. For more on citations, see Chapter 10.

Utilize APA feedback resources

An effective approach to plagiarism protection is to have your APA citations and references reviewed by available resources, primarily your professor and writing center. When you contact your professor (by email or before or after class), clarify that you're requesting 15 minutes during office hours for the exclusive purpose of verifying your citations and references. Bring your research notes and this book. Show how organized you are by annotating your research paper, for example, by highlighting the information taken from your source (summary, paraphrase, and quotations) and underlining the attribution and signal phrase (see Chapter 11).

Team assignments also require adherence to standards of academic integrity and present additional challenges, with each team member held accountable for plagiarism by other team members. For example, if one team member plagiarizes, all team members are responsible for having submitted a plagiarized assignment. Honor codes intensify individual responsibilities by mandating that you report team members who plagiarize (see the nearby sidebar for more about honor codes). Many professors preview plagiarism before team assignments and require identification of team responsibilities for each section of team assignments.

Steer clear of unreliable strategies

Some common practices by inexperienced researchers produce a higher probability of plagiarism. Avoid these unreliable research strategies:

>> **Super citations:** A misrepresentation of crediting sources includes locating a citation at the end of a large section and thinking, "This is a super citation that credits everything I referenced in the previous section." Citations need to clearly identify the information they're referencing. Chapter 10 explains citations in detail and the importance of citing immediately following the referenced information.

>> **Citation procrastination:** An inadvertent form of plagiarism — but student accountable — results from carelessly recording the citation in your notes, and being unable to accurately retrieve it to cite it. Accurate citations begin with accurate note taking.

>> **Conditional common knowledge:** Common knowledge is a classification of information that generally doesn't require citations. However, it also includes a number of exceptions that require citations such as statistical data, disputable facts, and information not specific to the audience. (I detail common knowledge in Chapter 10.)

TIP

If you need to defend yourself against plagiarism, your best evidence is in the form of detailed notes that show your source in question, your extracted information, your reference in your text, and your citation.

TECHNICAL STUFF

Plagiarism-detection software is available with a variety of features, such as the ability to identify words, phrases, and sentences that require citations and also to check grammar and perform editing. Some versions are free, and some require a subscription. Most universities provide plagiarism software for faculty use. Common plagiarism-detection software includes Turnitin, CheckForPlagiarism, Grammarly, PlagiarismCheckerX, Noplag, Copyscape, CopyLeaks, and White-Smoke. With the evolution of artificial intelligence software, the capability to write essays should be available in the near future that will present another challenge to universities' battle against plagiarism.

Resumes are designed to reveal organizational and visual aesthetics with a ten-second glance, an eye test. A quick glance at a research paper can reveal potential indicators of plagiarism. Table 4-1 shows some examples of what a quick glance reveals about indicators of plagiarism.

TABLE 4-1   **Plagiarism versus Academic Integrity**

Looks Like Plagiarism	Looks Like Academic Integrity
Majority of sentences look like an essay that doesn't require sources.	Majority of sentences begin with researcher's name and include a date in parentheses.
Lacks headings such as discussion, results, and recommendations.	Contains required and appropriate optional headings throughout.
Little or no signal phrases that introduce paraphrase or summary.	Clear use of signal phrases such as *argued*, *supported*, and *questioned* (see Chapter 11).
Contains undocumented language and ideas beyond the student's level.	Clear distinction among voices of sources and author.
Inaccurately formatted reference page that lacks hanging indentations (see Chapter 12).	Accurately formatted reference page with hanging indentations.
Lacks required elements for references and citations.	Includes required elements for references and citations.

PLAGIARISM POLICY CONSEQUENCES

Most universities publish an academic integrity policy that includes definitions of academic misconduct. The policy, which identifies academic integrity expectations, contains examples of policy violations. The policy also includes university disciplinary actions that correspond with violations.

Academic integrity policies generally include three to five violation levels, ranging from inadvertent and unintentional plagiarism to a violation such as falsifying final grades. Levels of discipline include a transcript notation, academic probation, suspension, degree revocation, and expulsion. Repeated offenses raise the level of consequences. Alleged violations are presented to a review board consisting of students, faculty, and administrators.

Some universities administer minor discipline for minor violations such as neglecting to acknowledge sources for a few words or a sentence. Minor disciplining may include writing the paper without receiving a grade and scoring the paper one grade lower than the grade it would have received.

Closing Cultural Gaps: APA Strategies for Nonnative English Students

Studying both the English language and APA documentation will frustrate you. It's like learning to drive in the dark in a foreign country — with the car stuck in reverse. I know I can help you succeed because I know your determination from teaching students like you in the past. I taught one student who wrote A-level freshman essays by checking the spelling of almost every word in the dictionary. That's determination. You're on the right track. You've achieved high-level English literacy skills because you're reading and comprehending this book. That's also determination.

Beliefs and indifferences toward crediting sources and expert opinions vary among Eastern Hemisphere cultures and countries. Differences conflict with Western Hemisphere standards of academic integrity. The following sections take a closer look at the differences and provide some strategies you can use.

Grasping cultural differences in education

Your challenge of understanding APA begins with comprehending conflicting cultural differences between needing to credit what you take and simply being able to use what is free. Eastern cultural academic beliefs are like a smorgasbord where you can eat all you want and someone else is paying for it. You don't need to credit anything. Conversely, in the Western culture, nothing is free. Payment is required for everything, cash or credit. With research writing, credit is required for everything you take from another source. APA calls credit a citation.

American and Western systems of higher education attract numerous nonnative English speakers and other international students who contribute to the diversity of classroom ideas. But some of those cultures also contribute to the academic divide between Western and Eastern education — crediting sources. What Western culture understands as a pillar of academic integrity, Eastern cultures see as a gift to be shared among society. Western cultures believe that identifying sources is a writer's ethical responsibility and that the writer should provide a path for readers to explore that source. Some Eastern cultures believe in an openness of ideas, to the extent that authors' names are frequently omitted from what they write.

In many Eastern cultures, memorization of sources represents the highest form of academic respect, and writing ideas is discouraged. Plagiarism and crediting sources are as foreign to many of these students as a college bonfire and pep rally.

Policies of academic integrity vary among cultures and present serious challenges for international students enrolled in American universities. Schools that recruit international students usually provide advocate programs to help with the transition. These students face the challenges of learning English as an add-on language, adjusting to policies of academic integrity, and learning APA as a writing style and guide for crediting and formatting sources.

REMEMBER

Approach researching with the plan that you'll give credit to everything you take from sources you read — words, phrases, sentences, and ideas. If you take exact words, enclose them in quotation marks and cite the quote at the end of the sentence (see Chapter 10 for details). Citing too much is better than citing too little, because it won't result in plagiarism.

Utilizing additional APA strategies for nonnative English students

Here are some other APA strategies that are specific to the needs of students of English as an additional language:

>> Begin researching with library databases, ensuring quality and credibility of sources and generally eliminating concern for inferior sources.

>> Every time you read a research source, record notes that include reference elements (see Chapter 12). Record source information as paraphrase, summary, and direct quotation. Identify page numbers from which you take information. These strategies represent the foundation of crediting sources.

>> Read sources for the purpose of understanding the source's application to your writing. When you research, keep in front of you a copy of the sentence that identifies the purpose of your paper.

>> Use past research papers for successful APA documentation. For example, if you correctly use an artifact as a source, identify that citation and reference as a successful template for future use.

>> When papers are returned, collaborate with peers to review APA documentation and formatting, and share successful uses of APA.

HONOR CODE CONTROVERSIES

University honor codes, credited with first being established at William and Mary College in the early 1700s, establish accountability among students for ethical behavior in the classroom and on some campuses outside the classroom. The earliest honor codes of conduct were established by the U.S. military academies, which developed a code not to lie, cheat, or steal — or to tolerate anyone who does. Honor code colleges encourage proctors to leave the classroom during tests.

The phrase, "or to tolerate anyone who does," represents part of the controversy. Honor codes mandate that students who are aware of another student's cheating must reveal the violation or also be accused of cheating. Students never know when they'll be confronted by the plagiarism police, and on some campuses the accuser has the right to confidentiality.

Another controversy is that many honor codes prohibit collaboration because it conflicts with self-reliance, the belief that learning is an individual experience and ideas should be developed individually. Discouraging collaboration contradicts new learning theories and reduces collaboration practice required in many workplaces today.

Current research on colleges with honor codes reported that

- Students felt more pressure to report violations.
- Compliance with reporting violations was very low.
- A majority of students reported cheating at least once.
- Proctors would reduce cheating during tests.
- Many students witnessed cheating and didn't report it.

2

Earning Applause: APA Writing for the Academic Audience

Understand why parts of speech aren't created equal and that your success as a writer parallels your effective use of verbs and nouns.

Discover page navigation conventions that pace readers through dashes and slashes, semicolons and colons, parenthesis and brackets, italics and ellipsis — and reveal the story behind the cases.

Find out how to create a plan for lifetime literacy success.

Recall childhood lessons that apply to understanding bias-free language that respects race, age, disabilities, gender and gender identity, sexual orientation, and social economic references.

Apply revision strategies like a professional writer — strategies that can help you say more with less.

Understand why Mark Twain allegedly said, "I would have written a shorter letter, but I did not have the time," in reference to word-reduction strategies for multi-word verbs, superfluous verb endings, "ly" adverbs, and adjective clauses and phrases.

Chapter **5**

Writing for Success: APA Writing Style

Some academics identify writing as the highest intellectual activity performed by humans, an argument not endorsed by math and reading teachers. Writing, a brain add-on skill, requires thinking, planning, organizing, and revising — creating meaning with 26 letters.

Writing also requires regular reading and the accumulation of life experiences. Successful writing demands the same type of commitment and practice as is required by an athlete or musician. Without commitment and regular practice, athletes, musicians, and writers lose rhythm, flow, and instinctual patterns. Without commitment, you're unlikely to become a successful writer, just as you're unlikely to become a successful athlete or musician. With commitment, you can become all three.

Peer-reviewed scientific journals represent the most common form of publication for professors and other scholars. Student papers represent the most common form of scholarly contributions by undergraduates and high school students. APA's standard for all scholarly papers includes "an original contribution" and "appropriate citations to the works of others."

APA writing emphasizes clear communication of scholarly ideas with precise and concise word choices, organized in a logical structure. Characteristics of successful academic writing for college and high school students include

» Information-based content

» Predictable structure and organization

» Subject-action-verb sentence patterns

» Appropriate graphic organizers

» Limited compositional risk strategies

Smooth-flowing, concise writing, recommended by APA and professional writing organizations, begins when you have identified your specific audience and a clear writing purpose. In this chapter, I explain academic writing strategies and how to adapt the APA writing style to your audience, purpose, approach, and focus. I also provide techniques for smooth-flowing text with appropriate tone and respectful language. Switch your phone to mute, position your water bottle, unstrap your backpack, and get your game on.

REMEMBER

Use the following Mount Rushmore of APA strategies in your writing:

» Address the academic audience with a formal, informational writing style.

» Design a writing message with laser focus.

» Use transitional strategies to connect ideas.

» Prioritize unbiased, respectful language.

Focusing on the Why and How: Audience and Purpose

No creative person knew his audience better than Apple co-founder Steve Jobs, whose biography is portrayed in Walter Isaacson's *Steve Jobs* (Simon & Schuster). Jobs created an iPhone for an audience who didn't know they wanted or needed one. He anticipated that his audience (the consumer) was willing to pay budget-breaking costs, sign contracts for expensive monthly plans, and upgrade as frequently as college tuition increases occur. Jobs addressed his audience by providing them devices they could navigate based on their background. You as a writer are similarly required to address your audience with the information they need based on their background on the topic.

As the author of this book, I anticipated your needs as my audience. I assumed that you know of Steve Jobs, and that you're one of 98 percent of adults who own a cell phone. I chose not to reference a brick phone, rotary phone, or can-and-string communication — technologies of your grandparents. I anticipated that you connected APA with GPA and that you realize the real world lacks spring break and class cuts. I'm confident you can write to fulfill your academic purposes, understand the basics of the research process, and comprehend APA vocabulary such as *citation*, *reference*, *source*, and especially *plagiarism*.

Most college writing assignments identify the audience and purpose, which then influences your language, style, tone, and supporting evidence. The following sections cover audience and purpose in more detail.

Academic and assignment audience

Because you're an academic writer following APA guidelines, your success depends on understanding your academic audience. First, you're writing for your professors who are knowledgeable and well read and who thrive on thinking about

» The challenge of new positions on a topic

» A new slant to an old position

» Answers to questions and questions to answers

» Challenges to the status quo

Your professors expect you to think at a college level. When you don't, you can expect one of two minimal grades that rhyme with "B."

In addition to having professors as your audience, you are frequently required to address a secondary audience for an assignment, including the following:

» **Community leaders** — for example, convincing them of the value of trash-to-steam plants

» **Government leaders** — for example, justifying to Congress the benefits of a national service plan that reduces college debt

» **School leaders** — for example, convincing your athletic department to fund e-gaming

» **The public** — for example, persuading (or dissuading) the public of the environmental benefits of plant-based foods

Your secondary audience expects language that speaks to them. Both that audience and your professors expect timely academic sources, evidence-based support, and topic analysis demonstrating critical thinking.

TIP

Avoid thinking that your professors comprehend your writing because they're smarter than you. You as the writer assume responsibility for expressing ideas clearly to your reader. The reader doesn't assume responsibility for deciphering the writer's message. Your writing ideas must be clear to you as a writer before they're clear to your readers. A peer editor can help you identify language that is unclear to your audience.

REMEMBER

The following questions can help you identify your audience and ensure that your writing is easy for them to understand (feel free to amend as you see fit):

>> Can your audience be identified by characteristics such as age, education, interests, and topic background?

>> Does your opening engage their interest in the topic?

>> Do you intellectually challenge your audience (including your professor)?

>> Is the audience background underestimated or overestimated?

>> What value does the topic offer your readers?

>> Is vocabulary consistent with their understanding of the topic?

>> Are writing examples and references relevant to them?

>> Does the writing answer their anticipated questions?

TIP

High-achieving students read extensively to complement their writing. They also reference their readings regularly in their writing, which impresses professors (their primary audience) and usually earns exceptional grades. Reading and writing are as important to high-achieving students as cell phones and keys; college students can't survive without either pair. (Flip to Chapter 9 for more on the importance of reading and writing.)

Purpose

Steve Jobs analyzed his audience and worked with a clear purpose; he valued an innovator legacy more than a financial portfolio. His purpose was to disrupt innovation, where art meets technology. He prioritized product coolness.

Your writing success also depends on a clear writing purpose, one that exceeds earning a grade. If you've sarcastically preceded an assignment with the question, "What's the purpose?" then you actually asked a useful question to focus your writing. Traditional writing purposes include informing, explaining, analyzing, persuading, arguing, and qualifying. Assignments frequently identify purpose as the key writing task, which usually includes a form of arguing or persuading. "What's the purpose?" isn't a question to ask your professor in class.

TIP

Determine your reader's purpose by completing the statement, "The purpose of this paper is to argue . . ." Examples of successful and focused purposes that complete the statement include

>> Environmentally friendly strategies for improving mass transportation

>> Influences of sibling position on leadership

>> Justification of payment to Division I collegiate athletes

>> Economic benefits of careers in the trades

>> Improvements in U.S. health care delivery due to the COVID-19 pandemic

REMEMBER

Answers to the following questions help determine your writing purpose:

>> Is the purpose focused, neither too general nor too specific?

>> Does the purpose appeal to the academic audience?

>> Does the purpose address a position that challenges the thinking of the academic audience?

>> Does the purpose offer the reader a new approach to a topic or a new way to look at an old approach?

>> Does the purpose fulfill readers' expectations?

Zeroing In: Assignment Approach and Focus

If APA were planning an awards party, *audience* and *purpose* would be invited because they're well connected and confident. But the guests of honor would be *approach* and *focus*, a pair of writing skills that know how to accomplish the goals they want to achieve it. Writing without a predetermined approach and focus usually results in a professor commenting that the paper "lacks focus," as well as a frustrated student. Determining approach and focus is like programming your GPS before a road trip. A successful approach and focus helps you enjoy the journey and celebrate the destination — writing a successful paper.

Approach

Begin your assignment *approach* by analyzing your purpose and key task. For example, if you're required to evaluate the psychological benefits of pets on college campuses (think a fluffy Golden Retriever named Boomer), you're arguing the importance of reducing stress on college students. Your approach dictates researching topics such as "psychological benefits of pets on campus" and "stress on college students." The approach helps develop the focus. And if your academic goal exceeds "C's get degrees," then offer your professor original thinking such as "a pet's stress reduction correlates with the pet owner's relationship with the pet," or "student stress reduction correlates with exercise frequency and social interaction." You may also discover that Boomer benefits intellectually.

REMEMBER

Professors teaching a course numerous times frequently identify patterns of past assignment misunderstandings and list approaches *not* to include, such as outlines, irrelevant content, outdated sources, and .com sources. Your logistical approach to the assignment should include identifying length, preliminary draft requirements, due date, and file submission formats. Also note APA optional requirements such as title page, table of contents, abstract, figures, and annotated references. As you begin your research, record source elements required for your APA reference page: author, source, title, date, volume, database, and so forth. You can review reference elements in Chapter 12.

The key task question sets into motion your assignment's sequential approach, such as drafting your purpose statement (called a *claim* or *thesis*), researching your supporting evidence, and critically analyzing your topic — the heartbeat of your grade. You then write the middle section, responding to the key question. After drafting the middle section, you write the ending, and finally the beginning. The beginning or introduction is written last, when you identify content to be introduced.

REMEMBER

If your learning style requires a sequential approach to writing, start at the beginning and write through the middle to the ending. But plan to revise the beginning after discovering your argument and analysis in the middle section. See Chapter 8 for more information on revising.

REMEMBER

Answers to the following questions help you determine your writing approach:

>> What's the general context of the assignment within course parameters?

>> What content does the assignment suggest for the beginning, middle, and ending?

>> What assignment questions are required to be answered?

>> What models are offered illustrating instructor requirements?

>> What assignment ideas suggest new thinking on the topic?

>> What approach to this topic appeals to the academic audience?

>> If you were the instructor, what would you expect students to learn?

>> What approach options does the paper offer: interviewing, surveying, or observing?

Focus

Focus is like your wireless connection to your online service, the thread that connects your device with your learning and gaming. No connection, no activity. Writing focus is the connective thread from your title through to your ending. It connects project development with paragraph purpose. It also connects the writing's beginning, middle, and ending. No connection, no focused message.

Answers to the following questions help you determine your writing focus:

>> Are the beginning and ending connected to the thesis of the middle paragraphs?

>> Does every paragraph enhance the thesis?

>> Does any paragraph appear to drift from the focus?

>> Does the development of focus follow a sequential and logical pattern?

A reverse outline validates your focus. Summarize each paragraph topic with three or four keywords, and verify that each summarized topic contributes to the development of the thesis. Also evaluate whether paragraph topics can be organized more sequentially and logically. Here are examples of a reverse outline that identifies paragraph purposes (bolded):

Evidence supporting the problem: Cooper's 2017 "Causes of Childhood Injuries" reported that among children, bicycle accidents are the most common cause of serious head injuries. She also found that most of these injuries in children are preventable, but helmet use among children nationwide is just under 50 percent. The National Highway Traffic Safety Association (NHTSA) reported that 857 bicyclists were killed in motor vehicle crashes in 2018.

Evidence supporting wearing helmets: Wearing bicycle helmets, especially among casually riding adults, ranks as popular as a colonoscopy. Carlson's 2020 "Serious Injuries Among Serious Bicyclists" found that more than 90 percent of cyclists killed in traffic wore no helmet. The same study also found that serious injuries among helmet users were as low as 15 percent.

Evidence supporting helmet use: The major contributors to increasing children's helmet use have been state legislatures and enforcement. Pennsylvania and New Jersey were among the first states to mandate helmet use for children.

Both college-level focus and your professor's expectation require critical thinking — analyzing information and making reasoned judgments. Questions for developing critical thinking include

» What's surprising about the topic?

» What related subtopics need additional exploring?

» What trends or patterns surfaced?

» Is this topic associated with other academic interests?

» Is the topic relevant to current events?

» How does discussion of this topic improve lives, organizations, and institutions?

» Is this topic relevant to course objectives, historical themes, or popular books?

TIP

Your early writing decision of topic approach frequently determines whether a writing project will be successful or unsuccessful. You increase your opportunity for a higher grade if you avoid topics that are too common, too narrow, too broad, too complex, too abstract, or too emotional.

Smooth Sailing: Transitions and Flow

Obsessed with watersports, I recently enrolled in Sunfish sailing lessons. I became proficient at climbing back into the boat after constantly flipping myself into the Gulf of Mexico. I transitioned from sailing with my instructor to sailing solo. I then transitioned to tacking, jibbing, and coming about — strategies that kept me sailing smoothly on the water rather than in it. Without transitions, I would have been dead in the water.

Writing, like sailing, requires successful transitions to remain on course. With transitions, your writing flows smoothly and clarifies relationships between ideas. Without transitions, readers lack guidance to build relationships among ideas, like a pile of unconnected toy-building blocks.

Smooth writing requires transitional strategies at the organizational, paragraph, and sentence levels. Professor comments indicative of successful transitions include *well developed, good flow,* and *good focus.* Comments indicative of being dead in the water include *lacks flow*, *choppy*, and *needs restructuring*. Additionally, if a peer reader expresses difficulty in following your flow of ideas, you have an organizational and transitional issue. The following sections explore transitional strategies in greater detail.

Organizational flow

Transitioning begins with a structural organization that flows throughout the writing — from the beginning, through the middle, and to the ending. You can initially establish flow by separating the beginning and ending from the middle. The beginning, or introduction, includes

>> **A title and first sentence that attract readers to the topic.**

>>> **Title:** Pulitzer Prize Author Illustrates Wright Brothers' Literacy-Rich Childhood

>>> **First sentence:** "Choose good parents and grow up in Ohio," said Wilbur Wright, offering advice for success in life.

>> **Information about the topic that teases out questions to be answered.**

>>> The names Susan and Milton (a bishop of the Church of the United Brethren in Christ) lack the notoriety of those of their famous sons, but the aviation achievements of their sons Wilbur and Orville are directly attributed to their parents' home environment, which encouraged curiosity, perseverance, problem solving, attention to detail, and intellectual development.

>> **An indication of the topic approach and focus.**

>>> In addition to their parents providing love and emotional security, they also modeled strong reading, writing, and inventiveness.

Ending strategies include summary, reflection, significance, and final message.

>> **Summary:** In the past few years, our differences as Americans have defined us on race, religion, social justice, and political beliefs. America owes more to those thousands of faces who were murdered pursuing the opportunities America has offered. We can't return to the carefree, spontaneous America of September 10th, but we can return to the compassionate and united America of September 12th.

>> **Reflection:** College freshmen and seniors reflect similar anxiety — freshmen fear the unknown coming into college; seniors fear the unknown going out.

>> **Significance:** FDR's leadership modeled building trust with voters, choosing effective leaders, reaching decisions collaboratively, trusting that Americans wanted to work, and intervening when capitalism failed. More importantly, he taught Congress that helping people was a higher priority than being Democrat or Republican.

>> **Final message:** The argument required to insist your child wear a helmet is less stressful than the nightmare if your child is involved in a bicycle accident while not wearing a helmet.

TIP

The middle section of the project, the argument development, represents your major challenge and the major influence of your grade. Begin your argument (the beginning of your middle) with a sentence that includes your claim or thesis. Present your support (your research) from worst to first, saving your best evidence for last — like ending a meal with dessert.

REMEMBER

Successful organizational flow includes a clearly delineated ending of the beginning, beginning and ending of the middle, and beginning of the ending — more beginnings and endings than the love life of a teenager. Within that organization, develop a plan for delivering content in patterns such as chronologically, general to specific, cause and effect, and support and implication. To maintain flow, connect your ideas and support them with your focus. I discuss these patterns in Chapter 8.

Transition strategies

Think of transitions as bridges that connect your paths on campus — shuttles, short walks, skateboards, bicycles, and elevators. Your day crashes if you miss a shuttle, walk into a detour, blow a wheel, or get trapped in an elevator. Similarly, your writing flow crashes if ideas fail to connect. APA warns that lack of transitions may indicate that "you have abandoned an argument or theme prematurely."

Key transitional strategies, and their applications that indicate continuing an argument, include

>> **Similarity** — *also, furthermore, likewise,* and *in addition to*

   Furthermore, Wilbur described their challenge as "the ability to ride with the wind, to balance and steer in the air."

>> **Contrast** — *but, however,* and *on the contrary*

   But surprisingly, Bishop Wright allowed the brothers to occasionally miss school if the boys were engaged in a worthy scientific project or an interesting book.

>> **Summary** — *finally, in conclusion,* and *to sum up*

> Finally, the Wright brothers' success was achieved with home education that encouraged intellectual curiosity and modeled the most basic literacy skills: "Everyone in the house read all the time."

>> **Time** — *next, afterwards, later,* and *initially*

> Later they built the first "man-carrying glider" for less than fifteen dollars in a room above their bicycle shop.

>> **Sequence** — *first, second, finally, next,* and *eventually*

> Eventually they achieved a series of successful manned flights.

>> **Cause and effect** — *consequently, therefore,* and *as a result*

> Their argument over propeller direction resulted first in each taking the other's side and then realizing that they needed two propellers rotating in opposite directions.

These strategies transition the development of arguments within paragraphs as well as between paragraphs.

Additional indicators of transitions include indentations, headings, subheadings, and sidebars. Transitions help your reader navigate your sea of ideas.

Answers to the following questions help you determine transitions and flow:

>> Does every paragraph contribute to the flow of the focus?

>> Does the topic flow follow an organized, logical pattern?

>> Does every paragraph show evidence of a transitional strategy, explicit or implied?

>> Do the paragraphs show relationships with preceding and succeeding ones?

TIP

As you read leisurely, read from the perspective of a writer. As you read, identify the writer's transitional strategies.

Writing with Attitude: Tone

As a child, when you talked with your parents, demonstrating attitude or tone earned you a reprimand; when you write to your instructors in the classroom, demonstrating attitude or tone earns you praise. If you're an athlete, tone is your post-score celebration. If you're a cook, tone is your presentation on the plate. Tone, your attitude toward your audience and message, is determined by your content and purpose.

Controlling your writing tone provides you with the flexibility to express yourself forcefully or in a friendly way, formally or informally, sarcastically or serenely, or dramatically or comically. APA's recommendation for achieving tone is to "imagine a specific reader you intend to reach, and write in a way that will inform and persuade that individual."

Writing an array of papers across a variety of college courses requires application of a range of tones. For example, a playful, humorous tone frequently applies to sports and music topics, a satirical, sarcastic tone frequently applies to pop culture topics, and a serious or sober tone frequently applies to health issue topics. For almost all social science topics, especially scientific topics, APA recommends an informational, formal, and confident tone — like a conversation with your professor after learning your emailed final project disintegrated in cyberspace.

TIP

Nonscientific papers (especially essays) allow tone flexibility ranging from serious to sarcastic. Content such as writing to an instructor almost always requires a serious, formal tone; content such as writing to a sibling and a peer frequently requires a humorous, informal tone.

APA recommends identifying researchers' differences of opinion with a "noncombative" tone. Note the difference in the following examples:

>> **Combative language** — "Gaven (2021) completely neglected . . ."

>> **Noncombative language** — "Gaven (2021) lacked referencing . . ."

Tone is frequently determined by one or two words:

> *Bridget introduced John, her **current** boyfriend.* (John shouldn't pay cash for Bridget's Valentine's Day gift.)

> *The professor's explanation was more bizarre **than usual**.* (Don't let the professor hear what you're thinking.)

REMEMBER

A powerful two-letter tone word in the English language is *no*. With no explanation, *no* can't be weakened or rebutted. Simply stated, *no* means no. The tone of *no* weakens when you add qualifications: *No, I am not comfortable.* Qualifications can be rebutted; an exclusive *no* can't be argued.

APA says that contractions, colloquialisms, and similar informal language "distract from a professional tone in academic writing." (*Note:* That differs from this book. The For Dummies brand uses contractions.) You should almost always avoid the following patterns of informal language:

>> *Contractions* (two words condensed into one with an apostrophe). If you're unfamiliar with contractions, see *English Grammar For Dummies* by Geraldine Woods (John Wiley & Sons, Inc.). You can include contractions in direct quotations.

>> *Colloquialisms* (informal language that should generally be avoided in formal writing). Examples include *beats the heck out of me, doesn't mean diddly-squat, gonna* (going to)*,* and *hoodwinked* (duped).

>> *Clichés* (overused expressions that should generally be avoided in formal writing). Examples include *searched high and low, proof is in the pudding, prime example,* and *on pins and needles.*

>> *Jargon* (specific language common to a profession or group that may be unfamiliar to general audiences). Examples include *the ball is in their court, bottom line,* and *due diligence.*

>> *Idioms* (spoken-language expressions whose meaning differs from the literal understanding of the words). Examples include *penny for your thoughts, burn the midnight oil,* and *jump on the bandwagon.*

Here's a real-life example of the importance of tone. During the COVID-19 pandemic in 2020, language describing states' request for people to remain at home frequently communicated an incorrect tone. Note how the tone changes with the following words:

>> **Shelter-in-place** (references threats)

>> **Lockdown** (references institutional emergencies)

>> **Quarantine** (references a health department's order to remain indoors because of a contagious disease)

>> **Hibernate** (references animals conserving energy)

Most states issued *stay-at-home* or *safe-at-home* orders, both of which have a more agreeable tone.

Tone also comes into play with project presentation. If a hard copy is required, establish tone with a well-organized, visually pleasing package containing a clean copy. If an electronic submission is required, submit the recommended file format (usually a PDF) with the recommended filename and appropriate hard page breaks. Email your assignment to yourself to ensure there is no loss of formatting. See Chapter 15 for details on formatting.

Recalling Sandbox Lessons: Respectful Language

The locations of some of the most important lessons you learned in your lifetime include the playground, the athletic field, and the sandbox. These environments are like laboratories where most parents try to teach their children to be kind, caring, and respectful. You're a considerate person today (also intelligent because you bought this book) because of numerous reminders from the significant adults in your life who regularly said: "Be nice." "Be kind." "Share your toys." "Wait your turn."

Adults' "nice" and "kind" reminders referred to your respectful words to your young peers. The hurtful meaning of words contradicts an age-old childhood chant: "Sticks and stones may break my bones, but names will never hurt me." Disrespectful language — biased references to appearance, race, religion, gender and gender identity, sexual orientation, socioeconomic status, and more — hurts longer than the healing time of broken bones.

You also learned respect by participating in sports and similar activities. Professional sports in the United States experienced a metamorphosis after historical patterns of racial discrimination. Most athletes on all levels today value teammates for their ability to perform, regardless of their background. Minorities experienced racial discrimination and were banned from participating in professional leagues.

"I am not concerned with your liking or disliking me . . . all I ask is that you respect me as a human being," said Jackie Robinson, the object of racial abuse and the first Black man to play Major League Baseball for the Brooklyn Dodgers at Ebbets Field on April 15, 1947. Major League Baseball honors Robinson's racial justice accomplishment on that date annually, with every Major League player wearing his number, 42. Using language that is respectful to all human beings also honors Robinson. APA's recommendation to use bias-free language represents a goal of every academic writer and every respectable writing community.

REMEMBER

General guidelines for unbiased and respectful language in APA include the following:

>> Using people-first language to identify people with disabilities. Avoid language highlighting their disability.

>> Preferring gender-neutral language to gender-specific terms related to business and selected occupations.

>> Avoiding perpetuating stereotypes that denigrate people according to race, age, disability, gender, and sexual orientation.

>> Avoiding extreme comparisons of groups using language such as *normal*, *the average person*, *most people*, and *the general public*.

>> Additional topics that require language sensitivity and respectful choices include marriage, religion, and politics.

REMEMBER

APA identifies bias-free language choices as guidelines and suggestions, not as recommendations or requirements. Language, like people, grows and evolves. Words appropriate to one generation may eventually become unacceptable to another generation. The language recommended in this chapter is generally acceptable to most people and groups, but some people and groups may disagree. Because rhetorical situations vary, choose the most appropriate words for the writing requirement. Choose language that is sensitive to your readers, and ensure that it is positive and respectful. If you question a word's sensitivity, seek a second opinion.

Racial and ethnic references

Principles for respectful racial and ethnic references include

>> Avoiding inappropriate and unnecessary references to race. If you're talking about children traveling with stuffed animals, for example, references to the children's race lacks relevance.

>> Avoiding racial stereotypes, as well as exaggerated mental images that negatively associate a race with dress, appearance, food, and so forth.

Age and disability references

Principles for respectful age and disability references include

>> **APA suggests "exact ages or age ranges."** Some examples are older adults, 60- to 75-year-olds, the over-80 crowd, septuagenarians, octogenarians, nonagenarians, and centenarians.

   • **Biased:** The *elderly* were seated near the elevators.

   • **Revised:** *Senior citizens* were seated near the elevators.

   Elderly implies too large a group of people. It also implies a stereotype of fragility, a reference unacceptable to senior citizens who skydive and run marathons.

Language offensive to some senior citizens includes *old people, older people, oldest, old, old timers, elders, the aged,* and *seasoned adults.*

>> **Emphasize the person and not the disability.** APA recommends the phrase, "a person with."

- **Biased:** *Diabetics* check blood sugar regularly.
- **Revised:** *People with diabetes* check blood sugar regularly.

Language offensive to some people with disabilities includes *disabled, handicapped, crippled, mental retardation, mentally ill, wheelchair-bound, victim, suffering with,* and *afflicted with.*

Gender and sexual orientation references

References to gender and sexual orientation also require the sensitivity of a psychologist. Apply the "self-test" — How would you feel if the words were written about you? — before going public by hitting the Send button.

Gender references

Principles for respectful gender references include

>> **Using parallel gender references.** For example, use *girl* where you would use *boy, woman* where you would use *man, lady* where you would use *gentleman,* and *female* where you would use *male.*

- **Biased:** The *girls* in the lab collected data.
- **Revised:** The *women* in the lab collected data.

Both *girl* and *boy* imply a younger age than *women* and *men. Girl* and *boy* also imply informal colloquialism. APA recommends formal language, such as *men* and *women* when referencing adults. Gender references to high school students include *boys* and *girls.* Gender references to college students include *men* and *women.*

>> **Use neutral pronoun references.** An easy way to do this is to use the plural rather than the singular as the subject of a sentence.

- **Biased:** Each manager must prepare *his* department for working virtually.
- **Revised:** Managers must prepare *their* departments for working virtually.

>> **Avoid gender-specific stereotypes for occupations.** Examples include construction workers, secretaries, doctors, nurses, letter carriers, police officers, business owners, and flight attendants.

- **Biased:** When the doctor arrived, *she* immediately examined *her* patient.

- **Revised:** The doctor arrived and immediately examined the patient.

The following table has additional examples of biased gender language and acceptable revisions.

Biased	Revised	Biased	Revised
mankind	people/humans	man-made	manufactured
man-hours	staff-hours	chairman	chair
salesman	salesperson	spokesman	spokesperson

Some gender language issues remain in transition, as in the following examples:

>> **Can a women's basketball team play man-to-man defense?** Currently, when most male and female basketball teams play pressure defense, they identify their style of play as *man-to-man* defense. Among coaches of female teams, the terms *person-to-person* and *player-to-player* defense are gaining in popularity. For basketball fans, playing zone defense doesn't resolve the gender language issue.

>> **What's the most feared alert at sea?** Crew members at sea drill to react to "man overboard." One-syllable *man* requires less time to alert the crew than the two-syllable *person* or *woman*. U.S. Coast Guard documentation is beginning to reflect gender-neutral *person overboard*. Gender-neutral *personal flotation device* (PFD) helps you if you fall overboard but does not resolve the *man overboard* alert issue.

Avoid activity that risks falling overboard. Also, keep dogs safe on board because no terminology addresses if they fall overboard. But if they do, they have a stroke named after them.

Gender identity and sexual orientation references

APA's general categorization of *sexual orientation*, a person's feeling and sense of identity, includes heterosexual, bisexual, and homosexual. APA identifies nonbinary gender such as genderqueer, gender-nonconforming, gender-neutral, agender, and gender-fluid. Gender identity, exclusive of sexual orientation, includes transgender men and cisgender women.

REMEMBER

Specific gender identities are relevant for researchers, usually graduate students, identifying participants in a study. The academic community, at all levels, values respecting all people.

Sexual orientation language that is APA-acceptable includes *lesbians* and *gay men* (preferred to homosexuals). Also avoid *sexual preference, he/she, (s)he*, and alternating male and female pronouns.

Socioeconomic references

Principles for respectful socioeconomic references include

>> Focusing on what people have, rather than what they don't have

>> Avoiding offensive stereotypes

APA identifies socioeconomic status as income and "educational attainment, occupational prestige, and subjective perceptions of social status and social class." Terminology in this section applies primarily to professional researchers in their Methods section, but also generally to undergraduates, following their professors' guidelines.

APA recommends avoiding derogative language such as *low income, the poor, inner city, the projects*, and *poverty*. They prefer positive language such as *people experiencing homelessness* to *the homeless* and *opportunity gap* to *achievement gap*.

Chapter **6**

Creating a Foundation: The Principal Parts of Speech, Structure, and Usage

My obsession with language began as an elementary school student, learning grammar lyrics to a famous college fight song:

Pronouns and nouns, we meet face to face,

Person, number, gender, and case.

A diagram we know is work,

From which we will never shirk.

My passion for language continued through John Mooney's English class at St. James High School, where I developed proficiencies such as ten basic rules for the comma, nine classifications of pronouns, eight varieties of nouns, seven uses of the colon, six characteristics of clauses, and five properties of verbs.

Through high school my obsession continued. I was fascinated with grammar fundamentals and *diagrams*, visual displays of sentences. I would never *shirk* learning grammar or creating images of sentences. My passion with grammar continues today as I adjust to changes of rules that have existed for centuries.

This chapter helps you capitalize on key parts of speech to add vigor to your writing, become sociable with disagreeable nouns and pronouns, and apply usage strategies to navigate potholes and pitfalls of written communication.

Shining the Spotlight on the Stars of the Show: Action Verbs

Every college semester, I ask my writing students to name the eight parts of speech. In two decades, only one student successfully responded — her mother was an English teacher. Most students named two: verb and noun.

Fortunately, no studies correlate knowledge of parts of speech with writing success, and English teachers appear to be among the few educated people who can name and explain them. Also, the fact that so many people understand verbs confirms American novelist Ernest Hemingway's emphasis on action verbs as writers' primary part of speech. Action verbs are what's happening. APA highlights the verb properties of voice, number (agreement), and tense, and I clarify what you need to know in the following sections.

Using your voice

When writing, you need to lose half your voice, the passive half. Verb *voice* identifies the subject as the performer of the action (*active voice*) or receiver of the action (*passive voice*). College writing departments recommend almost exclusive use of active voice. John Wiley & Sons, Inc., publisher of this book, clarifies their position: "Avoid using passive voice." APA warns that "many writers overuse the passive voice." You're probably not a vocalist, but take this voice lesson.

Active voice: Mariah prepared a margherita pizza.

Passive voice: A margherita pizza was prepared by Mariah.

The active voice example shows *Mariah* as the performer of the action. She *prepared* the margherita pizza — everyone enjoyed it. The passive voice example shows *pizza* as the receiver of the action. Passive voice verbs usually include a form of the verb *to be: am, is, are, was, were, be,* and *been.*

TIP

Action verbs, the oxygen of written communication, breathe life into your sentences and paragraphs. Professional writers' best advice to academic writers is to write with active verbs. Hemingway's World War I romance novel *A Farewell to Arms* exemplifies the use of active verbs.

Show verbs

American poet Edgar Allan Poe allegedly advised writers to believe half of what they see and none of what they hear; in other words, he wanted writers to use verbs that show action rather than tell action. In *The Raven*, he avoids telling readers he was tired and heard a noise, preferring to show them action by writing,

While I nodded, nearly napping, suddenly there came a tapping . . .

Here are some examples that tell the action and show the action:

Telling action (avoid): Scientists <u>were happy</u> after *Curiosity*'s landing on Mars.

Showing action (prefer): Scientists <u>cheered</u> *Curiosity*'s landing on Mars.

Telling: The dog <u>was angry</u>.

Showing: The dog <u>snapped</u>.

Telling: The customer <u>was displeased</u> with the salesperson.

Showing: The customer <u>shouted</u> at the salesperson.

Telling: The baby <u>was tired</u>.

Showing: The baby <u>napped</u>.

Neuroscientists discovered that active verbs "light up" the brain. Using functional imaging studies, they showed that brain activity is heightened when you read active verbs.

TIP

When you read from the perspective of the writer, identify the writer's successful use of active voice and action verbs.

Concise verbs

Successful writers practice word economy by saying more with less and using concise verbs. Avoid multi-word verbs and eliminate unnecessary words in your action ideas. Frequently, a verb idea with three or more words can be reduced as such:

Multi-word verb: Congress <u>made an objection</u> to proposed legislation.

Concise verb: Congress <u>objected</u> to proposed legislation.

The verb phrase *made an objection* contains two action ideas (*made* and *objected*). The verb *objected* includes the meaning of *making*.

Multi-word verb: The board <u>decided to approve</u> new marching band uniforms.

Concise verb: The board <u>approved</u> new marching band uniforms.

Multi-word verb: The committee <u>arrived at a conclusion</u> that uniforms were essential.

Concise verb: The committee <u>concluded</u> that uniforms were essential.

Being in agreement

People respectfully disagree, but verbs aren't as polite as people. Verbs dislike disagreement and stubbornly insist on agreeing with their subjects. Subjects and verbs agree in number (singular or plural). *Agreement proficiencies* require the understanding of singular and plural when phrases are positioned between the subject and verb, and recognition of number ambiguity of some nouns:

The first two <u>hurricanes</u> of the year <u>were</u> less damaging than predicted.

Hurricanes (the plural subject) requires agreement with the plural verb *were*. Avoid identifying the singular *year* (which is the object of the preposition *of*) as the subject.

The <u>phone</u>, including the service plan and upgrades, <u>was</u> above Carson's budget.

The singular subject (*phone*) requires a singular verb (*was*). Avoid identifying the subject as *upgrades*, which is part of the phrase *including the service plan*.

TIP

Examples of prepositions and prepositional phrases include <u>from</u> the south, <u>of</u> unknown origin, <u>at</u> the meeting, <u>in</u> the research, <u>with</u> accessories, <u>after</u> the meeting, and <u>during</u> January. Be sure to identify the subject as the performer of the action, not the object of the preposition.

Sentences beginning with *there* and *here* position the subject after the verb:

There <u>are</u> few valid <u>excuses</u> for missing class.

Guidelines for subject–verb agreement include

>> Two or more subjects joined by *and* require a plural verb.

Blueberries and bananas are my favorite cereal toppings.

>> Two or more subjects joined by *or* require a singular verb.

Running or cycling is my favorite outdoor exercise.

>> Some nouns appear plural in form, but require singular verbs: *mathematics, physics, news, measles,* and *civics.*

Mathematics is my third-favorite subject.

Measles was declared eliminated in 2000.

>> Some collective nouns are singular or plural, depending on their use, as in the following examples.

Singular: The orchestra is meeting for rehearsal at 6 a.m.

Plural: The orchestra are asked to store instruments in music lockers.

Singular: The family was committed to volunteer for flood victims.

Plural: The family were each committed to different projects.

Focusing on tense

College students experience many stresses in their lives; verb tense shouldn't be one of them. *Tense* simply refers to the time an action takes place: present, past, or future. APA recommends verb tenses for specific sections of papers that follow the APA documentation style.

>> Research components completed in the past require past tense.

Review of literature: Winn (2020) reviewed causes of declining attendance in Major League Baseball.

Methodology: Athletes completed extensive conditioning prior to participating in cognitive activities.

Survey results: The survey revealed weaknesses in the instrument.

>> Research components referencing past research require present tense.

Discussion and implications: College athletes earn better grades while participating in their sports.

Conclusion and projections: Research shows that students living on campus earn better grades.

Avoiding Anonymity: Nouns

Nouns would never be a candidate for a witness protection program. They talk too much, naming everything and everybody, including people, places, objects, and ideas. Lazy writers who choose general rather than specific forms frequently abuse nouns because general forms require less thinking.

General noun: In anatomy class, we studied the <u>thing</u> between the neck and the abdomen.

Specific noun: In anatomy class, we studied the <u>thorax</u>.

Nouns generate specific images in the reader's brain. For example, when you write, *An <u>animal</u> walked by the lake*, the reader may visualize an animal such as a dog, cat, rabbit, or fox. If *animal* were replaced with a more specific form such as *reptile*, you'd create more reader urgency. And if *animal* were replaced with the more specific *alligator*, you'd create reader alarm.

Table 6-1 shows a continuum of nouns as they progress from general to specific. For example, "book" represents a general classification of reading, "novel" represents a less general classification of reading, and *Moby Dick* represents a specific piece of reading. Specific nouns impact readers more than general nouns.

TABLE 6-1

General to Specific Nouns

General	Less General	Specific
person	athlete	LeBron James
vehicle	automobile	convertible
space	room	office
food	vegetable	lettuce
technology	device	tablet
entertainment	movie	*Rocky*
activity	sport	soccer
thing	tool	hammer
cover	hat	helmet

Designating Replacements: Pronouns

No part of speech experiences a greater identity crisis than pronouns, which are frequently misused with the nouns they represent, such as people, places, and events. Pronouns belong to a large family, with relatives identified as personal, relative, indefinite, intensive, interrogative, possessive, and demonstrative. Pronouns, like nouns, insist on being agreeable — one of the few pronoun properties you need to master. Table 6-2 defines these different pronouns. I break down what you need to know about pronouns in the following sections.

TABLE 6-2: **Types of Pronouns**

Type	Definition	Examples
Personal	Refers to people	I, you, me, they, them
Relative	Begins a clause (a group of words that refer to a noun)	who, that, which
Indefinite	Refers to an unknown number of people or things	someone, anyone, both, few, many, several
Intensive	Adds emphasis to a noun it refers to	itself, myself, yourself, themselves, ourselves
Interrogative	Begins a question	who, whom, what, which
Possessive	Indicates possession or ownership	his, my, their, our
Demonstrative	Points out a specific reference	this, these, that, those

Staying in agreement

Pronouns are highly compatible with nouns, so they agree with their *antecedent* (the noun or pronoun they replace) in person, number, gender, and case:

> The father of a <u>daughter</u> plays a major role in <u>her</u> development as a confident woman.

The pronoun *her* agrees with the antecedent *daughter* in person (third), number (singular), gender (female), and case (objective) — just as I learned in the college fight song.

Here are other pronoun properties you need to know:

>> **Person:** English has three *persons* (first, second, and third).

- *First person* refers to pronouns such as *I, me, we,* and *us*.

- *Second person* refers to the pronoun *you*.

- *Third person* refers to pronouns such as *he, she, it, they,* and *them*.

>> **Number:** *Number* refers to pronouns representing one noun or pronoun person or object (singular), or two or more people or objects (plural).

- *Singular* pronouns include *I* and *me*.

- *Plural* pronouns include *we, they,* and *them*.

- The pronoun *you* can be either singular or plural.

>> **Gender:** Gender identifies pronouns as male (*he*), female (*she*), or non-binary (*they, ze, ve, per, and hir*).

>> **Case:** Case refers to pronouns used as subjects (*I, he, she, they, it*) or objects (*me, her, them, us*).

>> **Subject pronouns:** <u>She</u> and <u>I</u> volunteered to tutor freshmen.

>> **Object pronouns:** Educational materials were given to <u>her</u> and <u>me</u>.

REMEMBER

APA recommends gender–neutral pronouns (which frequently include phrasing that avoids use of *he* and *she*):

After the study <u>participant</u> completed the forms, <u>they</u> were administered the survey.

The experiment showed that college <u>seniors</u> experience separation anxiety in <u>their</u> senior year.

Eyeing APA person preferences

When using pronouns in research, follow these APA guidelines:

>> Describe your research and your personal analysis in the first person (*I*) if you're the sole author:

<u>I</u> conclude that the results of the study corroborate the findings of Osterman (2019).

>> Use *we* if you're co-authoring. If you reference a co-author, use the person's name:

<u>We</u> validated our results with previous studies in the field. Jackson (2021) and <u>I</u> completed disclosure statements.

>> Avoid referencing yourself as *we,* and using third-person references such as *the researcher* or *the author*.

>> Avoid editorial *we* references to people in general. Replace *we* with a specific noun.

<u>We</u> advise incoming freshmen to participate in campus activities.

Campus <u>counselors</u> advise incoming freshmen to participate in campus activities.

Using the singular "they"

The Publication Manual of the American Psychological Association Seventh Edition endorses the use of the pronoun *they* (inclusive of all people) as plural, in addition to its singular use. Plural *they* has also been endorsed by advocacy groups, publishers, and the *Merriam-Webster Dictionary*. APA recommends the use of the plural *they* (and its forms) as singular for a person who uses *they* as their identified pronoun:

The <u>researcher</u> performed <u>their</u> study following accepted practices.

A <u>participant</u> must apply for <u>their</u> approval by June 14.

Building Basics: Structures

A writing idea without basic sentence and paragraph structure is like a course without a syllabus — it creates the potential for major misunderstanding. Sentences, the social media of the writing process, engage readers, build idea networks, capitalize on visual imagery, and share ideas with wider audiences. Sentences' powerful messages can cycle solo:

"If you can dream it, you can do it." — Walt Disney

"No one can make you feel inferior without your consent." — Eleanor Roosevelt

"You miss one hundred percent of the shots you don't take." — Wayne Gretzky

But sentences prefer going viral with other sentences and paragraphs. They fear insecurity and the isolation that comes from straying off topic. Their colleagues include unity, flow, and development.

Paragraphs, units of ideas, are the building blocks of successful writing. Good paragraphs flow like the wind in a sail on a breezy day. Major paragraph parts include the topic or central sentence, middle developing and supporting details, and the concluding transitional sentence. Paragraphs practice social distancing and begin with an indentation. Good sentences generate engaging paragraphs; engaging paragraphs generate ideas as contagious as a yawn in a boring lecture.

These sections show how to develop effective sentences and paragraphs and how to structure them with brain-friendly parallelism.

Sentences and paragraphs

Develop sentences with a general length of between 21 and 25 words, approximately one-and-one-half lines of standard text, or the length of this sentence. The heart of the sentence is the subject-action-verb sentence pattern:

> Division I college football generates millions of dollars for college athletic budgets.

Compose sentences by first identifying the subject or topic you're making a statement about (*football*), and follow with an action verb (*generates*). Add variety to that basic pattern by adding dependent thoughts:

> Division I college football generates millions of dollars for college athletic budgets, <u>creating the potential for overshadowing college academics.</u>

or

> Division I college football, <u>a fall Saturday ritual</u>, generates millions of dollars for college athletic budgets and <u>lifetime memories for passionate fans</u>.

When sentence structure fails, paragraphs fail, writing fails — and you fail.

Paragraphs demonstrate unity when they focus on one topic, with every sentence contributing to the development of that one focus. The number of sentences in a paragraph varies from one (an impact strategy in essay writing) to a half dozen or more in a complex research document. Paragraph development strategies include illustrating, exemplifying, explaining, contrasting, comparing, describing, and analyzing. Paragraphs befriend anecdotes, statistics, and specifics, and they focus on one powerful message, as in the following example:

You have brains in your head. You have feet in your shoes. You can steer yourself any direction you choose. You're on your own. And you know what you know. And YOU are the one who'll decide where to go...

— *Dr. Seuss, Oh, the Places You'll Go!*

Paragraph development strategies include adding the phrases *such as . . .* and *for example . . .*, as shown here:

> Professors are impressed with students who show initiative in writing projects and include references <u>such as</u> books, current events, experts' quotations, class lectures, and content from other courses.

TIP

Sentences and paragraphs thrive on specific references, such as the previous *21 to 25 words*, *Division I*, *millions of dollars*, *Dr. Seuss*, and *fall Saturday*.

Answers to the following questions help you develop your sentences and paragraphs:

» Is the sentence length generally between 21 and 25 words? Can longer sentences be divided into two?

» Do the sentences generally show evidence of subject-action-verb sentence patterns?

» Do all the paragraphs contribute to the central focus? Do any sentences or paragraphs stray from the central focus?

» Can an excessively long paragraph be divided into two?

» Does the paragraph development include illustrations, examples, explanations, and so forth?

» Does the sentence and paragraph development include specifics?

Parallelism

Parallelism is similar to when you synchronize your smart devices, thus allowing similar information to flow through your phone, tablet, and laptop. With parallelism, similarly structured ideas flow through sentences and paragraphs, adding writing rhythm, increasing readability, and helping readers to anticipate similar constructions.

For example, if your audience reads, "Researchers analyzed reading, writing, and. . .," then they anticipate construction and rhythm similar to *reading* and *writing*, a word ending in "ing", such as *calculating*. The three gerunds (verb forms ending in *ing*) also create pleasing sequential sounds.

Unparallel constructions break sentence rhythm and cloud comprehension:

Researchers analyzed to read, write nonfiction, and to calculate.

Parallel phrases add clarity and create additional rhythm:

Researchers analyzed reading novels, writing nonfiction, and calculating fractions.

Parallel structure requires the following components:

>> **Series of similar constructions:** Related nouns, phrases, and clauses require parallelism.

> **Unparallel:** The following can be done in the summer: reading on the beach, play tennis, and ride bikes.

> **Parallel:** Summer activities include reading books on the beach, playing tennis in the park, and riding bikes through trails.

>> Create parallel structure by identifying the sentence topic (*summer activities*) and following with the action verb (*include*). Structure items in a series to be parallel: *reading*, *playing*, and *riding*. Parallelism can be enhanced with phrases: *books on the beach*, *tennis in the park*, and *bikes through trails*.

> **Unparallel:** Earning advanced degrees requires determination to overcome adversity, friends and family who are supportive, and researching long hours and weekends.

> **Parallel:** Earning advanced degrees requires determination to overcome adversity, support of family and friends, and commitment to extensive research.

> Revise the three requirements with parallel nouns: *determination*, *support*, and *commitment*. Continue parallelism with phrases that follow: *to overcome adversity*, *of family and friends*, and *to extensive research*.

>> **Constructions joined with conjunctions:** Coordinating conjunctions (*and*, *or*, and *but*) and correlative conjunctions (*not only . . .*, *but also . . .*, and *either . . . or . . .*) require parallelism.

> **Unparallel:** Participants' options included walking trails or the bus.

> **Parallel:** Participants' options included walking or riding the bus.

> **Unparallel:** We not only compiled electronic results, but hand printed results.

> **Parallel:** We not only compiled electronic results, but also hand printed results.

>> **Listed related constructions:** Listed related constructions represent parallel structure challenges. Each listed construction requires parallel initial words, followed by consistent parallel wording:

Artifacts at the September 11 Memorial revealing the scope of the tragedy include a

- <u>Severed</u> NYFD Ladder 3 <u>fire truck</u> with spaghetti-like twisted back ladders
- <u>Battered</u> and <u>punctured</u> New York Fire Department <u>ambulance</u>
- <u>Garden hand rake</u> used during recovery to search for human remains
- <u>Ripped</u> airplane window <u>frame</u>
- <u>Granite slab</u> from the 1993 memorial containing the name *John*

Each bulleted item follows the pattern of an initial descriptive word followed by a noun: *severed fire truck, battered* and *punctured ambulance, garden hand rake, ripped frame*, and *granite slab*.

Creating parallel lists also includes deleting repetitious items and combining similar items.

Reducing Confusion: Problem Pairs

"The difference between the right word and the almost-right word is the difference between lightning and the lightning bug." This quote, attributed to American literary legend Mark Twain, references a myriad of similar word usage that challenges college writers.

From my teaching experience dating back to The Beatles' arrival in America, the following usage issues appear regularly in writing that I evaluated.

Problem pairs

APA highlights usage issues with the following pronoun pairs:

A lot, allot: *A lot* (adjective and noun) means plentiful; *allot* (verb) means allocate. *A lot* is frequently misspelled as one word. Remember, *a lot* is used to build a house. *Earning a college degree requires <u>a lot</u> of perseverance. Administrators were asked to <u>allot</u> resources equally.*

Accept, except: *Accept* (verb) means to receive or agree to; *except* (preposition) means other than. *We graciously <u>accepted</u> the award. Everyone <u>except</u> Jacob drove to the concert.*

Affect, effect: *Affect* (verb) means to influence; *effect* (noun) means the result. *The effect on participants was minimal but affected test results.*

An, a: Use *an to* precede words beginning with a vowel sound: *an* honor, *an* apple, and *an* earful. Use *a* to precede a word beginning with consonant sounds: *a* decision, *a* backpack, and *a* water bottle. *Participating in research was an educational experience. Lunch was provided at a local restaurant.*

Continual and continuously: These two time-sequence words affiliate with your two favorite parts of speech. *Continual* describes nouns: *continual texts, continual red flags.* Continuously describes verbs: *complains continuously, works out continuously.* Remember, *ly* indicates an adverb, and adverbs describe verbs. *After continual blue screens, Alexia bought a new tablet. His phone also shuts down continuously.*

Farther, further: *Farther* references a measurable distance; *further* references a comparable degree. *Jayne lives farther from campus than Laticia. Vijay is further advanced in biology.*

Fewer, less: *Fewer* references a countable quantity; *less* references a noncountable quantity. *Maine has fewer residents than Missouri. The less time spent on worksheets, the better for education.*

However: *However* used as a conjunction is punctuated with a semicolon (*; however,*). *However* used as a parenthetical expression is punctuated with a comma (*, however,*). *The study was completed before deadline; however, it was over budget. The study, however, lacked validation.*

It's, its: *It's*, a contraction, represents it is or it has; *its* is a possessive adjective. (*Its'* is not a word.) *It's time for new solutions to old problems. The puppy injured its paw.*

Then, than: *Then* (adverb) represents time; *than* (conjunction) indicates comparison. *We then studied another student population. The final study revealed more problems than the first.*

Problem pronouns

APA highlights usage issues with the following pronoun pairs:

That, which: *That* introduces clauses that are essential (restrictive) to sentence meaning. *Which* introduces clauses that are nonessential (nonrestrictive) to sentence meaning. Nonessential *which* clauses are marked off with commas. *The partition that separates the library was opened for the speaker. The library, which was built in 2000, was updated with a new sound system.*

Who, that: *Who* refers to people; *that* refers to objects and ideas. *The man who returned the gift was appreciative of the customer service policy. Businesses promote policies that preserve resources. That* can also refer to a group of people such as an organization. *I belong to an organization that supports amusement park safety.*

Who, whom: *Who* is a subject pronoun; *whom* is an object pronoun. If *he, she,* or *they* can be substituted, *who* is the correct pronoun; if *him, her,* or *them* can be substituted, *whom* is the correct pronoun. <u>Who</u> *compiles results of the control group?* <u>Whom</u> *should I speak with about receiving survey results?*

Who's, whose: *Who's,* a contraction, is short for *who is. Whose* shows possession. <u>Who's</u> *going to the library Saturday night?* <u>Whose</u> *backpack was left in the gym?*

Misplaced description

Logical word order in a sentence is as important as letter sequence in spelling. Misplaced description, the illogical order of words in a sentence (*We saw a bear driving through Alaska*), is as serious an error as misspelling your name on your resume. The following strategies correct misplaced description:

>> Position the performer of the action, the subject, as one of the first few words of the sentence.

> **Misplaced:** To complete the assignment, <u>two nonfiction books</u> must be read.

> **Revised:** Students are required to read <u>two nonfiction books</u> to complete the assignment.

> **Misplaced:** Who was the woman who repaired your laptop <u>in jeans</u>?

> **Revised:** Who was the woman <u>in jeans</u> who repaired your laptop?

>> Position prepositional phrases and other descriptions as close as possible to the noun or pronoun they describe.

> **Misplaced:** Dr. Marshall administered the survey to third graders <u>with a smile.</u>

> **Revised:** Dr. Marshall <u>smiled</u> as he administered the survey to third graders. (The idea of "with a smile" is repositioned as a verb following Dr. Marshall.)

> **Misplaced:** The child ate baklava <u>with a new shirt</u>.

> **Revised:** The child <u>with a new shirt</u> ate baklava.

>> Follow introductory participle phrases (*ing* and *ed* words and phrases used as an adjective) with the performer of the action.

> **Misplaced:** Anticipating icy highways, the writers' workshop was rescheduled by <u>administration</u>.

> **Revised:** Anticipating icy highways, <u>administrators</u> rescheduled the writers' workshop.

Misplaced: <u>We</u> stood watching the game on the roof.

Revised: Standing on the roof, <u>we</u> watched the game.

» Logically position awkward adverbs such as *only*, *almost*, *just*, *hardly*, *usually*, *scarcely*, *nearly*, and *even*.

Misplaced: People who are honest <u>usually</u> are happy.

Revised: Honest people are <u>usually</u> happy.

Misplaced: I <u>almost</u> revised half the report.

Revised: I revised <u>almost</u> half the report.

Meaning changes as challenging words are repositioned:

If only Clayton asks Alisha to dinner, she will accept.

If Clayton <u>only</u> asks Alisha to dinner, she will accept.

If Clayton asks Alisha <u>only</u> to dinner, she will accept.

If Clayton asks Alisha to dinner <u>only</u>, she will accept.

Only is as easy to misplace as a set of keys. It's used as an adjective or an adverb. *Only* used as an adjective means one or very few:

You are the <u>only</u> student reading your copy of *APA Style & Citations For Dummies*.

Our <u>only</u> car is parked in the garage.

Only used as an adverb means limited actions and is generally positioned in front of a noun:

<u>Only</u> a few students enroll in Advanced Chinese.

<u>Only</u> a few freshmen are invited into the honors program.

Only is also frequently used in spoken language to add emphasis:

<u>Only</u> you could offer an explanation like that.

<u>Only</u> a college senior would worry about getting a job.

» **Highlighting special effects**

» **Conforming with spelling**

» **Casing costly letters**

Chapter **7**

Navigating Pages: Conventions of Style

Y ou're successful as an adult and student because you follow rules and fulfill responsibilities. At school you register for classes, accumulate credits, and meet course requirements. Following rules helps you navigate school and organize your life.

Your writing has similar expectations, requiring that you follow rules to guide your readers. Content may be king, but successful writing requires accurate grammar, word usage, punctuation, spelling, and other conventions. And the consequences of misuse are as costly as neglecting a course requirement.

The richness and versatility of the English language includes stylistic conventions that guide readers and orchestrate meaning, showcasing the functions of dashes and slashes, colons and semicolons, parentheses and brackets, and the contrarian ellipses.

This chapter guides you through common conventions of style and identifies APA highlights with the precision of a fork searching for blueberries in a summer fruit salad. In addition, I identify minefields and mudholes of language issues that I have seen in student writing since *Star Wars* first hit the big screen. You also find out about the musical beats that readers need to navigate the printed page.

If you're obsessed with language conventions such as the evolution of the question mark, the conflicting demands of the comma, the abuses of the apostrophe, and rules for the dash, or if you have an English major friend who's celebrating a milestone, consider Lynne Truss' *Eats, Shoots & Leaves: The Zero Tolerance Approach to Punctuation* (Penguin Group).

Marking Cadence: Punctuation

I once asked a publisher his preference on the *Oxford comma* (the comma before *and* in a series) and other optional marks of punctuation. He surprisingly responded, "If you were paying my ink bill, you would avoid every optional mark of punctuation. I could save a million dollars a year." I learned that money drives punctuation and that punctuation rules aren't as strict as the nuns taught me they were. In this section, you discover that money also influenced the implementation of lowercase letters. Optional punctuation marks are like free points in your professor's gradebook: an opportunity to double down on your choices of being correct.

Punctuation, once arbitrarily aligned with the rhythm of music, offers a variety of beats to establish the cadence of writing that helps readers emphasize, de-emphasize, pause, stop, and connect meaning.

End punctuation and spacing

End punctuation (periods, question marks, and exclamation points) signals temporary stops on the printed page; it gives readers a quick refresh before moving forward.

The period as end punctuation signals the end of a sentence, a complete thought that either makes a statement or gives a command:

> **Statement:** The south rim of the Grand Canyon is located in Arizona.

> **Command:** Please assemble in the auditorium after lunch.

Other end punctuation marks are the question mark (?) and exclamation point(!):

> Have you read any Shakespeare sonnets?

> Finally, we have a return of college football!

Avoid excessive use of exclamation points, including multiple exclamation points!!!

APA's seventh edition reduced spacing after end punctuation from two spaces to one space. The spacing between the previous sentence and this sentence is an example of the new spacing — as well as end-mark spacing throughout this book. Spacing following a colon was also reduced to one space.

Comma

A *comma* is like a short pause in a workout, a breath in a telephone conversation, and a quick hello to a passer-by. It's a pre-COVID-19 handshake and a brief freeze on your computer screen.

Typical uses of commas include dates, addresses, and numbers. Additionally, commas used in pairs and multiples include the following:

» **Items in a series:** My favorite fruits are blueberries, bananas, and grapes.

» **A parenthetical word or phrase:** Alyson, by the way, was introduced last.

» **An appositive (an explanatory noun following a noun):** Isiah, team captain, scored the winning goal.

Additional comma uses include separating clauses:

» **Clauses in compound sentences joined by a conjunction:** The hurricane headed toward the coast, and residents were issued mandatory evacuation notices.

» **Introductory dependent clauses from the main sentence idea (independent clause):** When everyone arrived, the celebration began.

» **Long (four words or longer) introductory phrases:** During the presentation of awards, children in the audience became restless.

» **Names directly addressed:** Chelsea, you left your book on the table.

APA also emphasizes using a comma to separate the author and date in an in-text citation: (Sanchez, 2020).

Most stylebooks don't require commas for separating hours from minutes (*1 hour 15 seconds*) and feet from inches (*3 feet 6 inches*).

Semicolon and colon

A semicolon functions like a comma on steroids; a colon functions like a comma with attitude. Semicolons take on responsibilities that exceed the job description of a comma by separating complex ideas. Both specialize in making short rest stops on long journeys.

Semicolons are used to separate the following:

>> **Independent clauses without a conjunction:** We drove to the library; our friends drove to the party.

>> **A series of independent clauses:** The van was not damaged; no passengers were injured; no property was destroyed; and everyone felt relieved.

>> **Items in a series that contain clauses with commas:** Prepare for your senior year in college by meeting with your advisor, department chair, and college dean; by visiting the career planning center to update your resume, interview skills, and networking skills; and by ensuring you fulfill your credit requirements and financial obligations.

   The challenge of writing long sentences with clauses separated by semicolons is in maintaining parallel structure. See Chapter 6 for additional information.

>> **Connective words such as *however, therefore, for instance*, and *for example* when they connect two or more independent clauses:** I always enjoy a warm day at the beach; however, I like to make it academically productive.

TECHNICAL STUFF

If the semicolon is your favorite punctuation mark because it handles complex problems, read about its evolution in Cecelia Watson's *Semicolon* (HarperCollins). Find out why Herman Melville's *Moby Dick* contains 4,000 semicolons, one every 52 words.

The colon, one of the oldest punctuation marks and used as far back as ancient Greece, was originally a slightly raised period. It was first used with the dash (:–) and represented a pause in reading text. Its current use evolved from the 1600s, when it assumed its current role between the pause of a comma and the full stop of end punctuation.

A colon's job description includes introducing the following:

>> **Explanations:** Home-schooled children experience three benefits; reading more independently, studying longer hours, and solving more problems.

>> **Examples:** American Literature courses should include books by the following authors; Hemingway, Fitzgerald, Melville, and Steinbeck.

>> **Series:** To experience a variety of cultures in the United States, consider; a luau in Hawaii, a folk festival in West Virginia, salmon fishing in Alaska, a college football game in College Station, and a play on Broadway.

>> **Quotations:** Shakespeare wrote: "To thine own self be true."

>> **Follow-up thoughts:** Harrison confirmed the finding: Slides were contaminated.

Dashes and slashes

Dashes and slashes are the partisan politicians of punctuation; they interrupt and redirect the main idea of a sentence, with slashes sometimes causing more confusion than clarity. Dashes, lacking the job security of their own word processing key, can easily be replaced with a comma.

Dashes (formerly known by the pretentious *virgule*) come in two sizes: the en dash (–), nearly similar in appearance to the hyphen, and the em dash (—):

>> **En dash:** The en dash separates equal items.

The final score was *21–14*. He lived from *1918–1985*. The reference was located between pages *56–84*.

>> **Em dash:** The em dash indicates a digression or further explanation.

I recently upgraded my phone — a service plan upgrade is coming next — and blew up my monthly budget.

Foreign language study — declining in the United States — continues to grow in foreign schools.

Your education won't be considered deficient if you use the en dash and hyphen interchangeably.

Slashes are like overdraft protection on your bank account: You don't want to use it, but sometimes you can't avoid it. The forward slash (/), more than two thousand years old, is used in URL addresses and to separate lines of poetry and music. The slash should seldom be seen or heard because it frequently offers confusing choices:

If you plan to buy Max a sweatshirt, his size is small/medium/large. (Max's size includes too many options. A gift card contains one size that fits all.)

Max also has a pair of shoes he uses for walking/hiking/swimming/bicycling/painting. (Too many options can also result in foot problems.)

TIP

Avoid using slashes in situations like those shown here, and with "and/or." Replace the slash with "and" or "or."

Quotation marks

Quotation marks speak for themselves. They insist on impeccable accuracy and frequently complain of being misquoted.

Common uses of quotation marks include identifying the following:

>> **Speakers' or researchers' exact words (direct quotation):** Regarding the light bulb, Thomas Edison said, "I discovered 10,000 ways that that won't work."

>> **Titles of periodical articles and book chapters when used within text:** The sophomore's major argument was found in the periodical article titled "College Success Attributed to Overcoming Adversity."

>> **Partial quotations:** Vince Lombardi, legendary Green Bay Packers' coach, is credited with defining luck as "preparation meeting opportunity."

>> **Short stories, poems, and other minor works of art:** Did you read Frost's "The Road Not Taken"?

APA highlights the following use of quotation marks:

>> **Letters and words as literary examples:** Musical-sounding letters in the English language include "l," "m," and "s." One of the most pleasant-sounding words in the English language is "melody."

>> **Words or phrases used as "invented coinage":** Philadelphia Phillies fans who cheered their team during no-spectator games called themselves "phandemics."

A quotation within a quotation is identified with single quotation marks (Carole said, "My favorite Shakespeare line is 'All the world's a stage . . . .'"). You may also notice that single quotation marks are used within news headlines.

TECHNICAL STUFF

In the preceding examples, commas and end punctuation are positioned *inside* quotation marks. Colons, semicolons, and ellipses are positioned *outside* quotation marks.

REMEMBER

Quotation marks and quoted content represent high-maintenance content that you present to your readers. Misuse of quotations and conventions that support them, and careless inaccuracies presenting quoted content, can result in plagiarism allegations. A misused or neglected mark of punctuation or convention in this section can derail a dream.

Parentheses, brackets, and ellipses

Parentheses, brackets, and ellipses are the silent minority of punctuation, very polite but attention-seeking. They introduce themselves with an "excuse me" attitude and have much to say.

Truss' *Eats, Shoots & Leaves* credits Desiderius Erasmus as the originator of parentheses, also known as brackets. Erasmus named parentheses "lunulae" because they resembled the crescent moon.

Common uses of parentheses (literally "to put beside") include identifying the following:

» **In-text citations:** (Davis, 2021)

» **Afterthoughts or supplemental information remotely related to the central idea:** Graduating college seniors face many challenging decisions (spending gift money not being one of them), including employment options, housing arrangements, and continuing education.

» **Uncommon abbreviations:** The Government Printing Office (GPO) is located in Washington, D.C.

» **Directional information:** Economic indicators continue to progress (see Figure 7-6).

» **Use of *sic* (identifying a misspelled word) in authoritative sources:** The college newspaper reported, "The Iphone (*sic*) is the most creative invention of all time."

» **URL addresses:** (google.com)

Outside of in-text citations, excessive parentheses can interrupt the flow of text like a fire alarm during class.

When parentheses enclose a sentence, position end punctuation *within* the parentheses: (What is the strongest evidence that supports global warming?) When only part of the sentence is enclosed in parentheses, punctuate *outside* the parentheses: When you were in Atlanta, did you visit the Center for Disease Control (CDC)?

Brackets ([]), parentheses who like to play the angles, are referred to as square brackets by APA, while parentheses are identified as round brackets. During their formative years, brackets may have experienced separation anxiety because they're actually named *left bracket* and *right bracket*.

Brackets enclose information, as follows:

>> **Within parentheses:** (see Topez, 2019 [vol. 2])

>> **Within quotations:** Ralph Waldo Emerson, an American philosopher, said, "Nothing great [nor good] was ever achieved without enthusiasm."

Brackets, an additional writer's tool, help navigate the reader through complex research material. They have their time, place, and purpose, and they coordinate well with parentheses. If you don't confuse parentheses and brackets, they won't confuse you.

An ellipsis, the middle child of punctuation, marches to the beat of its own drummer. While most punctuation connects meaning and guides readers through a maze of meaning, an ellipsis says, "Something's missing; you figure it out."

Ellipsis marks (. . .), three dots or periods separated with spaces on both sides, show omission . . . and keep on rolling.

Ellipsis uses include the following:

>> **Continuation of similar content:** The cognitive test included reciting every other letter of the alphabet (A, C, E, ...).

>> **Omission of words in a quotation:** In the following passages, the first one shows an original selection. The second passage shows how a writer quoting the original passage might use an ellipsis to signal omission of content. Notice the four periods at the end of the sentence, three indicating the ellipsis and one ending the sentence:

> A few months after taking office, Hamilton issued a detailed document called Report on Public Credit. In it he proposed to fully pay off the government's $53.9 million debt (roughly $1.5 billion in 2019), about a quarter of which was owed to foreign creditors. Not only that, he proposed that future creditors always have first call on government revenues. A sound credit rating, he argued, was vital for establishing a stable financial system and earning international respect for the young country's economic practices — and attracting international investments to America (Wiegand, 2020).

> Hamilton issued a detailed document called Report on Public Credit. In it he proposed to fully pay off the government's $53.9 million debt ..., about a quarter of which was owed to foreign creditors. Not only that, he proposed that future creditors always have first call on government revenues. A sound credit rating, he argued, was vital for establishing a stable financial system and earning international respect. (Wiegand, 2020).

Seeking Attention: Special Conventions

Some language conventions stand out among their peers because of their special uses to pace readers through pages as they hear meaning from their internal voice: *John Norman III* (your internal voice whispers "the third") *served on many educational boards*. Other conventions create visuals highlighting content such as books, periodicals, poems, abbreviations, and numbers. Enjoy the sights and sounds as you explore special features that guide readers on their journey.

Italics

Italics, an aesthetic cursive font based on a form of calligraphic handwriting, first appeared in Italy around 1500. Italics belongs to the family of conventions that give special meaning to words.

Common use of italics includes identifying major works such as book titles, periodicals, webpages, court decisions, names of ships, poems, pieces of art, movies, television shows, and newspapers: *The Great Gatsby*, *Time*, *Enola Gay*, *Batman*, *American Idol*, *Thriller*, *Brown* v. *Board of Education*, *Challenger*, and *Hamlet*.

APA emphasizes that key terms are italicized when they require a follow-up definition:

> Science describes *active immunity* as vaccines that stimulate the immune system.

REMEMBER

Italics identifying titles and other major works of art doesn't include sentence punctuation that follows the title:

> Did you read Walter Isaacson's *Leonardo da Vinci*?

Italicize punctuation that's part of the title:

> I enjoyed reading *Who's Afraid of Virginia Woolf?*

TIP

When handwriting, italics is represented by underlining.

Some stylebooks endorse the occasional use of italics to emphasize words. Most professors prefer that you emphasize ideas with word choice, not font choice. For example, avoid writing, "Are you going to submit *that*?" Prefer language that specifies *that*: "Are you going to submit that half-completed paper?"

When you continuously emphasize words with italics, you're telling your professor that you choose not to take the time to consider better language. Also, patterns of italicized words designed to achieve emphasis provide evidence for receiving an unsuccessful grade.

Abbreviations

Let me be brief. Use abbreviations sparingly — about as infrequent as you lend a friend your credit card. APA advises that "writing is generally easier to understand when most words are written out. . .." Patterns of abbreviations are more likely to appear in scientific papers written at the graduate level.

When you use a term in text, APA recommends that you "present both the full version of the term and the abbreviation." For example, if using the abbreviation OSHA, write, "<u>Occupational Safety and Health Administration (OSHA)</u> ensures a safe and healthy workplace." After defining an abbreviation once, use only the abbreviation: "<u>OSHA</u> plays a major role in food safety."

Other APA guidelines for abbreviations include

>> **Use periods following initials in names,** such as Harry S. Truman and M.L. King.

>> **Use periods for abbreviations,** such as a.m., p.m., e.g., Mrs., Mr., Dr., Jr., Mon., and Jan.

>> **Don't use periods for abbreviations,** such as APA, IQ, PhD, EdD, MSW, MD, and RN.

>> **Use periods in citation and reference abbreviations,** such as p., 5th ed., and paras.

>> **Form plurals of most abbreviations by adding *s*** (without an apostrophe), such as URSs, vols, and IQs.

>> **Abbreviate time references (hours, minutes, and seconds) when accompanied by numbers,** such as 10 hr. 10 min. Don't separate hours from minutes with a comma.

>> **Use *v.* (versus) with court case references** such as Gross *v.* Lopez.

REMEMBER

Form the plural for "page" (p.) with "pp."

TECHNICAL STUFF

Use two capital letters for state abbreviations used exclusively as postal addresses: FL, PA, WA, TN, and AR. Use traditional state abbreviations for non–postal-addresses: Fla., Pa., Wash., Tenn., and Ark.

Numbers

In general, APA recommends writing words for numbers from zero through nine (one, two, three, and so on), and not spelling out the numbers 10 and above (10, 11, 12, and so on). Other stylebooks offer different guidelines.

APA numerical points of emphasis for numerical expression include the following:

» **Avoid beginning a sentence, title, or heading with a figure, including a year reference.** *Avoid:* 1969 was the year America landed on the moon. *Reword:* America landed on the moon in 1969.

» **Prefer words to express fractions.** Two-thirds of the pie was eaten.

» **Avoid commas in numbers such as page numbers, serial numbers, and model numbers.** The index begins on page 1001.

» **Form plurals of numbers by adding "s" or "es."** Please separate all fours and sixes from both decks of cards. Rock and roll began in the '50s.

» **Prefer figures to represent dates, ages, scores, and sums of money.** Your $200 refund will be mailed soon.

» **Combine figures and words to express back-to-back numerical values.** The Philadelphia Eagles scored four 2-point conversions in 2018.

Finally, APA suggests presentation approaches for combining numbers and text:

» If presenting three or fewer numbers, consider a sentence.

» If presenting four to 20 numbers, consider a table.

» If presenting more than 20 numbers, consider a figure.

Perfecting Appearance: Spelling

A book shouldn't be judged by its cover, and a piece of writing shouldn't be judged by its spelling, but both are. Just as the eyes are the window to the soul, spelling is the moral compass of a piece of writing. This judgment isn't fair, but many readers (including professors) correlate poor spelling with poor writing. As an academician, your writing proficiency will be judged by your spelling proficiency.

Many inconsistencies of English spelling resulted after the Norman Conquest in 1066, when numerous foreign words filtered into English. Spelling problems became so severe in America that President Theodore Roosevelt headed (unsuccessfully) a reform attempt to standardize spelling in 1906. Regardless of the challenge, patterns of misspellings are unacceptable among the academic community — and derail readers from the writer's message.

Teddy Roosevelt was right: English spelling lacks consistency and common sense. Educated people commit to achieving spelling success, and I offer some important spelling tips in the following sections.

Spelling strategies

Can you spell words generated by a search of the most commonly misspelled words? Here are some. If you can't, the following strategies will prepare you for achieving success. And if you want to compete for a national spelling bee championship, recruit a twelve-year-old to tutor you.

misspell	weird	handkerchief	nausea
bourgeois	knead	pronunciation	asthma
Australia	broccoli	mnemonic	phlegm

>> **Keep a list of words you frequently misspell or words you question when you write:** Note memorable patterns. For example, since people learn spelling by sight, note the shape of the ascender letters that surround "knead." The ascender letters "k" and "d" present the visual of goal posts encapsulating the word. Also note the unusual "mn" beginning of "mnemonic," which means a memory aid. "Mnemonic" also has an unusual configuration, lacking ascenders and descenders (letter formations extending up and down).

>> **Study a few spelling rules:**

- "Weird" is an exception of the rule that *i* comes before *e* except after *c* (*receive, deceive, ceiling*) or when *ie* sounds like long *a*, as in *neighbor* and *weigh*.

- Nouns ending in y preceded by a consonant form the plural by changing y to i and adding es: army / armies; nursery / nurseries; sky / skies; body / bodies.

- Some nouns maintain the same form for singular and plural: *pliers, moose, eyeglasses, scissors, sheep, deer,* and *tuna.*

» **Collect spelling oddities:** *nth* (lacks a vowel); *facetious* (vowels in sequence); *queueing* (five consecutive vowels); *almost* (all letters in alphabetical sequence); *bookkeeper* (three consecutive double letters); *asthma* (begins and ends with a vowel and no other vowels between)

» **Review homophones:** *its / it's; their / there / they're; two / to / too; stationary / stationery; alter / altar; hair / hare.* Chapter 6 details uses of problem pairs.

» **Master Spell Check:** Enter appropriate words, integrate manually, address any wavy red underscores, and activate appropriate features.

REMEMBER

APA spelling conforms to *Merriam-Webster.com* (`www.merrian-webster.com`). Spelling psychological terms conforms with the *APA Dictionary of Psychology.*

Each year produces only one national spelling bee champion, usually a twelve-year-old. Everyone else is challenged by the spelling of some words.

TIP

Pair with a peer and review each other's papers exclusively for spelling. Your campus may also have resources where your writing is reviewed before final submission.

Possessives

If you travel outside the United States, you'll experience the challenge of English language spelling and recognize that many retail signs contain misspellings, frequently possessives. Because foreign travel is likely on your bucket list, a few rules will help you recognize misuses and appreciate the challenge of English spelling for non-English-speaking people. If you don't travel abroad, you can still find possessive errors in your community. And when you do find them, practice the golden rule of grammar: Being polite is more important than being correct.

Rules for forming possessives (see Table 7-1) are as basic as unlocking your phone:

» **To form a possessive singular,** write the singular form (*building*) and add *'s* (*building's*): The building's exterior needed repair.

» **To form a possessive plural,** start by writing the plural form (*buildings*).

- **If the plural ends in s,** add an apostrophe (*buildings'*): The buildings' configuration formed a hexagon.

- **If the plural doesn't end in s,** add *'s*: The geese's habitat was not compromised by the event.

TABLE 7-1

Forming Possessives

Singular	Possessive Singular	Plural	Possessive Plural
pet	pet's	pets	pets'
tooth	tooth's	teeth	teeth's
child	child's	children	children's
man	man's	men	men's
woman	woman's	women	women's

Foreign forms

The English language is rich with words from Latin, Greek, and French. Forms of many of these foreign words often include plurals from their original language. Spelling foreign words challenges many educated people. Table 7–2 can help.

TABLE 7-2

Foreign Forms of Nouns

Singular	Plural	Singular	Plural
matrix	matrices	analysis	analyses
syllabus	syllabi	appendix	appendices
datum	data	hypothesis	hypotheses
parenthesis	parentheses	alumna	alumnae
crisis	crises	census	censuses

Hyphenation

The hyphen, near-identical twin of the en dash, represents one of the most versatile conventions in the English language. The hyphen, which moonlights in the number's department, also serves as a negative sign and formerly as a subtraction sign. It welcomes the work after being victimized by automation when word processing's word wrap feature replaced its use as an end-of-line syllable separator. The hyphen lives on the top shelf of the keyboard, sharing space with long-time friend "underscore." They enjoy the large picture window just above them.

Working in the compound industry, the hyphen clarifies meaning at the word level. Compound nouns are continually evolving from word pairs (*fire house*), to hyphenated words (*fire-house*), to single words (*firehouse*). *Email* was formerly *e-mail*.

The bad news for writers is that compound hyphenation rules lack consistency. The good news is that compounds offer three options (separate words, hyphenated words, and single words), and the better news is that almost all professors will accept any reasonable option. APA defers to *Merriam-Webster* for the defining word, and the dictionary says that forming compounds represents writers' most significant spelling challenge.

Hyphenation guidelines include

>> **Hyphenate to clarify meaning:** The parents supported their college twins living in <u>two student dorms</u>. Do the parents support each twin living in a different building (two student-dorms)? Or do the parents support their twins living together in "two-student dorms?"

>> **Hyphenate two related words serving as one adjective:** The <u>award-winning</u> teacher declined the opportunity to run for public office.

>> **Hyphenate numbers from twenty-one through ninety-nine:** The couple celebrated their <u>thirty-ninth</u> wedding anniversary.

Generally, avoid hyphenating the following:

>> **Foreign words:** We visited an <u>á la cart</u> restaurant.

>> **Clear and well-established compounds:** *High school athletes, math department policy,* and *present day standards.*

TIP

APA doesn't hyphenate the following.

>> **Compounds containing an "ly" adverb:** <u>Commonly</u> read books in college include Jon Krakauer's *Into the Wild* and Malcolm Gladwell's *Blink.*

>> **Fractions used as nouns:** Approximately <u>one third</u> of Americans earned college degrees.

Base-formation compounds (a word form to which prefixes and suffixes are added) vary their requirements for hyphenation. APA recommends hyphenating the following base-formation compounds:

>> **Capitalized base words:** We visited a <u>Pre-Revolutionary</u> War museum.

>> **Self- and ex- prefixes:** Many college business majors are <u>self-starters</u>. The <u>ex-president</u> of the automotive company visited the new plant.

>> **An -elect suffix:** The <u>captain-elect</u> addressed the team.

Standing Tall: Capitalization

For thousands of years, all letters were capitalized — royal, majestic, and tall. In approximately the ninth century, printers developed a smaller set of letters and stored them in the lower case, with the taller letters stored in the higher or upper case. For hundreds of years, printers preferred either all uppercase letters (called *majuscule*) or all lowercase letters (called *miniscule*). Some printers at the time recognized that smaller letters used less ink, thus saving money — possibly the first time that money drove punctuation and spelling.

Fast forward a few hundred years after the two-case alphabet, and letters in the upper case were reserved for beginning special words, capitalized words. Uppercase letters were well positioned until June 29, 2007, when Steve Jobs introduced the first iPhone, and the position of tall letters was once again pushed aside.

APA identifies their capitalization style as "down style," meaning lower case by default unless there is "specific guidance to capitalize them." For example, when beginning a sentence with a lowercase name such as da Vinci, APA recommends not capitalizing it: *da Vinci discovered the principles for flight 500 years before the Wright brothers.* However, APA also recommends rewording a sentence rather than beginning it with a noun such as iPhone, eBay, or da Vinci.

Familiar rules for capitalization include the first word of a sentence, people's names, and proper nouns such as the days, months, holidays, cities, countries, nationalities, historic events (Prohibition), time periods (Middle Ages), parts of the world (Arctic), government bodies (United Nations), special days (Mother's Day), scientific terminology (Theory of Relativity), and languages.

TECHNICAL STUFF

Most nouns naming diseases and medical terms aren't capitalized: *influenza*, *measles*, *smallpox*. Many nouns naming diseases and medical procedures affiliated with a person *are* capitalized: *Down syndrome* and *Alzheimer's disease.*

TIP

Don't capitalize *french fries* and *irish potatoes.*

APA highlights capitalizing the first word of a sentence following a colon. *The professor's directions were clear: A validated study was required to be submitted.* If a sentence doesn't follow the colon, capitalizing isn't required. *The professor's directions were clear: a rigorous academic paper.*

WARNING

Don't capitalize seasons or compass directions (unless the direction refers to a specific section of the country: *We travelled throughout the South.*).

Proper nouns

The largest group of words capitalized in English are classified as proper nouns, fittingly defined as "one only" in some dictionaries. Capital letters help readers visualize the difference between *university* and *University of Notre Dame*, between *mountain* and *Mount St. Helens*, and between *bridge* and *Golden Gate Bridge*.

APA recommends capitalizing the following proper nouns specific to research:

>> **Names of racial and ethnic groups:** The candidates for university president included ten <u>Black</u> women.

>> **Names of specific university departments and academic courses:** *Rowan University's* <u>Department of Writing Arts</u> *offers* <u>Writing as Managers</u> *as a requirement for management majors.* Don't capitalize "writing department" unless it's preceded by a proper noun: *Rowan University's Writing Arts Department offers a number of writing-related majors.*

APA also recommends capitalizing nouns followed by numbers or letters that are part of a group or series:

Chapter 5	Section C	Part 2	Figure 12
Row AA	Room 212	Series 3	Building 10
Level 7	Flight 3636	Trials 2–3	Error 404

Don't capitalize *paragraph* or *page* when followed by a number: *paragraph 2, page 3.*

Additional proper nouns frequently requiring capitalization are brand names and business names. Many college students dream of opening a business, an evolution of a childhood lemonade stand. A brand name identifies your product or service and contributes to your company's success: *Joe's Dough Shop.* Your business name is your business's legal name, the official name on company legal documents: *Pizza and Pasta Products.* Trade names and business names are generally capitalized: *Jeep, Kleenex,* and *Scotch Tape.*

TECHNICAL STUFF

Some brand names are trending against capitalization rules and searching to attract alternate audiences by changing their brand name to all caps, or all lowercase: *WALMART, amazon, target, facebook,* and *at&t.* Some brand names are starting their own trend: *iPod* and *YouTube.* Research shows that various letter formations attract different audiences.

TIP

Inconsistencies in capitalizing medical terms require validation in *Merriam-Webster.*

Titles and headings

While capital letters guide readers through daily life by highlighting proper nouns — names of streets, buildings, transportation centers, retail stores, restaurants, schools, housing developments, service centers, recreation centers, stadiums, and so forth — no emphasis is as important as capitalizing titles associated with names.

Imagine visiting your bank and seeing the capitalized "President Chesney" on the office door. You know you'll be speaking with the decision-maker to negotiate the rate of your student loan.

REMEMBER

Many style books recommend capitalizing high government positions that lack names (Senator, Secretary of State) and their prefixes (Vice President, Lieutenant Governor). Similarly, references to a deity and religious denominations are capitalized: God, Yahweh, Allah, Jehovah, Methodists, Christian Scientists, and Mormons.

APA recommends capitalizing job titles or positions when the title precedes the person's name:

> After World War II, <u>General Dwight D. Eisenhower</u> became the 34th President of the United States.
>
> I spoke with <u>Professor Rowan</u> after her film class.

Don't capitalize job titles that follow the name:

> President <u>Ulysses S. Grant</u>, a Civil War <u>general</u>, was inaugurated on March 4, 1869.
>
> <u>Lee Iacocca</u>, <u>president and chairman</u> of the board of Chrysler Cooperation, was known for the development of the Ford Mustang.
>
> While walking on Route 2, I saw <u>Don Stollman</u>, <u>professor</u> of journalism.

Avoid capitalizing a description of the person's position that doesn't name the title:

> Steve Jobs, <u>developer</u> of the iPhone and iPad, died at age 56.

Capitalize titles of organizations.

> World Health Organization, American Kennel Club, National College Athletic Association, and National Education Association

APA utilizes two capitalization styles for titles of works and headings within works:

» **Title case** requires capitalization of major words (nouns, verbs, adjectives, adverbs, pronouns, and all words four letters or longer). Minor words that aren't capitalized include conjunctions of three or fewer letters, prepositions, and articles. In title case, capitalize the first word of the title, heading, and subtitle (*The Great Influenza: The Story of the Deadliest Pandemic in History*). Title case is used for titles of books, periodicals, and reports used in text.

» **Sentence case** requires lower case for most words. Capitalize only the first word of the title (or heading) and subtitle, and the first word after a colon, dash (em dash), or end mark of punctuation (*The great influenza: The story of the deadliest pandemic in history*). ***Note:*** Sentence case is used in the reference list.

» Rethinking the big picture

» Pruning paragraphs and sentences

» Searching for precise words

Chapter **8**

Covering All Bases: Three-Level Revising

S ystematic revising, the motherboard of academic and career writing success, offers an opportunity to transition writing from good to great, to restructure a C-paper into an A-paper.

Writing professors generally agree that their best writers are their best rewriters. Successful writing results from major revisions of second, third, and sometimes fourth drafts. During these revisions, a shift happens as writers revise at the structural level, paragraph and sentence levels, and word level. Writers show improvement from draft to draft as they also fulfill a multi-draft requirement of many university first-year-writing programs.

APA recognizes the importance of revising manuscripts, saying, "Most manuscripts need to be revised. . .." This advice applies to all serious writing. (You decide the seriousness of your texting, emailing, and social posting.)

In this chapter, I guide you through an organized revision plan from a global approach through to a local approach. You see an improvement in your writing as you organize your argument, tighten your paragraph and sentence structure, and choose precise words. If you commit to revising every time you write, you'll see your writing improve with every new project.

WARNING

Don't equate revising with editing. Editing is like throwing a ball with a friend; revising is like teaching your dog to catch a ball. Editing and proofreading, lower-order skills, involve the correction of spelling, grammar, punctuation, and usage — mechanical skills that improve readability. Revising, a higher-order skill, is the recursive process of rethinking, 're-visioning', and rewriting.

HEADING TO THE OPERATING ROOM: TIME TO REVISE WITH "MAJOR SURGERY"

"It is no sign of weakness or defeat that your manuscript ends up in need of major surgery. This is common in all writing and among the best of writers," said E. B. White (1899–1985), author of *Charlotte's Web* and co-author of the iconic *The Elements of Style*. White emphasizes that "the best of writers" revise with "major surgery." Other legendary writers who promote revising include

- Robert Graves, British poet and novelist (1895–1985): "There is no such thing as good writing. Only good rewriting."

- Nora DeLoach, American mystery writer (1940–2001): "Writing is rewriting."

- Mark Twain, American humorist (1835–1910): "A successful book is not made of what is in it, but of what is left out of it."

- Patricia Reilly, American children's literature author (b. 1935): "Revision is the heart of writing."

- S. A. Bodeen, American young adult novelist (b. 1965): "It's easier to revise lousy writing than to revise a blank sheet of paper."

- Vladimir Nabokov, Russian-American novelist (1899–1977): "I have rewritten — often several times — every word I have ever published."

- Robert Cormier, American author (1925–2000): "The beautiful part of writing is that you don't have to get it right the first time, unlike, say, a brain surgeon. You can always do it better, find the exact word, the apt phrase, the leaping simile."

- Judy Blume, American young adult author (b. 1938): "I'm a rewriter. That's the part I like best . . . once I have a pile of paper to work with, it's like having the pieces of a puzzle. I just have to put the pieces together to make a picture."

- James Michener, American author (1907–1997): "I'm not a very good writer, but I'm an excellent rewriter."

Revising: Why Rewriting Is So Important

A wise person once said only fools and dead people never change their minds. You're neither a fool nor unable to revise your writing. Writers do change their minds. Successful writers have been revising since the invention of the eraser, which evolved into your deletion key. Revising is part of the creative process and common to the work of artists, architects, automakers, designers, and chefs — even spouses occasionally revise.

The goal of revising is improving performance. If the Wright brothers didn't continuously revise and improve, the invention of flight would have been delayed. If famous writers lacked their passion to revise, many famous literary works of art would not exist.

The value of revising to you as an academic writer includes

- >> Improves structural organization
- >> Clarifies development of ideas
- >> Eliminates unnecessary and overused words
- >> Corrects inaccurate use of language conventions

Experienced professors can easily identify one-and-done writing projects that lack commitment to revising. Red flags of one-draft writing include

- >> An unbalanced pace of argument development
- >> A loosely structured argument that lacks tie-in to the focus
- >> A pattern of longer sentences with excessive afterthoughts
- >> Editing errors resulting from limited manuscript readings
- >> Patterns of clichés and informal language
- >> Wordiness resulting from a lack of feedback
- >> A grade that won't please you

Revising may not have been a regular writing process strategy prior to college, but it's necessary for successful college writing. Professors not only hold you more accountable for your writing ideas, but their preparation hours allow them more time to evaluate your writing content.

The following sections show you techniques for getting feedback and how to apply that feedback to sections of your paper.

Seeking feedback when revising

Quality revision begins with quality feedback. Your primary source of feedback is your professor. Your most effective professor feedback strategy is scheduling a conference to review your writing. Ask questions using the language of writing: organization, tone, focus, development, and opening and closing. As you become familiar with sources (see Chapter 11) and citations (refer to Chapter 10), ask questions about them. If you lack understanding of your professor's comments, ask questions about how to address them. Keep your professor focused on the information you want. As you practice feedback and revising, you'll develop self-feedback skills to complement feedback from others.

REMEMBER

In addition, cultivate a dependable, trusted peer as a feedback partner. Peer feedback research shows that the person giving the feedback improves writing more than the person receiving the feedback. You give feedback on a peer's writing and you see a peer's approach that addresses assignment issues. You'll also follow your mom's advice that giving is better than receiving.

A successful revising strategy demands a 24- to 36-hour separation from a previous draft. The interval frees data from the brain's working memory, the most limited storage capacity of the brain. Another technique that frees memory is a short walk or run.

WARNING

Occasionally writers make false starts or experience writer's block. A false start, like losing your appetite for an overpriced menu item, can result from too broad or too narrow an argument or the unavailability of research to support the argument. Before committing to a topic, ensure sufficient research is available. If you experience writer's block or a temporary inability to create text, find another area of your project to continue with: revising, reading, researching, validating citations and references — something that progresses your paper. As you know, almost all college deadlines, like workplace deadlines, are set in stone. In many cases, asking your professor for a deadline extension is like telling your professor you mismanaged your time.

Rewriting in action: A real-life example

The following example (see Figure 8-1) of an unrevised college research paper was submitted by Grant Giampalmi, then a freshman at Boston College. The revision of the opening, middle, and closing appears in the sections that follow. The paper earned an A.

WARNING

Citations in this model have been fictionalized to avoid plagiarism, and the reference list is not included. Citations are detailed in Part 3. *Note:* The font sizes in the examples in this chapter aren't in line with APA style. They've been sized for this book.

Take Me out to the Ballgame

"We continue to struggle with the time of the game," admittedly claimed Major League Baseball Commissioner Rob Manfred when asked about the decreasing popularity in the sport (Baseball, 2020). With a 162-game season, it is difficult to maintain fan interest throughout the entire season. National viewership and popularity have decreased, especially in the younger generation when compared to the NFL and NBA (MLB Marketing, 2019). While part of the baseball experience used to be going to the ballpark, fans now want a more action-packed and faster-moving spectacle. To solve baseball's popularity problem, Major League Baseball needs to shorten the length of games by decreasing the time in-between innings and eliminating all pitcher's mound visits. Furthermore, the league needs to increase marketing through social media to improve national viewership.

Baseball's decreasing popularity results from its slow pace of play. As of 2017, the average MLB game spans over 3 hours and 5 minutes (Swanson, 2019). Paired with a grueling 162 game season, this sport seems laborious to watch compared to other major sports. The NFL owns a day of the week, Sunday, for five months of the year. The NHL and NBA each have 82 game seasons, nearly half that of Major League Baseball.

Major League Baseball should implement minor changes to eliminate "dead time" during the games. Casual baseball fans do not have the attention span to watch a meaningless, three-hour game. The solution of speeding up the game needs to balance between baseball purists and the fair-weather fan. That means no fundamental alterations of the original rules that have lasted since the late 1800s. Decreasing the time in between innings, or even eliminating this dead period and having an intermission period will help solve this problem. Similarly, prohibiting mound visits between coaches and pitchers will suffice.

Shortening the time in-between half innings will increase the pace of play and lead to more action and less wasted time. This change will help solve baseball's popularity problem. For locally broadcasted games, pitchers get two minutes and five seconds to throw as many warm-up pitches as they wish. This period extends an extra 20 seconds for nationally televised games, and an additional 50 seconds for postseason games (What is, 2019). These constant 2-minute interruptions every half-inning make the game longer. If Major League Baseball cut this time in half, the game would flow much more quickly. Locally broadcasted games would eliminate almost 18 minutes per game. The loss of advertising revenue could be balanced with more in-game advertisements. The NFL has enacted this type of advertising, partnering with Amazon Prime to offer in-game "Next-Gen Stats brought to you by Amazon Web Services" (Reddick, 2019).

Major League Baseball could take an even more drastic measure and eliminate in-between inning time accompanied by a half time period like other sports. Scrapping the two minutes in between innings saves 37 minutes and 30 seconds for local games. This increases to 43 minutes and 30 seconds for nationally televised games and an astonishing 52 minutes and 30 seconds for postseason games. Less dead time means more action. A five-minute intermission can occur in the fifth inning to allow for advertisements. The main revenue draw for Major League Baseball is ticket sales, accounting for nearly 30% of its revenue. Implementing these changes to the game will help solve another issue of declining attendance and will increase ticket revenue. With initial success in YouTube streamed games, the overall advertising market will most likely not decline substantially. Especially with increased ticket sales, the total revenue for Major League Baseball would certainly increase (MLB Revenue, 2020). With this proposed change, the average baseball game drops from over three hours to approximately two hours and 20 minutes.

Major League Baseball has implemented rule changes to help speed up the pace of play, however, these changes could use improvement. Starting in the 2020 regular season, relief pitchers will be required to face a minimum of 3 batters before being replaced. This rule change helps solve the issue of managers inserting pitchers every other batter, which adds time to the game. While this remains a suitable option for increasing the pace of play, pitchers still take up 2 minutes to throw warm-up pitches, even after they spend approximately 30 minutes warming up in the bullpen. Pitchers sprinting directly from the bullpen into live-action, without warming up again on the pitcher's mound, will not only increase the pace of the game but will add

FIGURE 8-1: An unrevised college research paper. Published with permission from Grant Giampalmi.

an extra element of excitement (MLB Announces, 2019). Another possibility to increase the pace of play in MLB would be to eliminate all mound visits from the coaches of the defensive team. The limit of mound visits was set at six in 2018 and reduced to five in 2019. Eliminating all mound visits from coaches, but still allowing players to converge at the pitcher's mound, will undoubtedly accelerate the game. Mound visits from the pitching coach are often used as a strategy to throw off the batter's rhythm or discuss how the pitcher should approach the batter. This work can be done just as easily in between innings.

To address Major League Baseball's decreasing popularity issue, the league must market to a younger audience. A 2017 Market Watch article found that the average baseball viewer is 57 years old (Vance, 2018). Even worse, the same survey found that just 7% of baseball viewers are below 18 (MLB Teams, 2018). Possible reasons for the lack of younger viewership is attributed to younger generations having a shorter attention span, as they spend more time on their smartphones. This past summer, MLB shifted 13 nationally broadcasted games to a YouTube stream. Tim Katz, head of YouTube's sports partnerships, discussed this new way of watching baseball: "Ease of access to the games is our number one thing; both making it free and making it available across as many device types as possible" (2018, p. 84). This partnership seems to be the start of new ways of attracting this younger audience. A July 2019 game between the Philadelphia Phillies and Los Angeles Dodgers saw nearly 2 million total viewers, with 200,000 concurrent viewers at its peak. The game featured zero commercials. Instead, fans saw in-game interviews with coaches and players in the dugout (The MLB/YouTube, 2019). Expansion to more accessible platforms for Major League Baseball will increase viewership and help capture a younger audience.

Major League Baseball must aggressively market their superstars to increase national viewership and popularity. Why would a viewer from Texas want to watch a game between the Philadelphia Phillies and the Los Angeles Dodgers if they have no association with either team? Other sports do not have this issue. LeBron James draws attention from fans of every city. Baseball players cannot say the same. Mike Trout is on pace to have the best career of any player in over 150 years, yet he is not an established household name. The market research firm Q-Scores found that only 22% of the US public is familiar with Mike Trout (2019). As for comparison, NBA star Stephen Curry and New Orleans Saints Quarterback Drew Brees are near 50%. Even among sports fans, Trout's recognition increases to 50%, which is minuscule compared to the near-universal recognition of Tom Brady and LeBron James (Mookie, 2019).

MLB Players, with the help of Commissioner Manfred, must market themselves better on social media to increase the popularity of the sport. Mike Trout's 1.2 million Instagram followers fall short to Tom Brady's 6.8 million, even though Brady joined the platform in 2017. Part of this issue is that Trout remains a more mellow and less vocal person. Houston Astros Third Baseman Alex Bregman, unlike Trout, is passionate about the general lack of interest for baseball compared to other sports. Bregman launched a YouTube channel, with videos ranging from a trip back to his alma-mater at LSU to his Spring Training routine, and had great initial success. His channel received 4.3 million social engagements this past offseason, which is 2.5 times the next highest MLB player, Marcus Stroman (MLB Media, 2019). The Opendorse marketing company that released these numbers also disclosed that Bregman's engagement numbers do not come close to the leaders on the NFL charts (Major League Baseball Marketing, 2019). Bregman's actions are the foundation of what the MLB needs: more social media engagement with personalities that care about the growth of the game. MLB Commissioner Rob Manfred refuses to accept blame for this marketing issue, particularly with Trout: "I think we can make [Trout's] brand very big. But he has to decide to engage" (MLB Brand, 2019). Manfred should be ecstatic to have a generational talent in this suffering time for baseball. While the individual players themselves are to partially blame for this, the commissioner's words are not exactly promising for the future (Mookie, 2019).

Baseball's popularity crisis is a result of the digital age. No fundamental and revolutionary changes to the rules are needed to revive the game. In its 150- year history, the rules have rarely been the cause of the problem. Adapting to the digitally-driven age we live in to increase the pace of play and social media engagement will lead back to the glory days of Major League Baseball.

FIGURE 8-1:
(continued)

Streamlining: Structural Organization

Revising begins at the structural level, just as building a car begins with the frame, building an education begins with books, and building a healthy body begins with diet and exercise.

Begin big-picture revising by ensuring that you've fulfilled rubric requirements for topic, length, readings, objectives, audience, and purpose. Review Chapter 5 for additional details.

Evaluate the following organizational questions and revise as necessary:

>> Structurally, did the paper deliver the argument articulated in the introduction?

>> Is the argument focused, logical, and clearly stated in the introduction?

>> Does the structure address audience objections to the argument?

>> Do paragraphs flow through a beginning, middle, and closing?

>> Does every paragraph develop the argument and clearly connect to that argument?

>> Does the flow of ideas contain specifics such as reasons, statistical data, facts, and researched evidence?

>> Does the overall structure contain author reflection on the factual content?

>> Does the argument lack dominance of author opinion?

>> Is the structure consistent with models provided and anticipated professor expectations?

>> Do the argument and research offer value to the audience?

REMEMBER

Comprehensive revising includes addressing professor comments on recent papers and past patterns of revision issues such as focus, development, wordiness, source engagement, and connecting support to the argument.

With your writing structure in place, like a foundation and roof, you can begin revising the interior elements of your paper: the opening, middle, and closing.

Opening: Working title, first sentence, and introduction

Shakespeare said, "All's well that ends well." He also could have easily said, "All's well that begins well." Writers know the importance of a good opening: the title, first sentence, and introduction. If writers fail to engage the reader with the opening, the middle and closing lack relevance.

Most writers begin papers with a working title, a title that maintains focus but will be revised when the project is completed and they know what they are titling. I discuss title strategies in Chapter 14.

Follow the title with a first sentence that engages the reader. The purpose of your first sentence is to engage the reader, your professor, and encourage them to begin thinking, "This paper interests me, and I am reading to justify evidence that it earns an excellent grade." The remainder of the introduction includes a few sentences explaining the importance of the topic and additional background. (See an example of topic background in the Revised College Research Paper: Title and Introduction.) Transition the introduction into a claim statement or focus statement that identifies the argument of the paper.

This section includes some strategies you can use when drafting your first sentences and openings, as well as an example research paper to illustrate an effective opening.

Drafting an effective opening: The how-to

First-sentence and opening strategies for research papers include

>> **Expert quotations:** "An expert knows all the answers — if you ask the right questions," said Levi Strauss, American businessman (1829–1920).

>> **Unusual information:** The Nation's Report Card, the National Assessment of Educational Progress (NAEP), reveals a startling fact about students who score high in all subject areas: They write more in school than students who score poorly.

>> **Series of questions:** What's the cause of high-performing students underperforming on high-stakes standardized tests such as the SAT, ACT, and GRE? What's the cause of a professional athlete underperforming on a game-winning play or a pressure putt? Do underperforming students and athletes share common characteristics for a "choke"?

Sian Beilock's *Choke: What the Secrets of the Brain Reveal About Getting It Right When You Have To* (Free Press) analyzes athletes' and students' approach to performance under pressure and offers strategies for success.

- **Emotional appeal:** Next to loving and caring about their child, parents' most important responsibility is to provide their child with the best education available. Fulfilling your child's educational needs requires active participation on your part. Making homework sessions a regular part of your routine at home together is an excellent way to do this.

- **Summary:** Is all work and no play synonymous with college success? Not according to a ten-year study by a team of Harvard researchers who analyzed academic habits of a successful college experience.

- **Anecdotes:** When I began drawing as a hobby in the late '80s, I asked experienced artists one piece of advice they would offer me as a novice artist. Each artist consistently gave me the same piece of advice: Draw, draw, and draw. When I started freelance writing in the late '80s, I frequently asked editors to recommend the best book for future writers. The book unanimously suggested, and the book that remains the foundation of my teaching and writing, is Strunk and White's *The Elements of Style.*

WARNING

Don't begin a research paper (or any other college paper) with a standard dictionary definition.

TECHNICAL STUFF

If you're opening a graduate-level research paper, focus less on reader engagement with the first sentence and introduction, and more on the rationale and importance of the thesis or hypothesis. Also, include a review of the literature in the opening section. Keep in mind, though, that many undergraduate professors don't require formal sections titled Statement of the Problem, or Review of the Literature, Methods, and Discussion.

The opening ends with clarification of the argument (a claim statement or thesis), a promise to the reader that foreshadows the development of the argument.

A real-life example: Revised opening

Here I include the example research paper and show how opening after revision strategies were applied.

Here is an overview of what was done during the revision:

- Revised the title with a focus that references the argument (*But Not a Boring Four-Hour Experience*). The author also deleted underlining from the title (underlining or italicizing signifies a book title).

- >> Added an engaging first-sentence quotation ("We continue. . .") that summarizes the major focus of the argument.

- >> Revised the argument statement to identify a stronger and more inclusive focus ("MLB needs to improve. . ."). The next-to-last sentence also identifies the argument, and the last sentence ("But baseball. . .") suggests signs of a self-recovery of popularity. This broader statement extends the argument beyond length-of-game issues and allows the introduction of solutions such as more attractive, special game experiences and expanded social media experiences, in addition to addressing game-shortening strategies.

- >> Added a brief history of baseball to the first paragraph. The author also added statistical support of the problem to the second paragraph.

- >> Changed all spacing after end punctuation from two spaces to APA required one space.

Figure 8-2 shows the revisions applied to the first draft of the opening of the paper. Citations in this model have been fictionalized to avoid plagiarism. Chapter 10 details citations.

Take Me Out to the Ballgame: But Not A Boring Four-Hour Experience

"We continue to struggle with the time of the game," claimed Major League Baseball Commissioner Rob Manfred when asked about the decreasing popularity of baseball (Baseball, 2020, p. 186). The game arguably invented by Abner Doubleday in 1839 and America's oldest professional sport, professional baseball began approximately a hundred years after American Independence with formation of the National League. America's pastime was played by soldiers during the Civil War. It survived an on-field death, world wars, a World Series scandal, the Great Depression, sign-stealing scandals and performance-enhancing drugs. It improved the social fabric of America with the emergence of Jackie Robinson, the first African American to play in a major league baseball game in 1947.

The popularity of Major League Baseball (MLB) faces the challenge of maintaining fan interest over a 162-game schedule, and games that approach four hours. National viewership and popularity has decreased, especially with millennials compared with the National Football League (NFL) and National Basketball League (NBA) (MLB Marketing, 2019, p. 15). MLB average attendance was below 30,000 for the first time since 2003 (businesstoday.com, 2019, p. 140). Attendance during the 2019 regular season was down 1.7 percent, representing a 14 percent decline from a high of 79.5 million total attendance in 2007 (Front Office, 2019, p. 25). While the traditional appeal of baseball was the sport itself and its ambiance, today's fans want a more action-packed and faster-moving spectacle. MLB needs to improve the ballpark experience, promote player and game visibility on the national level, and increase marketing through social media to appeal to the smartphone generation of fans. But baseball does show signs of a rally to support its claim of America's pastime to thrive through future decades.

FIGURE 8-2: Revised first draft of sample research paper.

Published with permission from Grant Giampalmi

Middle

The middle section of a research paper contains much more than ingredients sandwiched between the beginning and closing. It's the "show me the money" part of the paper, the support of the argument and refutation of the counter-argument. The middle develops background information introduced in the opening, and transitions to present the research evidence and citations. Chapters 10 and 11 explain how you support the argument, and Part 3 details support and citations. Solid supporting evidence fast-tracks you toward a B grade or higher, assuming accuracy of language skills and conventions such as those I describe in Chapter 7.

The following example (see Figure 8-3) shows the revisions made to the middle:

>> Included additional background information, transitioning from the introduction

>> Added paragraphs on marketing to children and past personalities of baseball

Closing

The closing, the final message to the reader, includes a summary and author reflection on that summary, which may include suggestions for further related research. The ending is your final opportunity to impress your professor with your critical analysis. Your last sentence contains the last words you write before your professor begins to grade your paper. A short three- or four-sentence ending paragraph tells your professor that you are in a hurry to end your paper, and don't expect an A grade. A successful paper not only includes a good first impression, but also a good last impression.

The following example (see Figure 8-4) of an effective closing shows the revisions made to the closing:

>> Added paragraphs on successful baseball promotions

>> Added paragraphs showing baseball's successful financial data and comparisons with other major sports

>> Added paragraphs justifying baseball's overall attendance, which exceeds a hundred million spectators annually

>> Ended with a sentence that references the opening sentence

Many baseball fans attribute baseball's popularity decrease to its slow pace of play. With a marathon game schedule, baseball to many seems laborious compared with other major sports. The NFL owns a day of the week, Sunday, for five months a year. The NHL and NBA each have 82 game seasons, nearly half that of MLB. But baseball's timelessness and eventual finality was considered an asset a generation ago when games were 45 minutes shorter. Covid-season time savers in 2020 included seven-inning double headers and the designated hitter in both leagues.

Speeding up the game needs to balance between baseball purists and fair-weather fans. That means no fundamental alterations of original rules that have existed since the late 1800s. Decreasing time between innings (a major source of commercial revenue time) is a change worth considering. For locally broadcasted games, pitchers get two minutes and five seconds to throw as many warm-up pitches as they wish. This period extends an extra 20 seconds for nationally televised games, and an additional 50 seconds for postseason games (Baseball Times, 2019, p. 15). These two-minute interruptions every half-inning extend games. If Major League Baseball cut this time in half, the game would flow much more quickly. Locally broadcasted games would eliminate almost 18 minutes per game. The loss of advertising revenue could be balanced with more in-game advertisements. The NFL has enacted this type of advertising, partnering with Amazon Prime to offer in-game "Next-Gen Stats brought to you by Amazon Web Services" (Reddick, 2019, p. 56)

Since the main revenue stream for Major League Baseball is ticket sales, accounting for nearly 30 percent of its revenue, these changes could increase attendance and ticket revenue. And with initial success offering YouTube streamed games, the overall advertising market will most likely increase also (MLB Revenue, 2020, p. 102).

MLB has implemented rule changes to help speed the pace of play and increase audience appeal; however, these changes are works in progress. Starting in the 2020 regular season, relief pitchers will be required to face a minimum of three batters before being replaced. This rule change helps solve the issue of managers inserting pitchers every other batter, which adds time to the game. While this remains a suitable option for increasing the pace of play, pitchers still take up two minutes to throw warm-up pitches, even after they spend approximately 30 minutes warming up in the bullpen. Pitchers sprinting directly from the bullpen into live-action, without warming up again on the pitcher's mound, will not only increase the pace of the game but will add an extra element of excitement (MLB Announces, 2019, p. 137). Another possibility to increase the pace of play includes eliminating mound visits from the coaches of the defensive team. The limit of mound visits was set at six in 2018 and reduced to five in 2019. Eliminating all mound visits from coaches, but still allowing players to converge at the pitcher's mound, will undoubtedly accelerate the game. Mound visits from the pitching coach are often used as a strategy to disrupt the batter's rhythm or discuss the pitcher's approach the batter. Strategy sessions can be done between innings. A trial time-saver introduced in the 2020 Covid season was seven inning double headers, which raises the issue of crediting pitchers for seven inning no hitters and perfect games.

To address baseball's decreasing popularity, the league must market to a younger audience. A 2017 Market Watch article found that the average baseball viewer is 57 years old (Vance, 2018, p. 78). The same survey also found that just 7 percent of baseball viewers are below 18 (MLB Teams, 2018, p. 34). The lack of younger viewership is possibly attributed to younger generations having shorter attention spans, as they spend more time on smartphones. This past summer, MLB shifted 13 nationally broadcasted games to a YouTube stream. Tim Katz, head of YouTube's sports partnerships, discussed this new way of watching baseball: "ease of access to the games is our number one thing; both making it free and making it available across as many device types as possible" (Whitby & Agnew, 2019, p. 323). This partnership seems to be the start of new strategies for attracting this younger audience. A July 2019 game between the Philadelphia Phillies and Los Angeles Dodgers attracted nearly 2 million viewers, with 200,000 concurrent viewers at its peak. In place of commercials, fans saw in-game interviews with coaches and players in the dugout (MLB/YouTube, 2019, 1:06.). Expansion to more accessible platforms for MLB will increase viewership and help capture a younger audience.

FIGURE 8-3: The revised middle of the research paper.

Published with permission from Grant Giampalmi

MLB must aggressively market their superstars to increase national viewership and popularity. Why would a viewer from Texas want to watch a game between the Philadelphia Phillies and the Los Angeles Dodgers if they have no association with either team? Other sports do not have this issue. LeBron James draws attention from fans of every city. Baseball players cannot say the same. Mike Trout is on pace to have the best career of any player in over 150 years, yet he is not an established household name. Market research firm Q Scores found that only 22 percent of the US public is familiar with Mike Trout. Comparatively, NBA star Stephen Curry and New Orleans Saints Quarterback Drew Brees are nearly 50 percent. Even among sports fans, Trout's recognition increases to 50 percent, minuscule compared with the near-universal recognition of Tom Brady and LeBron James (Mookie, 2019, p. 45).

Baseball also needs stronger marketing directed towards kids, their future lifetime fans. The Phillie Phanatic represents a new age mascot who entertains children during games. The Phanatic also entertained cardboard cutouts during Covid games. Baseball also needs to return to attractions such as two-inning youth league games played in stadiums before major league games, teams in uniform admitted free, and player appearances (for a reasonable cost) at community events. And World Series games need to be scheduled at reasonable starting times to accommodate children's bedtimes.

In addition to baseball's lack of marketing, baseball also lacks yesteryear's eccentric personalities such as Mark Fidrych, Ozzie Guillen, Manny Ramirez, Reggie Jackson, Willie Stargell, and Ken Griffey, Jr. Baseball also lacks the drama of closers such as Al Hrabasky, Mitch Williams, Rollie Fingers, and Mariano Rivera. Also lacking are broadcasting legends such as Mel Allen, Vince Scully, Harry Caray, and Harry Kalas.

MLB players, with the help of Commissioner Manfred, must also market themselves better on social media. Mike Trout's 1.2 million Instagram followers fall short to Tom Brady's 6.8 million, even though Brady joined the platform in 2017. Part of this issue is that Trout remains a more mellow and less vocal person. Houston Astros Third Baseman Alex Bregman, unlike Trout, is passionate about the general lack of interest for baseball compared to other sports. Bregman successfully launched a YouTube channel, with videos ranging from a trip back to his alma-mater at LSU to his spring training routine. His channel received 4.3 million social engagements this past off-season, which is 2.5 times the next highest MLB player, Marcus Stroman. The Opendorse Marketing Company that released these numbers also disclosed that Bregman's engagement numbers do not approach NFL social media leaders (Major League Baseball Report, 2018, p. 89). Bregman's actions are the foundation of what the MLB needs: more social media engagement with personalities that care about the growth of the game. MLB Commissioner Rob Manfred refuses to accept blame for this marketing issue, particularly with Trout: "I think we can make [Trout's] brand very big. But he has to decide to engage" (Major League Baseball, 2019, p. 83).

FIGURE 8-3:
(continued)

Regardless of the grand-old-game's shortcomings, baseball is not on life support. Baseball's approximate 2,430 regular-season games produces major income compared with the NFL's 256, and the NBA's 1,230. Baseball Fan reports MLB games in 2019 attracted 68.5 million spectators, a 1.7 percent decline from 2018 (MLB Brand, 2019). And baseball's minor leagues sold nearly 50 million tickets in 2017 (New York Times, 2019), totaling well over a hundred million fans attending professional baseball games in recent years—hardly a lack of interest in baseball.

One of today's baseball personalities, Bryce Harper, recently signed a $330 million contract, increasing Philadelphia Phillies' attendance to 2.72 million fans his first year in Citizens Bank Park. On the West Coast, the Los Angeles Dodgers averaged 49,066 fans in 2019 and set single-game attendance records with special night attractions, including Cody Bellinger Bobblehead Night, Fernando Valenzuela's Legends of Dodger Baseball Night, and Mexican Heritage Night. Dodger Stadium's largest crowd since renovations in 2013 was LGBT Night attracting 54,307 fans (Baseball Report, 2019).

Noah Garden, MLB Executive Vice President of business and sales, explains that MLB in 2018 "invested more into digital platforms like MLB At Bat mobile applications and Ballpark Pass," reaching over two billion users and increasing monthly ticket options and other purchases by 49 percent (Front Page Sports, 2018). *Athletic Journal* lists the NFL as the most profitable sports league in the world, generating $13 billion annually. MLB is second, generating $10 billion and the NBA third, generating $7.4 billion (2019). Baseball is as financially healthy as our technology toy makers. MLB Commissioner Manfred may struggle with the time of baseball games, but the league does not need to spend time worrying about its finances.

FIGURE 8-4:
The revised closing of the research paper.

Published with permission from Grant Giampalmi

Paring: Paragraphs and Sentences

Revising paragraphs and sentences is like organizing your desktop where you're deleting files and apps, eliminating clutter, and reorganizing folders. Paragraphs and sentences are like a good friendship: They connect tightly, flow smoothly, and fulfill a variety of needs. Paragraphs in research paper writing introduce new ideas, explanations, and evidence, and strongly connect to the argument.

The lifeblood of a paragraph is its topic sentence — its focus, its reason for existence. The body of the paragraph (short or long) develops that one focus and thrives on details, examples, evidence, and definitions.

REMEMBER

Revise paragraphs by reflecting on answers to the following questions and applying revisions as necessary:

>> Does the paragraph contain a topic sentence and a focus?

>> Does the paragraph topic add to the development of the focus?

>> Is the paragraph positioned appropriately in relation to other paragraphs?

>> Is the paragraph length appropriate for the importance of the topic?

>> Does the paragraph contain development strategies such as details, examples, evidence, and definitions?

>> Does the paragraph transition from the previous paragraph and into the next paragraph?

>> Can any paragraph sentences be eliminated because they are repetitious?

>> Can any paragraph sentences be condensed because they contain similar ideas?

The following section offers classroom-tested strategies for revising paragraphs, sentences, and words. Embrace them with American philosopher Ralph Waldo Emerson's approach to life: "Nothing great was ever achieved without enthusiasm."

Sentence starters

A default sentence-creation strategy includes starting sentences with patterns such as "It is," "There are," and "It becomes." These patterns delay identifying the topic of the sentence, and therefore delay reader understanding. Almost any sentence can begin with a sentence starter. Revise sentence starters by identifying the sentence subject or topic, usually found within the sentence, and following the subject with an action verb.

Sentence starter: *There are* dozens of college websites to support essay writing.

Revised: Dozens of college websites support essay writing.

Revise *There are* by identifying the performer of the action as the subject of the sentence: *Dozens (of college websites)*. Follow the subject with the action verb *support*.

Sentence starter: *It becomes* difficult for freshmen to manage time during fast-paced college semesters.

Revised: Freshmen struggle with managing time during fast-paced college semesters.

Revise *It becomes* by identifying the performer of the action as the subject of the sentence, *freshmen*. Follow the subject with the action verb *struggle*.

Sentence starter: *It was* hot today.

Revised: Today's temperature soared to 100.

Revise *hot* with specific language *temperature soared to 100,* which offers the reader visualization. Follow the subject with the action verb *reached*.

Sentence-starter patterns may also appear in the middle of a sentence:

Sentence starter: With a 162-game season, *it is* difficult to maintain fan interest throughout the entire season.

Revised: Baseball struggles to maintain fan interest throughout a 162-game season.

Avoid the confusing sentence starter "it" in "it is" and so forth with pronoun references to previous ideas. For example, Dickens' "It was the best of times, it was the worst of times," references "it" as the 18th century, not as a sentence starter.

Apply Microsoft Word's "Find and Replace" feature to locate sentence starters.

Spoken-language wordiness

You may have been taught to write like you talk. But because a person speaks approximately 125 words per minute, spontaneous conversation lacks writing's precision and word economy, and includes a library of superfluous language. Compose sentences by identifying the sentence topic (the subject) within the first three to five words and following the topic with an action verb. The written language frequently includes unnecessary spoken expressions that provide the speaker with thinking time: *by the way, I believe, permit me to say, if you ask me, it's no wonder,* and *in my opinion.*

Wordy: *If you ask me,* college success requires better time management than high school.

Revised: College success requires better time management than high school.

Wordy: *By the way,* Immaculata University won three consecutive AIAW (later NCAA) Women's National Basketball Championships in 1972, 1973, and 1974.

Revised: Immaculata University won three consecutive AIAW (later NCAA) Women's National Basketball Championships in 1972, 1973, and 1974.

Wordy phrases and clauses

The spoken language encourages wordiness because speaking time lacks the word limit of a printed page or computer file. Spoken-language wordiness encourages unnecessary words to filter into writing.

Apply the following strategies to revise wordy phrases and clauses:

>> Revise adjectival phrases and clauses into single adjectives.

Wordy: Turn left at the house with the red paint.

Revised: Turn left at the red house.

Revise *house with the red paint* to *red house*. *With* phrases signal revision opportunities.

Wordy: The player who was injured left the game.

Revised: The injured player left the game.

Revise *player who was injured* to *injured player*. *Who* clauses signal revision opportunities.

>> Revise and condense wordy expressions such as the following.

Wordy Expression	Condensed Revision
in the event that	if
at this present time	now
for a long time	historically
come in contact with	meet
on the occasion of	when
in this day and age	now

Wordy: College students *in this day and age* are expected to contribute toward their education.

Revised: College students *today* are expected to contribute toward their education.

Whittling Words

The English language contains a little more than a million words. The average English speaker navigates daily life within a range of 20,000 to 35,000 words and writes with approximately a thousand words. No academic writer should experience a word shortage, but many academic writers neglect to practice word diversity and overuse a smaller selection of words — like excessively repeating a favorite spoken expression.

REMEMBER

Precise writing results from deleting unnecessary words and revising overused words. Excessive words are like excessive calories: they're unhealthy for the writer and the reader. Writing becomes precise with accurate and economical words. A healthy vocabulary includes a daily diet of action verbs and specific nouns. Because excessive and overused words bore and distract readers, fewer and precise words produce clearer meaning and add power to writing, like 5G wideband service.

Whittle your words, and say more with less as you apply these word-revision strategies.

Unnecessary and overused words

Inexperienced writers incorrectly believe increasing sentence length improves writing clarity. Unclear ideas with twenty words are not clarified with forty words, just as wearing additional shoes does not improve dancing. Figure out how to say more with less as you apply word-level revising strategies that eliminate unnecessary words, avoid overused words, and prune verbs.

Word-level revision strategies include the following.

>> **Delete unnecessary words** by applying the "need test" — evaluating the need for every word contributing to reader understanding.

>> **Unnecessary words:** Cover up all the plants.

>> **Revised:** Cover up all the plants.

>> Is *cover* needed for reader understanding? (yes) *up*? (no) *all*? (no, unless emphasis is needed) *the?* (yes, for fluency).

>> **Unnecessary words:** The driving rule of no texting while driving is strictly enforced in all states.

>> **Revised:** No texting while driving is strictly enforced nationally.

- Avoid the redundancy of *The driving rule of* and the rule itself. *In all states* can be reduced to *nationally*. Please avoid texting while driving.

» **Avoid overused words.** Overused words (such as nice) lack precision and cloud reader comprehension. For example, a nice day in Alaska differs from a nice day in Hawaii by about 40 degrees. An awful research grade could be C, D, or F, and in some circumstances, B. Avoid overused words such as the following:

Adjectives: beautiful, great, grand, super, amazing, tremendous, fantastic, terrible, awful, horrible, pretty (good), cute, adorable, awesome, outstanding, and phenomenal

Adverbs: very, really, truly, even, extremely, and fine

Nouns: thing, gadget, factor, aspect, way, case, individual, and stuff

Verbs: seems, appears, claims, went, got, affected, and did

» Revise overused words with specific words.

Overused: We had an awesome day at the amusement park.

Revised: Our day at the amusement park included swimming, volleyball, music, pizza, and, of course, the state's highest roller coaster.

Overused: The roads were extremely treacherous.

Revised: The roads were covered with snow and ice.

Overused: What's that thing on the table?

Revised: What's that tool on the table?

» **Avoid the following clichés common to college writing:**

- in this day and age
- level playing field
- time and time again
- take one for the team
- worst nightmare
- eye for an eye
- one in a million
- perfect example
- moment of truth
- my whole life
- bottom line
- smell the roses
- last but not least
- prime example
- made my day
- back in the day

>> **Avoid repetitious word combinations.** For example, "illegal" means not according to law. The phrase "under the law" used with "illegal" is repetitious. Avoid repetition in the following examples:

- illegal under the law
- baby puppies
- long-lasting durability
- two twins
- combine together
- perfect square
- very unique
- repeat again
- the month of June
- striped zebra
- six years of age
- adequate enough
- big in size
- both of them

- argued back and forth
- red in color
- six a.m. in the morning
- repeat again
- round circle
- nod in agreement
- close proximity
- added bonus
- protest against
- sat down
- visible to the eye
- expensive in cost
- true facts
- null and void

>> **Avoid vague, fashionable words.** Some words appear, disappear, and reappear as often as clothing styles. Avoid coined words ending with the following.

- **-wise:** weather-wise, money-wise, job-wise
- **-oriented:** summer-oriented, math-oriented
- **-conscious:** grade-conscious, car-conscious
- **-ish:** sixish, sickish, smoothish
- **-happy:** clothes-happy, concert-happy
- **-type:** outdoor-type, gaming-type
- **-phobia:** chemistry-phobia, car-phobia
- **forced plurals:** the Harvards and the Ben Franklins

Revise vague words with specific words.

- **Vague:** <u>Weather-wise</u>, driving east was good.
- **Revised:** We drove east during sunshine and warm temperatures.
- **Vague:** College students are <u>grade-conscious.</u>
- **Revised:** College students work hard for their A's and B's.

Verb and ly-adverb combinations

Verb and "ly" adverb combinations are words that signal a need for a precise verb. Reduce combinations such as the following:

Wordy Expression	Condensed Revision
look quickly	glance
think quietly	meditate
read quickly	skim
drink quickly	gulp
look closely	examine
dislike intensely	hate
cook slowly	simmer
drive quickly	speed
act irrationally	panic
run quickly	sprint
hold tightly	clench

Wordy: Please *quickly read* this assignment.

Revised: Please *skim* this assignment.

Wordy: Drinking water *too quickly* can cause choking.

Revised: *Gulping* water can cause choking.

TIP

The road to C-level college writing is paved with adverbs and adjectives. The road to A-level college writing is paved with action verbs and specific nouns. Choosing good roads makes writing and life smoother.

Superfluous verb endings

Avoid superfluous verb endings. Delete verb tails such as the following:

>> divide up	>> cover up
>> write down	>> connect up
>> rest up	>> head up
>> join up	>> pay up
>> cool down	>> start up
>> join with	>> fall down
>> stand up	>> polish up
>> finish up	>> clean up

Wordy: After hours of outdoor play, the young children were asked to settle *down*.

Revised: After hours of outdoor play, the young children were asked to relax.

Wordy: The bursar's office expects students to pay *up* before registering for classes.

Revised: The bursar's office expects students to pay before registering for classes.

TIP

Because you also learn language from your sense of hearing, read your paper aloud (with what your elementary teacher called your "one-foot voice") and listen for expressions that sound too familiar, overused, and exclusively used in the spoken language — the previous examples of wordiness.

Analyze the sentence revisions in the following examples and see if you recognize wordy patterns common to your writing. Word count for unrevised and revised sentences appears in parentheses. Challenge yourself to revise the revisions and further reduce their word counts.

>> **Unrevised:** Eliminate all words in a sentence that can be crossed out without losing any of the meaning in that sentence. (20)

Revised: Eliminate wordiness. (2)

The sentence subject is understood to be *you*. Reduce *all words in a sentence that can be crossed out without losing any of the meaning in that sentence* to *wordiness*. The pronoun *that* signals potential wordiness.

» **Unrevised:** Parents were happy at their children's college graduation. (8)

Revised: Parents cheered their children's college graduation. (6)

Revise *were happy* to *cheered,* which shows the *happy* action.

» **Unrevised:** The game of baseball changed because of analytics. (10)

Revised: Analytics changed baseball. (3)

Analytics caused the change. Follow the subject with the completed action *changed. The game of* can be deleted because *baseball* names the game.

» **Unrevised:** She made another shot into the net. (7)

Revised: She scored another goal. (4)

Scored offers a more specific reader-visual than *made.* Revise *another shot into the net* to the precise *goal.*

» **Unrevised:** Following all these steps will have a high impact on whether or not the team will be successful. (18)

Revised: These steps will determine team success. (5)

Steps (the subject) performs the action. Reduce *will have a high impact on whether or not the team* to *determine.*

» **Unrevised:** Feeling that I knew what I could do, I enrolled in advanced calculus. (13)

Revised: Feeling confident, I enrolled in Advanced Calculus. (7)

Reduce *that I knew what I could do* to the precise *confident. That* identifies a revision opportunity. Capitalize course names.

» **Unrevised:** Because of the way things were done in the past, graduation was once again scheduled off campus. (17)

Revised: Because of tradition, graduation was scheduled off campus. (8)

Reduce *the way things were done in the past* to the precise *tradition.*

» **Unrevised:** Before a graduation date is determined, the board of trustees and student government must be in agreement. (17)

Revised: Trustees and student government must agree on a graduation date. (10)

Trustees and student government, the sentence subject, are performing the action. Reduce *must be in agreement* to *must agree on.*

» **Unrevised:** The person who was sick was taken out of the stadium. (11)

Revised: First responders assisted the sick spectator from the stadium. (9)

Because the performer of the action is unidentified, determine that *first responders* assisted the sick person. Revise general *person* to specific *spectator*, assuming the person was attending a stadium event. Reduce *was taken out* to *assisted*.

» **Unrevised:** Washington D.C. is the capital of the U.S. Eleven Smithsonian museums are located there. (15)

Revised: Washington D.C. houses 11 Smithsonian museums. (6)

Assume your audience knows Washington D.C. is the capital of the United States. Revise *are located* with specific *houses*. Review APA rules for numbers in Chapter 7.

» **Unrevised:** It is a sport that is heavily mixed with the ancient culture of Japan. (14)

Revised: Sumo wrestling incorporates Japan's ancient culture. (6)

Revise *it is* by identifying the performer of the action and the sentence topic *Sumo wrestling*. Revise wordy *that is heavily mixed with* to precise *incorporates*. Reduce the prepositional phrase *of Japan* to the adjective *Japan's*.

» **Unrevised:** Rappers made their way into the fashion world. (9)

Revised: Rappers invaded the fashion world. (5)

Replace the wordy verb idea *have made their way into* with the precise and active *invaded*. Alternate verb choices include *infiltrated* and *burst*.

Chapter **9**

Achieving Your Personal Best: Student Improvement Plan

U p to now, the two major academic skills that have contributed to your school success are reading and writing. They're the same two skills that will help you to earn your degree, land you a successful job, promote you in your career, provide lifetime enjoyment, increase your income, improve your health, add interest to your social life, and navigate you through daily life.

You're currently performing one of those skills by reading to derive meaning from a series of lines, curves, and spaces that you translated into complex ideas. The other skill is the reason why you're reading this book — to write a paper that follows APA style and citations. Reading and writing are complementary skills: Reading improves writing, and writing improves reading. Additionally, by valuing reading and writing, you are also likely to instill that value into your children.

A body of brain research shows that reading and writing improve speaking, listening, spelling, vocabulary, and comprehension of all academic courses and topics. Additional advantages of regular reading and writing include an increase in the following:

>> Focus and concentration

>> Discipline needed to complete academic projects

>> Exposure to new ideas

>> Literacy among family members

A successful college education requires an in-depth approach to reading and writing, rather than the surface approach that is common to high school academics.

This chapter guides you through strategies for college-level literacy that meet APA standards. Here I model a plan that prepares you for lifetime literacy. In this chapter, I also reference books for your reading enjoyment. (My success as an author depends on motivating you to read at least one of those books.) Book choices are also adaptable to a college student's budget, because they're available for free from college and community libraries.

REMEMBER

Here is a trifecta of college success strategies:

>> Reading at least 25 pages daily

>> Writing a few paragraphs daily, including summarizing class notes

>> Creating connections among academic topics in your daily life

Understanding What Makes a College Reader

High school reading is like going to the movies; college reading is like planning a spring break vacation. Reading requires focus and commitment. You can't educate yourself without committing to regular reading. Just as college requires upgraded skills for organization, socialization, and technology, it also requires upgraded skills for reading. Prior to college, your reading demands involved summarizing and identifying *who* and *what*; now your demands include synthesizing and identifying *how* and *why*. Reading books, the signature activity of educated people, represents the brain's most intensely focused intellectual activity.

Similar to writing, reading development requires daily practice. If you break your reading rhythm, your academic performance declines. Daily practice improves proficiency and develops college and career reading skills.

In addition to your college courses requiring more reading and more complex reading materials, they challenge you to reflect on that reading. Reading without reflecting is like exercising without sweating. College readers show evidence of their reflecting when they speak and write. The academic person you are today is the product of past words you've read and heard. The academic person you become in the future will be the product of words you read and hear today and in the future.

Finally, a reader is never bored. You can enjoy reading in a hammock, on a beach, in an airplane, under a tree, on a balcony, beside a rock, waiting for someone — anywhere. You're the best academic "you" when you are the best reading "you."

REMEMBER

Characteristics of highly proficient college readers include

>> Reading everywhere when time is available

>> Hanging out in libraries, bookstores, and coffee shops — with a book in hand

>> Socializing with friends who are also readers

>> Referencing books and authors in class discussions and writing projects

>> Coming from a family of readers

>> Enjoying the smell and feel of a new hardback book

>> Attending author lectures

>> Enrolling in reading-concentrated courses

>> Demonstrating an extensive spoken vocabulary

>> Graduating with honors and a good job

TIP

A recent study showed that 72 percent of undergraduates rarely or never completed reading assignments on schedule. If this lack of reading applies to you or if you lack confidence in your reading ability or skills, your academic institution offers trained and patient professionals to help you. Your decision to buy this book shows your determination to improve your academic skills. Take an additional step toward that goal by talking with professionals who can improve your reading.

READ TO GIVE YOUR BRAIN A GOOD WORKOUT

Is your brain due for a book workout? Don't lift it; read it. Scientists imaging the brain found that reading enhanced development of the *occipital lobe,* the part of the brain that processes visual information. Reading was also shown to increase imagination and creativity and to improve decision-making and planning. Imaging also revealed that reading developed the *parietal lobe*, the part of the brain that translates letters into words and words into thoughts, skills that are relevant to writing. Scientists also learned that reading reduced stress, enhanced social skills, and improved memory.

A recent study showed that students who read self-selected literature for pleasure averaged higher grades in English, mathematics, science, and history than their non-reading peers. That same study reported that many famous celebrities and leaders are also avid readers and that reading for pleasure was a greater academic influence than having a parent with a college degree.

Developing Lifetime Literacy Skills: Reading for Success

You've achieved your academic success today because your family recognized the value of reading and teaching you reading skills at a young age. Studies show that successful readers are happier, healthier, and more economically secure. Reading on level by about fourth grade predicts academic and career success, regardless of socioeconomic background. Add if you need more evidence, readers make better choices of a significant other. Why do you think college libraries are so popular?

Reading to learn

Trying to educate yourself in college without reading is like trying to swim without water; oceans of knowledge are inaccessible. In addition to reading for pleasure, college students also read as their primary source of learning and absorbing information. Reading-to-learn strategies and content-specific approaches to engaging with information differ for nonfiction sources such as textbooks, research articles, technical materials, and math and science content. Intense content, such as that found in textbooks, requires a deliberate pace and frequent re-readings. I discuss these strategies in greater detail in the following sections.

Engaging with critical thinking skills

College reading not only requires that you learn and discover skills that are common to high school reading, but also that you engage with the following critical thinking skills:

>> **Applying:** What other topics are similar to what you read? How is the topic applicable to current events, other books you are reading, topics in other courses, and your life in general?

>> **Questioning:** What questions does the topic raise? Who or what is affected? . . .

>> **Evaluating:** What are the topic's assets and liabilities? Does it have more pluses than minuses? Is any part of the topic an outlier?

>> **Validating:** Is the topic mainstream and generally accepted as believable? Is the publication source accepted as valid in the field?

>> **Speculating:** How does the topic respond to what-if scenarios? What if the topic was relevant a hundred years ago, or will be relevant a hundred years in the future?

>> **Articulating:** What one sentence clarifies the topic? Can that sentence be revised following the strategies discussed in Chapter 6?

>> **Synthesizing:** How does this information fit into the big picture?

REMEMBER

You can develop your critical-thinking skills by responding to the following questions before, during, and after reading:

>> What are the author's background (including financial affiliations), positions on the topic, and level of respectability within the field? Is the author considered mainstream or an outlier?

>> Do the date and source of publication increase or decrease relevance to the topic?

>> What did you learn from skimming titles, headings, subheadings, and figures? What information is revealed in the abstract, glossary, notes, or appendix?

>> What do you identify as a purpose for reading? Why was the topic assigned? How does the reading align with course content?

>> What background information do you know about the topic? What could you briefly read that provides additional background information? Do the citations and references add to this information?

>> What's a one-sentence summary that identifies what you learned from the reading?

>> What books offer additional follow-up on the topic?

>> What questions and clarifications need follow-up?

READ TO LIVE LONGER

Scientists have discovered that people who read novels live longer. Strategies for reading novels and similar fiction include the following:

- Skim a plot summary to familiarize yourself with the setting, plot, and characters. Also read a short background on the author, time period, and location.

- Recognize the focus, concentration, and attention to detail required to read the novel — which also represents your mental growth. Acclimation to the story may take 50 or more pages.

- Read with a pencil and record notes, questions, and clarifications. Draw diagrams to connect characters and ideas. Record page numbers for future reference. Frequently stop, think, and record thoughts. End a reading session at the end of a chapter. Capitalize on the author's use of interpretation of events.

- Identify how the author's use of literary devices (flashbacks, foreshadowing, symbolism, and repetition) applies to the plot or theme.

Talking to yourself: Annotation

Annotation, another read-to-learn strategy, is self-conversation where you discuss your reading. Like any conversation, reflecting increases learning. Sometimes called *active reading*, annotation creates connections among an author's ideas. The purpose of annotation is to locate key information to recall and react to for class discussion and writing reference. Strategies for annotation include

- ❯❯ Identifying relationships among ideas
- ❯❯ Locating main and supporting points
- ❯❯ Paraphrasing main ideas using familiar words
- ❯❯ Identifying new vocabulary, terms, and concepts
- ❯❯ Applying, speculating, and questioning

TIP

Highlighting lacks the effectiveness of annotating because it does not require handwriting, a brain-engaging activity. Annotating can be completed in book margins or by writing on sticky notes.

The following figure contains a sample paragraph.

The late Steve Jobs (1955–2011) is remembered for many technological innovations, including starting Apple with Steve Wozniak and creating the iPhone. But he may be underestimated for his greatest achievement, rebounding from failure. The Reed College dropout was forced out of Apple in 1985 after a power struggle with the board. That same year he founded NeXT, a platform development company aimed at the higher-education and business markets, which ended up as a $12-million failure. He moved on to Pixar and partnered with Disney to produce new-generation 3D animation and the successful feature film *Toy Story*. Apple, on the verge of bankruptcy, acquired NeXT, along with Jobs, who restored the company's domination in the industry with the iMac, iTunes, the Apple Store, the App Store, the iPad, and the iPhone. As an elementary school student, Jobs loved math and reading, but was bored with school. As a business leader at Apple, he frequently inspired employees to achieve beyond their expectations, but with a style that could be easily described as bullying. The child who was given up for adoption, followed the beliefs of Buddhism, was obsessed with attention to detail, designed like an artist, and was not intimidated by failure, achieved his goal of putting a dent in the universe. He died from complications of pancreatic cancer in 2011.

Here is a sample annotation for this paragraph.

* Argues resilience after failures at college, Apple, and NeXT

* Tone supports Jobs' resilience

* Good use of specifics

* Jobs' creativity compares with Edison, da Vinci, and the Wright brothers

* Can Jobs be successful as a spouse?

* Is his boredom with school a failure of the school system?

* How did Buddhism influence his creativity?

* What do the experiences of Jobs and Gates say to college students about dropping out of college?

* When does manager "encouragement" become bullying?

* Can learning resiliency be traced to his childhood?

* How would Apple be different today if Jobs were alive?

* Would Jobs have worn a mask during the COVID-19 pandemic?

STRATEGIES TO READ TEXTBOOKS

Textbooks represent some of the most challenging materials you'll be required to read, and frequently the most expensive, sometimes requiring a mortgage. However, like a house, textbooks represent a good investment, and many textbooks will be lifetime treasures. As you become more experienced with college academics, you'll develop a sense of how to approach textbooks — like a gentle lamb or a ferocious lion, either reading for general ideas and concepts, or attacking it for facts and fundamentals. Read textbooks with the confidence that you can understand concepts. Textbook reading strategies include

- Reading the Preface to identify the author's approach

- Previewing titles, headings, and other organizational aids

- Studying to align content with the type of text, such as fiction or nonfiction

- Creating and answering test questions

- Reading study questions at the end of a chapter, and previews at the beginning

- Explaining what you read to someone in your class

- Learning new vocabulary, terms, and concepts

- Reading at a slow pace and in small chunks

- Ending textbook sessions with notes and annotations for future review

A recent study identified the benefits of reading textbook chapters backward, beginning with study questions and working toward the front of the chapter.

Improving your reading plan

You may not be surprised to hear that not all college students work with the same intensity; some students approach academics like a lamb, and some like a lion. But in the world of higher education, lambs can become lions. If you're a lamb — and your reading skills are producing grades lower than a B-level GPA — then you can transform into an academic lion by modeling the reading behaviors of your school's best scholars.

With a few weekly hours committed to additional reading, you can become an academic predator, achieving higher reading proficiency, improving your performance in all courses, earning a higher GPA, and increasing your career and lifetime opportunities. The following sections discuss some strategies you can include in your reading improvement plan.

Be committed

To rule the reading jungle, schedule at least one 2-hour reading block every week. Logistics of that commitment include the following:

>> **Identifying your ideal time, location, and environment for scheduling reading sessions.** Determine if your reading energy is highest in the morning, evening, or nighttime. Select a convenient location that motivates you — outdoors, near a window, or in a study room. Separate yourself from devices. Your social media empire won't collapse in two hours.

>> **Creating a reading-session plan.** Establish length and content goals for the reading you want to accomplish. Read the most challenging materials first. Annotate or summarize. Finish with a reading accountability strategy such as writing the purpose or application of the reading.

>> **Determining a reading purpose.** Establish a reading purpose, in the form of a question, for each section you read.

TIP

Begin every academic project with 30 minutes of background reading on the topic. Read for topic history, approaches, positions, relevancy, and implications.

Incorporate reading in your everyday life

Long-term strategies (around your semester workload) to improve your college reading skills include

>> Exploring a variety of formats and genres, such as poetry, plays, science fiction, short stories, biography, memoir, and technology

>> Talking with people who read similar books or authors

>> Browsing large bookstores and small local bookstores and searching for books on Amazon

>> Researching topics that interest you, such as music genres, finance, languages, cooking, travel, and do-it-yourself skills

TIP

In addition to academic reading, read for leisure about 30 minutes daily, which provides additional practice and information. Read current events, which can provide background and context for classroom discussion and writing.

Your daily functional reading will require another 30 minutes: directions, schedules, forms, signs, websites — anything college students need to navigate through their day. As you read, reflect, speculate, evaluate, and apply.

READ LIKE STEVE JOBS

The late Steve Jobs, the celebrated college dropout, developed an obsession for reading as a young student. Books that he recommended everyone read include the following:

- *1984* by George Orwell
- *Diet for a Small Planet* by Frances Moore Lappé
- *Moby Dick* by Herman Melville
- *The Innovator's Dilemma* by Clayton Christensen
- *King Lear* by William Shakespeare
- *The Collected Poems of Dylan Thomas* by Dylan Thomas

A recent study found that benefits of leisure reading each day included improvements in the following:

- » Mental stimulation . . .
- » Memory
- » Focus and concentration
- » Analytical skills
- » Vocabulary
- » Writing skills

Read and read some more

Books that are popular among your peers and required reading at many universities include the following:

- » *Drive: The Surprising Truth about What Motivates Us* . . . by Daniel H. Pink (Riverhead Books)
- » *Hidden Figures: The American Dream and the Untold Story of the Black Women Mathematicians Who Helped Win the Space Race* by Margot Lee Shetterly (William Morrow)

>> *Garbology: Our Dirty Love Affair with Trash* by Edward Humes (Avery)

>> *The Immortal Life of Henrietta Lacks* by Rebecca Skloot (Crown)

>> *Stuffed and Starved: The Hidden Battle for the World Food System* by Raj Patel (Melville House)

>> *Educated: A Memoir* by Tara Westover (Random House)

SELF-EDUCATED LEADERS

Can reading be a sole source of education, without a formal degree? Becoming "educated" is an achievement people work for, not a status based on who they are and how they were born. Some self-motivated people earn their education and notoriety solely through reading rather than in a credentialed institution.

Your familiarity with the following autodidacts reflects your reading background.

Technology Leaders	Political Leaders	Business Leaders	Literary Leaders
Steve Jobs	Abigail Adams	Andrew Carnegie	Edgar Allan Poe
Bill Gates	Grover Cleveland	Ray Kroc	J.D. Salinger
Michael Dell	Frederick Douglass	John D. Rockefeller	Maya Angelou
Orville Wright	Patrick Henry	Walt Disney	Walt Whitman
Wilbur Wright	James Monroe	Henry Ford	Bob Dylan
Paul Allen	George Washington	Estée Lauder	Samuel Clemens
Steve Wozniak	Eleanor Roosevelt	Ted Turner	Herman Melville

For a limited number of highly motivated and disciplined people, reading offers a path to self-education without a college degree. The autodidacts listed here are examples of the result of obsessive book reading. "Although I dropped out of college and got lucky pursuing a career in software, getting a degree is a much surer path to success," wrote Bill Gates in a recent blog post. "College graduates are more likely to find a rewarding job, earn higher income, and even, evidence shows, live healthier lives than if they didn't have degrees." Also, you have the opportunity to experience an event that Bill Gates never experienced, a college graduation and family party.

Additional books that are frequently required for college writing reference include the following:

>> Thinking, Fast and Slow by Daniel Kahneman (Farrar, Straus and Giroux)

>> *Big Data Baseball: Math, Miracles, and the End of a 20-Year Losing Streak* by Travis Sawchik (Flatiron Books)

>> *The Geography of Genius: Lessons from the World's Most Creative Places* by Eric Weiner (Simon & Schuster)

>> *Blink: The Power of Thinking without Thinking* by Malcolm Gladwell (Back Bay Books)

>> *Give and Take: Why Helping Others Drives Our Success* by Adam Grant (Penguin Books)

>> *The Female Brain* by Dr. Louann Brizendine (Harmony)

Writing As a Skill for Lifetime Success

Writing is sometimes called the gatekeeper skill. It opens gates to your college admission, college degree, job interviews, and career opportunities. Currently, your college writing proficiency can help you to avoid becoming one of the 57 percent of students who start college and fail to graduate — 31 million over the past two decades who were also burdened with an average of $14,000 in student loan debts. Without college writing skills, gates are closed on degrees, job opportunities, careers, and lifetime financial opportunities.

Businesses are pressuring colleges today to place more emphasis on writing, resulting in an alphabet of programs: writing across the curriculum (WAC), writing in the disciplines (WID), and writing-intensive (WI) courses. Your campus has a writing center (WC), and you may have a Writing Department, separate from your English Department.

Writing, the pulse of the academic process, is difficult because it requires and shows thinking. Your writing products offer a window into how you analyze, problem-solve, implicate, apply, evaluate, and conclude. These critical thinking skills are revealed in research when you develop and support an argument using a research formatting style such as APA.

Writing is also visual evidence of understanding course content. College writing skills enable you to respond to an essay question such as, "What did the world learn about global healthcare from the COVID-19 pandemic?" The writing that you produce demonstrates your level of understanding of lessons learned about global healthcare. . ..

Your college writing also demonstrates your persistence and resilience. In addition to writing requiring regular practice and revising, it also requires determination and confidence when facing every new challenge. Writers at all levels experience rejection and failure, including J. K. Rowling, Stephen King, and Agatha Christie.

You'll face writing challenges and writing failures — and professors who don't connect with your writing. If you do not experience some academic failures, you are not experiencing enough academic risk. The life lesson of writing is motivating yourself to turn failures into success. To paraphrase Thomas Edison, you haven't failed, you've found many ways that it won't work.

Developing Lifetime Literacy Skills: Writing for Success

The purpose of most college writing is to communicate ideas and information. But writing is also a tool to discover, learn, and develop ideas. To paraphrase English novelist E. M. Forster (1879–1970), you don't know what you're thinking until you see what you write. And sometimes you write information you didn't know you learned. What follows are strategies for writing to learn.

Writing to learn

Because the brain likes to be primed like a water pump, writing-to-learn (WTL) strategies prompt the brain to create meaning. For example, if asked to list career choices, you might respond with salesperson, teacher, and manager. But if asked to respond alphabetically, you might instead respond with acrobat, barrister, coach, deckhand, and so forth. Try identifying careers beginning with E, F, and G.

The premise of WTL strategies is to prompt the brain to connect known information with unknown information. WTL strategies include the following:

>> **A hypothetical** (or to hypothesize) suggests ideas based on assumed conditions.

(If . . ., then . . .) If people worldwide spoke one language, then the world would have fewer conflicts.

>> **Speculative** (or to speculate) offers a theory based on fact. . . . .
(*What if . . .*) What if Leonardo da Vinci invented the airplane before the Wright brothers?

What if the Earth's rotation were one second slower?

What if the Earth's temperature increased by one degree?

What if the same book were read by every person in the world?

>> **Application** (or to apply) shows relationships, such as similarities and differences.

Similarities: College freshmen are like books. They have a story to tell, and each day is a different chapter.

Differences: College freshmen differ from college seniors. Freshmen fear coming in; seniors fear going out.

>> **Mythical** (or a myth) is a factitious narrative with symbolic meaning.

A conversation between Earth and Mars

A diary entry of a comma travelling through freshmen essays

A letter from Isaac Newton's first law to his third law

An obituary of the college essay

>> **Freewriting,** an unstructured free flow of ideas from the brain, shows what your brain is thinking.

In ten-minute sprints, handwrite or type to data-dump your working memory. Begin with a prompt sentence such as, "What do I think about smart cars?" Or, begin with a self-greeting such as, "Hi, it's me. What are you thinking about?"

>> **Mapping,** a visual display of words and ideas, uses circles and lines to connect related ideas.

Write your topic in the middle of a piece of paper and circle it. Around that word, write major subheadings of that topic. Connect the major topic and each subtopic with a line. List other words related to the subtopics, and connect those related words. The map of your words is worth a thousand pictures.

These right-brain activities elicit uncommon information about the topic. Try an A-to-Z list on the topic of animals. Did you surprise yourself with your responses? Did you arrive at *anaconda* for "A"? Writing is a strategy for discovering information.

In addition to your daily functional writing (forms, lists, class notes, email, texts, and social media), write at least a paragraph a day, such as course note summaries, test preparation, a blog post, and other writing projects. Every minute of writing is another minute of thinking.

Putting together your writing improvement plan

The purpose of a writing improvement plan is to develop your college writing, and any level beyond that you desire to achieve. If your goal includes publication, work to make it happen. If your goal includes proficient college writing and career writing, such as writing a company newsletter, go for it.

Similar to college readers, college writers are also either lambs or lions, approaching writing passively or aggressively. And some lambs experience malnutrition because college writing requires more effort and more thinking than reading.

The good news here is that improving your writing improves your reading more than improving your reading improves your writing. Improving your writing is like a get-one-free coupon. Because you're demonstrating college writing success by being enrolled in a course that requires the use of APA style and citation, you should view improving your writing as a DIY (do-it-yourself) project. The key to improving writing, similar to reading, is commitment.

A writing improvement plan begins with scheduling time and executing strategies. Various short-term strategies for writing improvement are detailed in Chapters 5 through 11. Long-term strategies (beyond semester workloads) for writing improvement include the following:

>> Soliciting writing feedback from multiple sources

>> Reading books about the craft of writing

>> Exploring writing in a variety of genres

>> Writing experimentally using various tones

>> Publishing online

>> Writing daily

Studying in Small Groups: Literacy and Socializing

Have you struggled solving a problem, asked for help, and received — not the solution — but an idea you developed into the solution? Collaboration to problem solve represents the advantage of working in small groups. Any group of you is smarter than any one of you. Working in study groups offers more brain power while providing much-valued socialization. Learning is a participation sport, and socializing is a fun and effective strategy for learning.

Advantages of study-group learning include the following:

» Academic and social support

» Reminders of course communications

» Content explanations in the language of your peers

» Student models of course requirements

» Nonjudgmental feedback

Small study groups (ideally four to six students) offer opportunities to extend learning beyond the classroom. This style of learning is research-supported and commonly practiced in higher education. Its popularity and effectiveness have resulted in dedicated small-group rooms being included in college construction plans. These rooms include functional furniture and technology necessary for group study.

Small-group study is ideal for literacy-rich courses and also math and science courses that may not be as reading- and writing-concentrated as humanity courses. If you're using this book to write an APA-formatted paper for a math or science course, then you have a professor familiar with current learning theory.

REMEMBER

A study group needs a leader. (Thank you for volunteering.) Study groups are most effective with students from the same class, but they can also work with students from the same course. Early in the semester, ask two or three students in your class if they're interested in forming a study group to meet once a week or once every two weeks. Explain that your purpose for meeting is to provide feedback on reading and writing assignments. Choose a day and time that is convenient to the group. Then, each of you ask another two or three students, telling them the day and time you plan to meet.

Your first meeting will require logistical planning, but a workable 60-minute timeline includes the following:

» 5 minutes socializing

» 45 minutes discussing content

» 5 minutes asking questions and clarifying

» 5 minutes summarizing

Focus the discussion on critical thinking questions that are related to reading and writing to learn. As the group leader, take notes and send summaries with reminders each time you're meeting.

REMEMBER

Your parents probably told you that a successful life results from successful choices. None of those choices are more important to you at this time than . . . improving your literacy skills. It's a life-altering decision. Remember that the future *you* will be the product of the words you read and write today.

3

Practicing Safe Cites: Writing and Citing Sources

Discover what to cite, when to cite, why to cite, and why not to cite — which also includes source preparation techniques such as summaries, paraphrases, and quotations.

Investigate the missing elements department: citations with unknown authors, page numbers, dates, and titles.

Remember first impressions are important, but don't underestimate last impressions — references that coordinate citations and provide retrieval information.

Examine the long and short of DOIs and URLs and other streamlined updates in APA's seventh edition.

Experience errors with source engagement, just as costly as errors with the other engagement.

Chapter **10**

Gaining Insight: To Cite or Not to Cite

G rowing up, your mother told you many times, "Give credit where credit is due." Her advice applies to you today as a college student. Credit is due for the sources you reference in your research papers.

Citing sources is like the college admission process. You cite sources to validate your preparation for college. Your application, interview, essay, and ACT scores show your ability to articulate your academic credentials, interact with college officials, and display literacy skills in high-stakes testing. Citing sources in a research project shows your ability to locate academic evidence, evaluate it, support it, and document it according to APA standards.

Additional justification for crediting sources includes the following:

>> Adding credibility to research by showing knowledge of APA requirements

>> Respecting scholarship by recognizing works of experts in the field

>> Preventing plagiarism and avoiding misrepresentation

>> Valuing readers by supporting an argument with reliable information in a standard academic format

>> Providing a reference list with information for locating sources and following up information

>> Establishing the work ethic of a scholar who values accuracy and attention to detail

Locating scholarly sources also adds diversity of support from experts in the field. For example, if you're arguing characteristics of successful writing, would you argue your claim using references such as Jim Brogan, Molly O'Brien, Karen Shinn, and Ray Datsun? Or would you argue using references such as Ernest Hemingway, J. K. Rowling, Stephen King, and Harper Lee? You'd choose the names that add credibility to the argument, the experts.

In this chapter, I explain why to cite, what to cite, what not to cite, and how to cite. I also provide guidelines addressing questionable information to cite. (Meanwhile, Chapter 11 explains how to incorporate and engage sources into your argument.)

This chapter also addresses the following changes made in the APA seventh edition regarding citations:

>> Sources with three authors or more are cited with the name of the first author followed by "et al."

>> Oral traditions and traditional knowledge of indigenous peoples are identified as a distinct source category and cited as "personal communication" requiring no reference listing.

>> References to indigenous groups and tribes are capitalized.

>> Avoid the phrase, "Retrieved by . . .," unless the source has regular updates, such as on Wikipedia.

TECHNICAL STUFF

A citation is half the process of identifying the source origin. The other half is the full description that appears in the reference.

DIFFERENTIATING BETWEEN PRIMARY AND SECONDARY SOURCES

Research sources are classified as primary and secondary — like the professors who you ask to write you recommendations. The foundation of strong research is primary sources, original information.

Your research will be supported by two kinds of data sources, primary and secondary. Some research topics are more dependent on one than the other. For example, some historical topics are more dependent on primary topics. Here is an overview of the two types:

- *Primary sources* are data collected by the researcher directly from the source, such as novels, art collections, diaries, letters, autobiographies, government documents, photographs, videos, and speeches.

- *Secondary sources* are data collected after it has been analyzed and interpreted: literary analysis, textbooks, and blog posts. Secondary data loses authority the more the information becomes removed from the primary document. If your research includes a senior project, master thesis, or similar credential-seeking requirement, emphasize primary sources.

Occasionally, secondary sources contain information unavailable in the primary source, and so the secondary source requires citing. For example, if you read in Mason that Carlson used a painting technique, you'd cite the source as (Carlson, 2019 as cited in Mason, 2020).

Crediting Sources: General Guidelines

Crediting sources is one of the few times in the life of a college student when credit is better than cash. APA requires that you cite "ideas, theories, or research" that "directly influenced your work." If you read a source and reference any ideas in your work, you're mandated to cite that source.

WARNING

Cited sources must appear in the reference list; sources that appear in the reference list are required to appear in in-text citations. Not citing a source represents a serious academic violation that could result in your dismissal from school. (I discuss plagiarism and its implications in Chapter 4.) If you master the fundamentals of citing now, you'll reduce the stress of mastering the fundamentals of plagiarism later. All errors aren't created equal, and citation errors can disrupt an academic career.

How many sources do you cite? APA recommends citing "one or two of the most representative sources for each key point." A traditional undergraduate research paper contains four to five major points. An additional two or three sources are required for background. If you're required to write a review of the literature, representative of a survey of sources on the topic, expect to reference another eight to ten sources.

TIP

As you research, in addition to recording reference data (author, title, source, copyright, and [if applicable] volume number, URL, DOI, and edition), also record in-text citations as you write. (See DOI in this section's "Citing Electronic Sources: Websites, Periodicals, Software, and Visuals.")

The following sections focus on guidelines for sources requiring in-text citations.

Full and partial quotations

If you're referencing an expert's words (full sentence or partial sentence), an in-text citation is required. Here are examples of full and partial quotations:

» **Full sentence quotation:** "At the village of Lexington, the British force was confronted by a group of about 74 militia members under the command of John Parker" (Wiegand, 2020, p. 117).

» **Partial sentence quotation:** McKensey (2021) argued that children who come from homes with adult academic role models learn resilience to "overcome academic adversity" when they face challenging topics (p. 286).

Block quotations

Long quotations of 40 words or more are formatted as a "block." APA guidelines for block quotes include the following.

» Don't enclose a block quote within quote marks.

» Begin the block quote on a new line.

» Indent the complete block quote 0.5 inch from the left margin.

» Indent the first line of additional paragraphs an additional 0.5 inch.

» Double-space the entire block quote.

» Cite the block quote in either parenthetical or narrative style. (See the section, "Citing author-date format," later in this chapter.)

In either style, don't add a period at the end of a block quote.

Here is an example of a block quote:

> Charles II was a witty fellow. When a court minister joked that the king never spoke foolishly and never acted wisely, Charles is reported to have retorted the paradox was easily explained, "for his discourse was his own; his actions were the ministry's." He also didn't order the minister's tongue cut out. (Charles's good sportsmanship did have its limits: After being crowned, he had Cromwell's body dug up and beheaded, in revenge for his dad's execution.)
>
> Both the king's humor and tolerance were marked departures from the reign of Cromwell, who was puritanical enough to have ordered all the theaters in London closed. Charles not only reopened them, but allowed female parts in plays actually played by females (Wiegand, 2020, p. 61)

REMEMBER

Although this chapter explains layout and formatting of a block quote and other quotation styles (as well as summarizing and paraphrasing), Chapter 11 explains how to incorporate those strategies into the development of your argument.

REMEMBER

When block quotations, or any quotations, contain citations, include those citations within the quotations, but don't include those citations in the reference list.

Summarizing and paraphrasing

A *summary*, a shorter version of the main points of an idea, requires an in-text citation. A *paraphrase*, restating an idea in your own words, also requires an in-text citation. Summaries are generally longer than a paraphrase:

>> **Summary:** Breslin (2019) explains that children can develop into successful academic students when their pre-school home experience includes

- A literacy-rich environment with adults reading and children having their own desk and bookcase

- Attendance at cultural events

- Visits to bookstores, museums, and historical locations

- Emotionally stable adults

REMEMBER

>> **Paraphrase:** Breslin (2019) explains that children need a stable home life with cultural and literacy experiences, and adult role models (p. 287).

APA doesn't require page numbers in the citation with a paraphrase, but many professors prefer page numbers with paraphrases.

Statistical data within the context of research

Cite statistics within the context of their source, because sources may bias their data. For example, the view of the nutritional value of alternative meat products varies between the alternative meat industry and the meat industry. Take a look at these two examples:

>> The alternative meat industry reports that their products contain ten percent less sodium than traditional meat products.

>> The meat industry reports that alternative meat products contain ten percent more sodium than traditional meat products.

Terms specific to a field

When a few words are used within a source that differ from its traditional meaning, the term requires citation. Such terms are usually identified with quotation marks. For example,

The National Foundation of Educational Assessment clarified that "special student populations" in the long-term study included "gifted and talented" populations, and that they were underrepresented in the data (2015, p. 215).

Reference to "special student populations" and "gifted and talented" requires citing and identification in the reference list because these terms are quoted in the source.

Tables, Internet images, and clip art

If you didn't create it and you use it, you're required to cite it. Executing your word processor's copy and paste function during your research should alert you that you need to cite.

Facts and figures that aren't common knowledge

You're familiar with the existence of oceans as being common knowledge, and you've probably seen at least one. Knowledge that the Pacific Ocean is the largest on Earth and covers 30 percent of the Earth's surface may not be common to you, but it's easily found uncited in general references. But more obscure statistical data unfamiliar to most readers qualifies that the fact needs to be cited. For example, if your Pacific Ocean fact includes the meaning of the word *Pacific*, the percentage of the Earth's surface covered by it, and its deepest point, then you need a citation.

REMEMBER

Common knowledge, vaguely defined as information common to most readers, doesn't require citing. It includes uncited facts, events, and ideas that are easily available online and in encyclopedias. Here are some examples of common knowledge:

>> Lansing is the capital of Michigan.

>> The Great Lakes are the largest supply of fresh water in the world.

>> Shakespeare wrote histories, comedies, and tragedies.

>> Harvard University is the oldest institution of higher learning in the United States.

>> The Earth's population in 2020 was estimated at almost 8 billion people.

>> A pandemic prior to 2020 occurred in 1918.

Controversial information that contradicts generally accepted truths

Common knowledge excludes controversial factual information. For example, you would need to cite sources of conspiracies such as the following:

>> The attacks on 9/11 were perpetrated by the White House.

>> The landing on the moon did not occur.

>> Osama bin Laden was not killed.

>> Earth was invaded by aliens in 1935.

REMEMBER

When your instincts question the validity of information, listen. You can also impress your professor by showing evidence that refutes controversial statements.

Less common information requiring citing includes examples like these:

» Another student's work

» Papers written for another course (see Chapter 4)

» A person's spoken ideas

No citations required

Information that doesn't require citing includes the generation of new knowledge that follows citing a source. For example, if you reference Allen's source explaining that participation in scholastic sports improves socialization skills, teaches respect for teammates, increases confidence, and improves grades, you may reflect on that cited information (without citing) as in the following example:

> My experience playing high school sports confirms Allen's research. When I played soccer, I became friends with teammates I never would have met. I felt confident with a larger group of students and I earned good grades. Sports provide a fun environment for learning about people.

TIP

You may have doubts about which sources to cite. When doubt daunts you, cite and sleep tight. APA warns to avoid undercitation and overcitation. Given the choice of two bad practices, most professors would prefer that you overcite rather than undercite because you're showing you researched sources.

WARNING

Is Wikipedia a creditable source for college research? The answer is both "yes" and "no." Ask your professor. If your professor says "yes," it's a creditable source. If your professor says "no," it's not a creditable source. But by asking your professor, you're saying that Wikipedia is easier to locate than scholarly sources. Although you can read Wikipedia for background, you should locate better sources, because your professor has higher expectations. Wikipedia is gaining popularity, but avoid it at this time.

Coordinating Citations: Common Elements

Coordinating citation elements is like getting everyone on the bus when it's time to return from a road trip. You can easily misplace someone or something. Coordinating citations requires knowing your options — no author, no date, and no title? No problem. These sections show APA preferences (and options) for citing and when citing elements are unavailable.

Meanwhile, Table 10-1 shows how to cite when key information is missing.

TABLE 10-1

Citations with Missing Elements

Missing Element	Replacement Option
No author	Use title in position of author.
No page number	Use broader available reference such as section label or part number.
No date	Use n.d. (no date) in position of date.
No title, such as with an image	Use general description such as "four adults dressed in 1920-style clothing."

Citing author-date format

The author-date format is one person and date you don't want to miss. APA requires the author-date format for in-text citations. The in-text citation consists of the author's last name and the source's publication date. The template looks like this: (author, date).

Citations are written as a *narrative style* (the author's name written as part of the narrative and the date written in parentheses) or *parenthetical style* (both the author's name and the date written within parentheses). Note that end punctuation is positioned after the parentheses.

>> **Narrative-style examples:**

- Windstorm (2015) explains rammed-earth building is an environmentally friendly technique adaptable to conditions in the Northwest.

- Hennessy (2019) found that the percentage of fresh water in the Great Lakes has remained stable in recent decades.

>> **Parenthetical-style examples:**

- Rammed-earth building is an environmentally friendly technique adaptable to conditions in the Northwest (Windstorm, 2015).

- The percentage of fresh water in the Great Lakes has remained stable in recent decades (Hennessy, 2019).

WARNING

Positioning end punctuation outside the parentheses represents punctuation accuracy, an expectation valued by your professor. Take a look at the end punctuation in the last two parenthetical examples.

Citing repeated narratives

Repeating offenders need to be silenced. When repeating a narrative citation in the same paragraph, avoid repeated uses of the date. Use that author's name only. The following example paragraph shows repeated narrative citations and represents an informal APA adaption in an essay that is acceptable in many first-year university writing programs. Similar to all citations, the complete source is required in the reference list. This example of narrative style citation contains repeated author references (DeCarlo) that avoid repeating the date:

> DeCarlo (2019) endorses LinkedIn as the premier social networking site for reaching business professionals and establishing contacts for job searchers. DeCarlo suggests posting a profile with information similar to resumes. She references a recent social networking survey that says 95 percent of recruiters use LinkedIn in their recruiting process.

Sections of a source

May the source be with you. Some citations reference a specific section of a source such as page sequences, chapters, figures, and tables. Include a brief description with the author–date citation. Here are some examples:

> (Sitwell, 2007, Part II)
>
> (Newson, 1981, Chapter 4)
>
> (Wellington & Jackson, 2012, Author's Note)
>
> (Winston, 2008, Glossary)
>
> (T. Beall & S. Beall, 2020, Appendix B)
>
> (Wills, 2019, Notes)
>
> (Callow, 1995, pp. 35–67)
>
> (O'Donnell, 2001, References)

This citation strategy also applies to referencing text for quotations and paraphrases when page numbers are unavailable, such as in some converted electronic documents.

Citations are written as either narrative or parenthetical, as I discuss in the section, "Citing author-date format," earlier in this chapter. The example citations are shown in parenthetical style, but are easily converted to narrative style.

Citing an unknown author

APA doesn't send an APB (All Points Bulletin) for missing or anonymous authors, but it does employ replacement elements. When the author is listed as anonymous, use "Anonymous" in the author position in the citation and reference list. If the author is a known group with an abbreviation for its name, use the abbreviation. When the author is unknown, such as in a periodical or magazine that's staff written, the periodical title becomes the first element of the citation and reference entry. Because most titles are long, professors generally accept the first three words of the title followed by an ellipsis. If the citation includes a page number for a quotation, include the page number. Here are some samples of citations without author names:

> (Anonymous, 2020)
>
> (CDC, 2020)
>
> (Financial Instruments Accounting, 2020)
>
> (Campaign Strategies of Special Interest Groups, 2020)
>
> (Escaping Cold Weather. . ., 2014)
>
> (*Activities for Inactive Hearts*, 2020, p. 358)

Citing numerous authors

When a research reference is written by a pair of authors, write both names joined by an ampersand (&). In the world of APA, three or more's a crowd, but APA calls in the romans (et al.) for crowd control. When a reference is written by three or more authors, write the name of the first author and the Latin abbreviation "et al." (and others):

> (Fisher & Young, 2006)
>
> (Brown et al., 2002)

When two authors are written in narrative style, "and" is used in place of ampersand, like this:

> Fisher and Young (2006) argue . . .

The abbreviation "et al." is used in both parenthetical style and narrative style.

Citing works by multiple authors looks like this:

(Bicker et al., 2015; Conway & Dixon, 2017; Kitchens, 2017)

Citing same author, same date

Some productive authors write two books in the same year. To distinguish each of two books in the same calendar year, cite and reference one book with the year, followed by lowercase "a," and the second book with the year, followed by lowercase "b." For example, if author Giampalmi wrote a second book in 2021, the in-text citation would appear as follows:

(Giampalmi, 2021a)

(Giampalmi, 2021b)

Citing authors with the same surname

If two authors share a surname, APA has you covered. Write each author's first initial with the date.

(J. Giampalmi & B. Giampalmi, 2015)

Citing organization authors

Many organizations write group documents. For example, the charitable organization CFC (Citizens for Citizens) regularly publishes research documenting its work. The first use of the citation appears with the full name (Citizens for Citizens, 2012). Subsequent citations appear abbreviated (CFC, 2012). In the reference list (see Chapter 12), spell out the organization's name.

Addressing Special Approaches: Personal, Authoritative, and Legal

Similar to some pets demanding special attention, some citation categories demand special approaches. Unique citations are required for personal communications, experts in the classroom, and legal references.

Personal communication

A variety of personal communications are often used as supporting research sources. Many professors are pleased to see student initiative that includes interviews, email, text messages, online chats, and telephone conversations — sources of nonretrievable information. Here's an example of a citation for personal communication:

(Stover, personal communication, March 17, 2015)

Academic authorities

Your professor and your textbook represent two authoritative sources for research (in addition to professors' being impressed that you recognized their expertise and application of their textbook source). Class lectures and notes are hyperlinked to support research topics in the course. Here's an example of a citation for a classroom lecture:

(Miles, personal communication, January 17, 2020)

Legal reference

Legal evidence provides strong support for many arguments, and many professors recognize students' initiative in researching U.S. Supreme Court decisions, federal statutes, amendments to the U.S. Constitution, and other legal documents. Citations for legal documents follow the format of the name of the document and the year. Legal citations look like this:

(*Bush v. Gore*, 2000)

(*Marbury v. Madison*, 1810)

(*Civil Rights Act*, 1991)

(*Lilly Ledbetter Fair Pay Act*, 2009)

Additional legal documents that you may find helpful in your research include the following:

Senior Citizens Right to Work Act, 2000

The Help America Vote Act, 2002

Miranda v. Arizona, 1966

Brown v. Board of Education, 1954

Roe v. Wade, 1973

Obergefell v. Hodges, 2015

Citing Electronic Sources: Websites, Periodicals, Software, and Visuals

Citing online sources is like putting together a puzzle after your dog ate some of the tastiest pieces. You can't get angry at your dog, and APA expects the same love. Electronic sources (including websites, webpages, podcasts, databases, and YouTube) follow the same pattern as print sources, but they frequently lack elements such as page numbers and complete date information. Also, the last elements of electronic sources in the reference list include a URL and sometimes a DOI. But again, APA has you covered. Although the complexity of electronic sources is reserved for the reference list (see Chapter 12), the simplicity of electronic sources is reserved for general references — as simple as feeding your dog a snack.

APA allows you to generally reference an electronic app with language as simple as the following:

Infographic was created at Graphics To Go (Graphicstogo.com).

As a general rule, electronic sources are cited similarly to print sources. Cite the author's last name followed by the date of publication:

(Jung, 2020)

Similar to print citations, when the author's name is unavailable, use the sponsoring organization or the first few words of the title of the article or page:

(Citizens for Citizens, 2019)

(Secrets of Successful Socialization, 2020)

Citations for quotations from an e-book or other electronic document without a page number are identified with available information:

(*Degrees Without Fees*, 2020, para. 12)

(*Degrees Without Fees*, 2020, "Costs of College")

(*Degrees Without Fees*, 2020, Part 4)

TED Talks, television shows, audiobooks, podcasts, and similar audiovisual works require a time stamp following the author and date:

(Riviello, 2015, 3:06)

The citation format of the author (creator) followed by the date also applies for visuals such as photographs, clip art, images, charts, tables, graphs, and maps. If the author is unknown, use the name of the object. Here's what citations of visuals look like:

(Scoops Clip Art, 2020)

(Universal Photographs, 2019)

(Academic Images, 2020)

What is a DOI? A *Digital Object Identifier* is a unique alphanumeric string that helps identify online documents similar to a URL (uniform resource locator). A DOI, located near the source's copyright notice, identifies content and provides a link to sources. A publisher assigns a DOI to almost all digital documents.

Evaluating Sources

When notorious criminal Willie Sutton was asked why he robbed banks, he responded, "Because that's where the money is." I'm obviously not encouraging you to rob banks, but I am encouraging you to go to where they keep the sources that will make your paper successful. Search where your choices are good or great.

Just as life is about making good choices, so is your college research dependent on how you choose your sources. You can't produce a quality research paper without quality sources. C-level sources can't produce A-level grades.

Major decisions early in your research include where to look for sources, how to recognize them, how to validate them, and how not to be fooled by them.

Determining what makes a reliable source

Scholarly sources help you develop your best argument, engage with experts in the field, avoid propaganda and politicization, and demonstrate scholarship in the section of your research where most professors first look to evaluate your paper — the reference list.

How do you find high-quality sources? Would you drop your fishing hook in a pool of water to catch a big fish? Fish for sources where you increase your chances of finding the big fish — college library databases, scholarly journals, and Google Scholar.

Scholarly sources are written by recognized academic authors who generally have published multiple books and articles in peer-reviewed journals (textbooks are peer-reviewed; websites aren't). Your most convenient scholarly sources, in addition to textbooks, are required course readings.

Characteristics of successful sources include

>> **Authority:** The author is credentialed and affiliated with creditable institutions and organizations.

>> **Accuracy:** The information is unbiased and error free. Author conclusions and assertions aren't influenced financially.

>> **Relevancy:** The information adds importance to your topic.

>> **Currency:** The information is up to date and technologically stable.

Here are questions to ask when evaluating sources:

>> Does the author appear as a credible authority in the field? What's the author's expertise?

>> Are spelling, grammar, and other conventions perfect?

>> Is the presentation perfect?

>> Does the author write in a scholarly tone that respects the reader?

>> Does the author provide retrievable citations that lead to additional information? Are links active?

>> Are quotations cited?

>> Is the website sponsored? By whom?

>> Is the domain *academically* focused, preferably not a .com?

Assessing the quality of the sources cited

In addition to determining the quality of sources cited by the source's extrinsic characteristics (author credibility, authoritative publication, and current date), quality of sources is also determined by intrinsic characteristics such as the following:

>> **Evidence fairness:** Evidence isn't slanted and avoids taking a position that lacks logic or support.

>> **In-depth analysis:** Evidence includes critical thinking such as evaluating implying, contrasting, and comparing.

>> **Topic relevancy:** Ensure that the source cited adds relevancy to your topic by further developing, agreeing, disagreeing, raising a related issue, or providing background.

Sources cited also need to pass your professor's eye test with a visual evaluation that includes the following:

>> Citations in APA format that include author and date

>> Some single-sentence quotations and partial quotations

>> Limited use of block quotations, which avoids the appearance of filling space

>> End punctuation of citations positioned outside parentheses

>> Accuracy of citations with unknown elements

REMEMBER

Many universities and individual professors vary in their APA requirements for sources and citations. Ask your professor the following questions about sources and citations:

>> How do you feel about Wikipedia being used for a source?

>> What's your preference for the ratio of primary and secondary sources?

>> Do you require page numbers for paraphrase citations?

Table 10-2 lists some common research domains where you can locate quality sources.

TIP

Referencing .com sources doesn't impress your professor and underestimates the expectations of most high school teachers. These sites are as impressive as a dog playing in a mud puddle and are as messy to clean up.

TABLE 10-2

Research Domains

Domain Extensions	Topic
.edu	Education
.org	Organizations, usually nonprofit
.gov	U.S. Government
.mil	U.S. Military
.net	Internet services
.k12	K-12 U.S. schools
.com	Commercial

Here are some top scholarly journals:

» *International Journal of Social Sciences and Humanity Studies*

» *International Journal of Humanities and Social Sciences*

» *New England Journal of Medicine*

» *American Literary History*

» *Journal of Music Theory*

» *Business Ethics Quarterly*

» *Cell*

» *Nature*

» *Science*

» *Journal of Finance*

» *The Lancet*

» *Advances in Physics*

» *Journal of Financial Economics*

» *Review of Financial Studies*

» *Digital Humanities Quarterly*

Meanwhile, here are some top scholarly websites for academic journals, articles, and books on a variety of academic topics:

>> Google Scholar

>> Science Direct

>> Google Books

>> Microsoft Academic Search

>> JSTOR

>> PubMed

>> Web of Science

>> Library of Congress

>> PsycINFO

>> African Journals Online

>> Arts & Humanities Citation Index

>> National Archives Catalog

>> Book Review Index

>> WorldWideScience

>> IEEE Xplore

In addition to scholarly sources, other types of evidence include personal experiences, observations, interviews, and surveys.

Chapter **11**

Preparing for Conflict: Source Engagement

icture this: You just aced a test you thought you failed — a common occurrence among nerds. You're back working on your research paper and you have at least a week before it's due. You're continuously researching and asking yourself what's the most productive part of your paper to do next. You asked the right question, and the answer is engagement — critical thinking, also known as critical engagement. It's like your first time sitting at the adult table and participating in conversation, but it's the conversation of the academic world, called *discourse*.

Chapter 10 discusses strategies for citing, formatting, and evaluating sources. In this chapter, the discussion of researching continues and sources get a workout as they transition into evidence that supports your argument. You add new insight to the academic community. This chapter, similar to annotating in Chapter 9, requires a conversation with yourself. It requires that you create interaction among your sources to support your argument. When you complete this chapter, the heavy lifting will be history, and only your reference list and formatting will remain.

Pre-Gaming: Gathering Sources

Your sources determine the success of your argument. If you think of scholarly sources as money in the bank, then you can think of lack of scholarly sources as a form of bankruptcy. Chapter 10 examines locations of scholarly sources and how to evaluate them.

REMEMBER

You're writing an argument and justifying the importance of that argument. You aren't trying to impress your professor with data overload, which is a strategy for an unsuccessful high school research paper. You're presenting a position (claim), arguing that position with scholarly sources, refuting the opposition, and offering reflection on the argument.

In addition to researching scholarly sources, continue researching library materials on the topic: books, journals, newspapers, PowerPoint, and multimedia. Research the implications of your topic, such as economic, social, legal, and cultural. To help focus your search, convert your claim into a question. Search with keywords that identify topics that support your claim. Table 11-1 shows some examples.

Identify eight to ten sources that support your argument, one or two sources that take a contrary approach, and one or two sources that add background.

TABLE 11-1   **Topic Questions and Keyword Searches**

Sample Topic Questions	Sample Keyword Searches
Does distance learning result in an inferior education for most students?	Distance learning and special populations
	Distance learning and disadvantages
	Distance learning and economics
Do plagiarism policies punish unsuspecting students?	Plagiarism and unintended consequences
	Plagiarism and discrimination
Is the Electoral College outdated?	Electoral College and the popular vote
	Electoral College and relevancy today
	Electoral College and economics
Is workplace bullying common in large retail companies?	Bullying and the workplace
	Bullying and large retail chains
	Bullying and cultural influences

TIP

You can use a source for a variety of argument purposes, including background, support, rebuttal, comparison, contrast, illustration, and opening and closing.

Create an outline of sources that builds your argument. Here's what an outline would look like arguing that the World Health Organization (WHO) should create a worldwide pandemic response team:

>> Naomi (2020) argues that preparation for COVID-19 was insufficient and that organizations have a moral obligation to take a leadership role.

>> Coffman (2019) supports all nations investing "medical capital" into a worldwide pandemic response team.

>> Isabel (2020) explains how uncoordinated international COVID-19 approaches cost tens of thousands of lives worldwide.

>> McCann (2020) compares 1918 pandemic approaches with 2020 pandemic approaches.

>> Gallo (2019) analyzes pandemics and politics.

>> Radson (2020) explains the challenge of discerning various strains of influenza.

TIP

When you write your argument, organize your evidence from weakest to strongest. Save the best for last.

Include one or two rebuttal sources with your outline:

>> Blick (2020) questions the ability of the international community to create the synergy necessary for an effective worldwide response.

>> Preston (2019) opposes attempts at a worldwide response, saying that past models of cooperation were unsuccessful.

Rehearsing: Preparing Sources

Preparing sources for engagement is like preparing for a trip to the beach. The planning and effort to get there are worth the reward upon arrival. Source preparation includes the following:

>> Summarizing each source and paraphrasing highlights

>> Determining the use of each source (or parts of sources) as background, evidence, or refutation

>> Identifying the development position of sources used as evidence

>> Selecting quotations that produce an impact

The most crucial preparation of sources involves analyzing source summaries for similarities, contrasts, and common patterns. An analysis of sources on the topic of government-supported tuition for higher education looks like this:

>> Phillips (2018) and Brennan (2019) endorse government-supported plans that include one year of national service following graduation.

>> Franklin (2017) and Hicks (2019) support plans requiring that a student be in the top 5 percent of high school class ranking to qualify.

>> Stillwell (2019) disagrees with a government-sponsored plan, but supports a loan forgiveness plan in return for one year of working in selected public service fields.

>> Auburn (2019) and Smith (2020) propose government-sponsored tuition at selected state universities.

>> Only Franklin (2017) supports a plan that doesn't require students to "give back."

>> Harkins (2019) and Slovak (2020) oppose any plan that provides tuition for students from families with income above $40,000.

The following sections offer you tools for preparing sources for use in your research writing (summarizing, paraphrasing, and quotations) and then citing those sources in your research.

Refer to Table 11-2 as you read the following sections to get a better picture of when to summarize, when to paraphrase, and when to quote sources.

TABLE 11-2 **Guidelines for Summarizing, Paraphrasing, and Quoting**

When to Summarize	When to Paraphrase	When to Quote
Need an overview of a book	Need highlights of a book	Need the impact of a single-sentence quotation
Need an overview of a large document, such as a legal reference	Need highlights of a large document	Need the impact of an explanatory multiple-sentence block quotation
Need an overview of a complex event, such as the Civil War	Need highlights of a complex event	Need the wording of a partial quote to clarify meaning

Using signal phrases

Signal phrases, like a GPS, determine the direction and purpose of a source. They also distinguish your words from the source's words and alert you that a citation is needed. Signal phrases introduce summaries, paraphrases, and quotations — strategies that build your argument and integrate your critical thinking.

To generate successful signal phrases and source references, do the following:

» **Begin your signal phrase sentence with the author's last name in narrative style.** *Barrett . . .*

» **Follow the author's name with the citation date in parentheses.** *Barrett (2021) . . .*

» **Follow the citation date with relevant biographical information.** *Barrett (2021), an industry leader in wind power, . . .*

» **Follow any biographical information with the appropriate signal phrase.** *Barrett (2021), an industry leader in wind power, supports . . .*

» **Follow the signal phrase with the reference to the source.** *Barrett (2021), an industry leader in wind power, supports gradually transitioning to wind farms as a pilot for assessing wind as an alternate form of energy.*

TIP

Many professors prefer to begin signal phrases with the narrative form citation style (see Chapter 10) because doing so identifies the author's name at the beginning of the sentence and clarifies that you, the student, are talking about the researcher. The citation in parentheses that follows shows your professor that you understand citations. Generally, you should avoid preceding the author's name with a wordy phrase such as "According to . . ."

Author credentials add credibility to your research, especially when no in-text background is included. An author outlier statement may require that you research the author's background. Credentials may be relevant, for example, when affiliations may represent a conflict of interest.

Here are some sample signal-phrase sentences that include author-credential information following the name and citation:

» Jones (2020), the chief financial officer at a large retail chain, *agrees* with cost-of-living wage increases.

» Murphy (2019), a well-known advocate of hybrid transportation, *opposes* sharing hybrid technology with competitors.

>> Clark (2020), a CEO in the soft drink industry, *denies* the sustained harmful effects of decades of sugar-water drinks.

>> Goodwin (2020), a nationally renowned educator, *supports* pre-K education for all children.

>> Caldwell (2018), a nationally known philanthropist, *questions* public funding to support professional sports stadiums.

Here are some source references in citation style:

>> The economic value of a college education exceeds one million dollars over a lifetime (Whitcom, 2019).

>> The healing power in music has been verified in numerous studies (Williams, 2015).

>> Financial security over a lifetime is the result of more saving than investing (Barbaro, 2018).

>> Lifetime success results from average intelligence and above-average work habits (Glassman, 2017).

Examples of signal phrases include the following:

Agree	Disagree	Question	Introduce
argues	contradicts	challenges	explains
endorses	refutes	doubts	adds
acknowledges	disputes	contests	analyzes
recognizes	neglects	debates	highlights
concurs	negates	queries	emphasizes
embraces	disapproves	quizzes	simplifies
approves	rejects	interrogates	proposes

TIP

Post in your work area a copy of your research question to ensure you maintain your focus.

Summarizing and citing correctly

Summaries are like reservoirs; they capture large quantities of information that sustain the life of your argument. They're a staple strategy for converting large quantities of information (books, studies, chapters, and multiple ideas) into a manageable format that contributes to the development of an argument.

A chapter summary for a Sanson (2021) book analyzing Greek life on campus looks like this:

> Sanson (2021) supports restructuring Greek life on campuses because it adds value to the college social experience, supports the local community, and provides lifetime career networking opportunities. She strongly believes that the rushing process and alcohol abuse associated with Greek life needs a new model. Sanson cites local newspaper stories in a number of college towns that describe incidents of hazing and criminal neglect that were affiliated with campus fraternities and sororities. She recounts two incidents that resulted in deaths. She offers a plan for restructuring Greek life on campuses and restoring their traditional service values (pp. 240–280).

Sanson's summary cites evidence to argue the value of Greek life organizations and the need to restructure them within the context of hazing incidents. Information in the summary could also be used to argue against continuation of Greek life organizations. The narrative style citation begins with the author's name followed by the citation date in parentheses. The end of the summary includes the page number citation in parentheses inside the end punctuation.

Paraphrasing and citing correctly

Paraphrasing, expressing a source's words in your own words, is your go-to tool for referencing sources. It allows you the flexibility to take (with citing) as much source reference as needed and to easily insert it into your text. Here's an example of paraphrased evidence to support restructuring educational funding:

> Lockland (2017) recommends eliminating educational funding on the local level because "local economically deprived school districts contribute to educationally deprived school programs." He cites a pattern of poorer school districts lacking programs in the arts, advanced sciences, and foreign languages. Lockland suggests replacing the local property taxes model with a combination of increased state and federal funding. He recognizes that the shift from local property tax would result in increased state taxes, but says that "investments in education today yield economic benefits tomorrow" (pp. 84–85).

Lockland's paraphrase outlines a plan to replace the local property tax model to support public education. The paraphrase and two partial quotes in this example add impact to his plan. The narrative style citation begins with the author's name, followed by the citation in parentheses. The end of the paraphrase identifies the page number citation in parentheses inside the end punctuation. Page number citations are optional with paraphrasing.

Correct use of paraphrasing (with citing) is the key to avoiding plagiarism. Study paraphrasing in your research reading and apply it in your research writing.

APA identifies page numbers with paraphrases optional, but many professors prefer page numbers as good research practice. Ask professors' preferences for page numbers with paraphrases.

Quoting and citing correctly

Use quotations of a few sentences or shorter to highlight memorable information that creates reader impact that would be unachievable by using a summary or paraphrasing. To avoid quotations that appear as popups, the quotations need a lead-in sentence and a follow-up sentence.

Here's an example of a few quotations highlighting the decision to fight the British and start the American Revolutionary War:

> Many American colonists were undecided about starting a war with the mighty British Empire, so a Virginian statesman provided the encouragement. "Gentlemen may cry, 'Peace, Peace' but there is no peace. The war is actually begun!. . . The next gale that sweeps from the north will bring to our ears the clash of resounding arms!. . . Is life so dear, or peach so sweet, as to be purchased at the price of chains and slavery? Forbid it, Almighty God! I know not what course others may take; but as for me, give me liberty or give me death!" (Weigand, 2020, p. 326). Patrick Henry's speech on March 23, 1775, convinced an audience, which included George Washington and Thomas Jefferson, to take arms against the British — and the rest is history.

The dramatic and historical quotation contains more impact than the paraphrase, "Patrick Henry convinced the American colonists to fight against the British." Note the lead-in sentence, which sets up the quotation: "Many American colonists were undecided . . ." and the follow-up sentence: "Patrick Henry's speech . . ."

Journalists, using the quotation strategy, "Don't bury a quote," begin a paragraph with a quotation. Here's an example:

> "Nothing important happened today," journaled King George III on July 4, 1776 (Weigand, 2020, p 327).

Sometimes, no news is more dramatic than fake news.

Synthesizing: Engaging with Sources

Source engagement is like a party where guests talk with the host, talk with each other — and everyone goes home happy. Think of source engagement as a conversation, not an argument. Your goal is to create a linguistic symphony that extends, refines, and implicates ideas.

The tone (see Chapter 5) of source engagement is professional and conversational, avoiding the shouting and assertiveness of a party. It avoids strong language such as "must," "should," and "needs."

REMEMBER

This list includes some immediate questions to ask your professor about source engagement:

>> Are both narrative style and citation style source references acceptable?

>> Which tense is preferred for signal phrases, present or past?

>> Which tense is preferred for source engagement, present or past?

>> Which tense is preferred for summary and paraphrasing?

>> Are page references required for paraphrase citations?

Here's a sample of synthesized source engagement:

> Tipton's long-term study of profit sharing in the workplace found that even the most marginal profit-sharing environment increased profits, improved work morale, and reduced absenteeism. He further found that employees interacted more outside the workplace than employees in traditional environments (2019). Jayson's studies focused on employee retention in profit-sharing environments and reported similar successes (2018). Larson analyzed owners of profit-sharing businesses and found some reluctance because "owners risk the capital and deserve financial rewards for those risks." Larson also found that employees showed very little compassion for owners who relinquished profits to employees (2019, p. 128).

REMEMBER

The previous synthesized source engagement model contains examples of narrative–style source references; the author's names begin the sentences (Tipton, Jayson, and Larson). Refer to the section, "Rehearsing: Preparing Sources," earlier in this chapter for more about source reference styles (narrative and citation).

Tipton's study of profit-sharing in the workplace is summarized. Jayson focuses on one phase of Tipton's study, employee retention. Larson approaches Tipton's study by focusing on the reluctance of business owners. The paragraph synthesizes a conversation among three sources, with each one adding a dimension of discussion.

The following sections demonstrate types of source engagement ("conversations" between and among your sources) that critically analyze your sources and support your argument.

Author and source

The most common form of source engagement is you, the author, engaging with the author of the source.

Here's a sample of author and source engagement:

> Romano (2021) argues that scholastic teams provide a venue for successful social interaction among teenagers. He explains that encouragement from teammates provides "a supportive environment for social interaction risks" (p. 142). My high school athletic experience supports Romano's research. I was an introvert until my participation on the co-ed volleyball team. My peers accepted me as a dependable teammate, which was especially important to me since I was not a gifted athlete. Their acceptance of me built self-confidence to interact with my peers outside the athletic environment.

The signal phrase "argues" introduces the paraphrase of the source: "scholastic teams provide." The source engagement begins with the change to the first person "My. . . research," indicating that you, the author, are telling the anecdote about your scholastic team experience, supporting Romano's research. The anecdote extends the paraphrase.

Here's another example in citation style:

> Scott introduced a plan of backburning hundreds of acres of national forestland serving as a *reservoir* to "prevent sweeping wildfires." He explained that the burning would follow environmental procedures established by the federal government (Scott, 2020, p. 241). I am a proponent of active forest management, a strategy that can save lives and thousands of dollars of property.

The signal phrase "introduced" initiates Scott's plan to backburn forests. Source engagement begins with the change to the first person (I) and agreement with the forest management strategy.

Source and source

Your symphony of source engagement also includes sources talking with sources. Here's an example of a source-and-source engagement:

> Broad (2020) supports equal privately funded campaign spending for all political candidates, believing a candidate's economic advantage is their political advantage. She proposes a pool of private funding divided equally among political candidates. Spruce (2020) agrees with Broad, but opposes federal funding. Spruce wants to avoid political expectations of private donors.

The signal phrase "supports" identifies Broad's commitment to "privately funded campaign spending." The signal phrase, "agrees . . . but," identifies Spruce's position and qualifies his agreement.

Here's another example of citation style:

> Boundaries for offshore fishing rights are often established with sensitivity toward protecting wildlife as well as protecting fishing industries (Daley, 2018). Established fishing boundaries in recent years have resulted in overfishing, unsatisfactory wildlife protection, and financial pressures on the fishing industry (Kingsley, 2018).

Daley introduces the neutral statement identifying guidelines for establishing fishing boundaries. Kingsley enters the conversation by expressing dissatisfaction with the boundary establishment plan.

Source, source, and author

A complex form of source engagement is a conversation between two sources and the author. Here's a sample:

> Diego (2020) analyzed affordable universal healthcare and concluded that it's "the most basic responsibility of a government showing care for its citizens" and that after five years, it pays for itself in the form of a healthier workforce working more productive hours (p. 234). Cinelli (2020) opposes affordable healthcare, arguing that costs will become uncontrollable because of medical conditions of an aging population with pre-existing conditions. I agree with Diego's belief that providing universal affordable healthcare for its citizens shows government's responsibility to protect basic life. I disagree with Cinelli's calculations that medical costs of an aging population cannot be controlled. People are living longer because they are practicing good health habits.

The signal phrase "analyzed" identifies Diego's overview of universal affordable healthcare. The signal phrase "opposes" shows Cinelli's opposition to Diego. The switch to the first person "I" clarifies you, the author, in the conversation. You extend the conversation and "disagree" with Cinelli.

Source, source, and source

Another variation of source engagement includes a conversation among three sources. Here's an example:

> Schultz (2020) studied student loans and discovered that increases in student loan availability parallel increases in tuition at major private universities. The Center for Economic Responsibility (CER, 2019) found that the college graduating class of 2015 entered the workplace with an average of $45,000 in student debt on an average starting salary of $43,000. Fifteen percent of their annual income was allocated to student loan repayment. Vissor (2019) reported that loss of economic power of five classes of graduates produces a ten-percent annual reduction in the Gross National Product. Schultz supports universities' temporarily capping tuition and temporarily capping increases in student loans until both can be studied. The CER endorses reducing interest on student loans, thus increasing students' buying power.

The signal phrase "studied" introduces Schultz's discovery related to student loan and tuition increases. The signal phrase "found" introduces the CER's finding of students' loss of earning power attributed to student loan debt repayment. Schultz extends the conversation, offering a plan to increase students' spending power. The CER enters the conversation and "endorses" an additional plan to increase students' buying power.

Primary sources as engagement

Primary sources are original accounts of a creation credited by experts who had direct connection with the source, such as original photographs, diaries, interviews, surveys, works of art, government documents, and speeches. Topics such as historical research and art appreciation frequently depend on primary sources. Primary research sources are uncommon for most college research topics. Verify with your professor their inclusion for topics such as historical research and art appreciation.

TECHNICAL STUFF

Original research, such as studies that include controlled groups, are also identified as primary research of primary sources. Original research is frequently required for theses and dissertations, requirements for advanced degrees.

Primary sources represent another variation of source engagement, such as you, the author, engaging in "conversation" with a comparison of two pieces of art. What follows are examples of primary sources used in engagement:

> The poultry industry released a survey ("The Yoke's on You") showing the increasing popularity of eggs over the past five years (Ryan, 2020). A number of healthy heart organizations question the unhealthy value of too many yokes (Schutts, 2021).

The poultry survey is introduced, followed by the author's engagement, questioning the unhealthiness of eating too many eggs.

> The Civil War diary revealed archaic medical practices (by today's standards) for treating battlefield injuries. Adam O'Brien, a private in the Union army, wrote that "a doctor's bag of instruments included a bloody saw as his primary tool for treating gangrene" (Morris, 2018, p. 243), as cited in Simms, 2015, p. 254). Fortunately, trauma treatment has improved over time. Still, trauma could be significantly reduced today if countries stopped fighting wars.

The diary entry, which includes a partial quote, describes Civil War trauma treatment. Author engagement includes commenting on the archaic treatment, followed by an opinion about war in general.

> The original 1939 photograph showed men, women, and children wearing oversized wool clothing, waiting in food lines. Many adults appear to be socializing as children play in small groups around them (Coleman, 2019), as cited in Herman, 2015). The photo shows the connection between unemployment at the time and the need to provide food for those who could not afford it.

Description of the photo is followed by engagement of the author, who comments on unemployment and food lines.

Post-Gaming: Verifying Information

Fact-checking is as important to a writer as a kitchen is to a cook. You can't cook up fake facts on a hotplate. In today's world of fake facts and unverified information on social media, facts cohabitate with fake facts. Readers need strategies to evaluate information on social media. If a story or fact appears too good to be true, listen to your instinct and find another source for verification.

REMEMBER

Your professor won't tolerate fake facts and unverified information. If you submit inaccurate information in one paper, your professor will question your accuracy of information in every subsequent paper that you submit.

In addition to citing and evaluating sources, you need to verify the information, which is a different skill application from revising. Information accuracy for research writing requires answers to the following questions:

- Are websites sponsored, indicating a conflict of interest for the writer of the information?

- Does cited information include a summary, paraphrasing, quotations, terms, statistics, and information that transcends common knowledge?

- Are sources scholarly and source elements accurate?

- Are citation and reference list items accurate and formatted according to APA standards? Are punctuation and abbreviations accurate?

- Are names spelled correctly, with proper titles, abbreviations, and punctuation?

- Is content-specific language spelled correctly? Are proper nouns spelled and capitalized correctly?

- Are major and minor works of art punctuated and spelled correctly?

- Is title page information accurate, including spelling and punctuation of the professor's name and title, course name, and affiliations?

- Is outlier information verified with at least two sources?

- Are URLs authentic?

Chapter **12**

Formatting Last Impressions: Reference List

Picture this: You finished writing your argument and you're ready to begin your final back section, your list of sources. The correct way to prepare your sources is to bold and center the word **References** at the top of a new page that follows the end of your text. If your professor asks for an annotated list of sources, use the APA-required bolded heading, "**Annotated Bibliography**". The reference list represents another lesson you learned in the sandbox: sharing — in this case, sharing the resources in your references with the academic community.

REMEMBER

For many professors, your reference list is the resume of your research. With a quick glance, it reveals your qualifications as a college student. Your reference list shows the quality of the sources in your research, your knowledge of APA formatting, and your commitment to the world of scholarship.

In this chapter, I explain new reference guidelines from APA's seventh edition (2019), guidelines for coordinating reference elements, and conventions and abbreviations that are specific to references. Additionally, I provide you with dozens of reference entry samples that you can use as models for listing your sources.

This chapter addresses the following new APA seventh edition changes for reference list entries:

>> References are revised and standardized.

>> Audiovisual entries such as YouTube videos, PowerPoint slides, and TED Talks are expanded into a new category.

>> Social media sources are addressed in a new category.

Playing by the Rules: General Guidelines

If you're a rules follower and you like details, creating a reference list will please you as much as racking up another 15 credit hours. If you don't like following rules, creating a reference list will be as unappealing as sardines on your pizza. The purpose of the reference list is to show your respect for scholarship by providing details of information that you take from experts' sources.

APA updated their reference guidelines with the recently released *Publication Manual of the American Psychological Association, Seventh Edition*. Reference list updates clarify past issues and reduce reference entry requirements. Here's a look at the updates:

>> Personal communications such as email, interviews, texts, and lectures are cited in the text only and aren't required in the reference list.

>> General references to websites, webpages, common software, and apps are cited in text only and not in the reference list. General references to

inspirational quotations by famous people aren't usually cited and don't appear in the reference list.

>> Authors included in a reference item now number up to 20.

>> DOIs (digital object identifiers), when available, are preferred to URLs.

>> Journal article references always include the issue number. Locations of publishers are eliminated from reference entries. New examples are included for YouTube videos, PowerPoint slides, and podcasts.

>> Social media, webpages, and websites are re-categorized to standardize formatting with blogs and other online platforms.

Formatting guidelines specific to the reference list include

REMEMBER

>> Center and bold **References** at the top of a new page following the end of the text of the paper.

>> If you're required to annotate your references, type **Annotated Bibliography** in place of **References**.

>> Alphabetize entries by authors' last names. If an author or group name is unavailable, enter the title in the position of the name.

>> Alphabetize multiple authors by the last name of the first author listed:

- Cronway, E., & Applebaum, R.

- Davis, B., & Carson, J.

- Ellis, J., & Smith, K.

>> Create a hanging indentation alignment by indenting successive lines a half inch from authors' names.

>> Formatting annotations are aligned with reference entries.

Here's what some typical reference entries look like.

References

Saulter, W. S. (2014). *Power of the graphic arts: A humanistic approach*. Olney. https://doi.org/10.0000084-111

Touey, P. S. (2015). *Success on the fast track: A five-step program to career success*. Parkside Press. https://doi.org/10.0000056-333

Zimmerman, J. S., & Caldwell, R. S. (2018). Wait time is the time learning takes place. *Journal of Applied Learning, 132*(8), 356–394. https://doi.org/10.0000084-222

Coordinating Reference Elements: Author, Date, Title, and Source

APA organizes reference entries by groups and categories. Format your entry by duplicating the pattern of the sample in the group and category. It's like grocery shopping. To find a can of soup, you look for the aisle with the "soup" sign and search the shelves for the kind of soup you're looking for. APA's groups, and the category of works and samples in each group, include the following:

>> **Textual works group:** periodical articles, books, reference works, edited book chapters, journals, magazines, newspapers, newsletters, blogs, reports, gray literature, dissertations, and reviews of other works

>> **Data sets, software, and tests group:** data sets, computer software, mobile apps, surveys, and polls

TECHNICAL STUFF

The term *gray literature* identifies reports that may or may not be peer-reviewed and includes grants, policy briefs, and press releases. A *data set* (or dataset) is a collection of data specific to a topic from a single source: prediction data from the National Weather Service, climate data, and Google trends. Data sets are a form of analytics.

>> **Audiovisual media:** YouTube videos, speech audio recordings, podcast episodes, and PowerPoint slides

>> **Online media:** social media, webpages, and websites

APA's categories of groups and works contain materials common to graduate-level research (theses, scales and inventories, unpublished raw data, and unpublished and informally published works) that you may have occasional use for in your undergraduate research. A general sequential pattern for entering almost all elements of reference items is author, date, title, source, additional source information if available, and DOI or URL if available and applicable. Here is what the different elements look like individually and then as a reference item:

Author(s): Scully, P. J., & Schwartz, D. W. (A comma precedes the ampersand.)

Date: 2018

Title: The long-term effects of music and learning: A study of prodigies

Source: *American Journal of Classical Musicians*

Additional source information: Volume 38, Issue 14

Page numbers: 210–243

DOI: https://doi.org/10.0000091-333

Scully, P. J., & Schwartz, D. W. (2018). The long-term effects of music and learning: A study of prodigies. *American Journal of Classical Musicians, 38*(14), 210–243. https://doi.org/10.0000091-333

REMEMBER

If you don't like shopping in a grocery store for cans of soup, here's a classroom-tested strategy: If you're looking to format a webpage entry in the reference list, follow a model format of a webpage entry. If you're looking to format a podcast entry, follow a model format of a podcast entry. Almost all APA sources of information include a variety of model reference entries. Numerous model entries are included at the end of this chapter.

But because APA reference entries have as many variations as there are paths to graduation, over-achievers like you need to understand the exceptions. APA identifies four elements for entering a source in the reference list: author, date, title, and source. Knowing the definitions of key elements helps you to address variations. For example, *author* can be defined as "producer" or "host." The following sections examine how APA defines each element.

Author

APA defines *author* as the name of the person or group that created the work, such as the editor, co-producer, host, and staff. Here are some guidelines for formatting the author element in reference entries:

REMEMBER

>> Enter the author's last name(s), followed by a comma and first and middle initials, followed by periods (Adams, J. L.). Spell out the full name of group authors followed by a period (Academy House Staff.).

Use one space between initials.

>> Provide last names and initials for up to 20 authors. If the source has between two and 20 authors, use an ampersand (&) before the final author's name. If the source has 21 or more authors, include the first 19 authors' names, insert an ellipsis (but no ampersand), and then add the final author's name.

>> If an author is credited using the word *with*, include them with the reference item in parentheses: Davis, M. N. (with Torres, M. L.).

>> If a work is designated "Anonymous," use "Anonymous" as the author:

Anonymous. *Future of plants indigenous to Central Europe: An unbiased analysis.* Preston. https://doi.org/10.0000054-222

>> If the author has one name (Tulip), use that name in the citation and reference:

Tulip. (2019). *Indigenous plants in moderate temperatures.* Binders. https://doi.org/ 10.0000054-222

>> Avoid titles and academic ranks with names.

>> If no author or group is listed, begin the reference entry with the title of the work:

Power of the graphic arts: A humanistic approach. (2014). Olney. https://doi.org/ 10.0000084-111

Date

APA defines *date* as the time period in which the work was published and includes terminology such as this:

March 22, 2020; February 2020; Fall; 2020–2022

ADDITIONAL FORMATTING OF AUTHOR ELEMENT ENTRIES

Here are some of the less obvious formatting guidelines that are specifically for the author element, in addition to the seventh edition upgrades (one even contradicts rules of standard English):

- Use a comma to separate an author's initials from additional author names.

- Use the serial comma before an ampersand (&) with three or more authors: Tole, E. S., Carpenter, V. M., & Cromwell, H. W.

- Also, surprisingly, use the serial comma before an ampersand with two authors: Wagner, B. J., & Cunningham, J. L.

- Use one space after initials.

- Use commas to separate initials and suffixes: O'Day, P. R., Jr.

- If secondary authors are credited using "with," include them in parentheses after the name: Donnelly, J. E. (with O'Keith, J. J.).

Most date element guidelines apply to graduate-level research projects, such as date designations for "summitted for publication," "work in progress," and "in press." Here are a few guidelines for date elements that apply to you as an undergraduate scholar.

>> Enclose the date entry in parentheses, followed by a period: (1989).

>> When a last-update date is available for an online source, use the updated date rather than the overall website date.

>> For frequently revised publications with changing dates, such as Wikipedia articles, a retrieval date is needed. When information changes less frequently, a retrieval date isn't needed.

Title

APA designates a *title* as the name (title) of the work being cited. Titles are categorized into two general groups. See the section, "Capitalizing references," later in this chapter that explains "title case" and "sentence case."

>> **Works that stand independently:** Books, journal articles, reports, videos, films, TV series, podcasts, social media, websites, and web pages

Guidelines for independent works include the following:

- Italicize the title.

- Use sentence case; capitalize only the first word (and the first word after a colon) and proper nouns.

>> **Works part of larger source:** Periodical articles, book chapters, datasets, and media episodes

Guidelines for works part of a larger source include the following:

- Avoid italicizing the title and using quotation marks.

- Use sentence case; capitalize only the first word (and the first word after a colon) and proper nouns:

  Successful homework strategies: Parents' perspective.

- For works part of a larger source, use italics and sentence case. Use title case for the independent source:

Scully, P. J., & Schwartz, D. W. (2018). The long-term effects of music and learning: A study of prodigies. *American Journal of Classical Musicians, 38*(14), 210–243. https://doi.org/10.0000091-333

For example, the part of a larger source journal article (The long-term effects of music and learning: A study of prodigies) appears in an independent journal (*American Journal of Classical Musicians*).

Source

APA defines *source* as the location where the cited work can be retrieved. Sources, similar to titles, are categorized into independent works and dependent works. If no source is available, such as when there are no available sources for texts, email, and classroom lectures, then no problem — use only the in-text citation and no reference entry.

Source elements are formatted according to their classifications:

>> A source element of a reference with one part, such as a book source without a DOI, requires only the listing of the book publisher:

Highspire, J. (2021). *Psychological approaches to remedial instructions: A ten-year study*. Folsom.

THE LONG AND SHORT OF IT: DOIs AND URLs

If you like technology choices (and you like to impress your friends with your technical knowledge), then APA offers you options on shortened URLs and DOIs. If you don't know the meaning of those abbreviations (uniform resource locator and digital object identifier), then those options aren't for you. If you follow the advice of good writers that shorter is better and you don't like lengthy URLs and DOIs that don't word-wrap neatly, then shortened versions can make your day.

Relatively new DOIs are replacing URLs. DOIs are expressed as alphanumeric (letters and numbers) strings that begin with "https://doi.org/" or "https://dx.doi.org" and are followed by the number 10. DOIs contain a prefix and suffix separated by a slash (backslash). Shortened DOIs are available from the International DOI Foundation (http://shortdoi.org/).

APA recommends shortened URLs for student papers written by undergraduates, which probably applies to almost anyone reading this book. Shortened versions aren't recommended for scholars intending to publish their research because shortened links are not as stable.

>> A source element of a book reference with a DOI requires a listing of two parts:

Conway, R. (2020). *Language deficiencies common to extreme climates.* Jackson & Sons. https://doi.org/10. 1007/0000084-000

An eLocator is a contemporary equivalent of page numbers on many e-print documents. It appears as a combination of numbers and lowercase letters. When an eLocator is available, use it in place of page numbers in a citation and reference.

Clarifying Elements: Reference Conventions and Abbreviations

Punctuation, abbreviations, spelling, spacing, and formatting required in reference entries represent the most detailed and complex language in the academic community. The complexity of this language exceeds that of your resume. But you can chill. Do your best to construct a perfectly accurate reference list, and recognize that your professor isn't looking to penalize you for incorrect spacing between volume numbers and issue numbers. Violations in formatting become a grading issue when your professor identifies big-picture issues such as lack of hanging indentations, weak sources, a vague argument, or disrespect for APA style and citations.

Show your pride as a scholar by nailing formatting requirements. Proof it, have it peer reviewed, have it reviewed by your writing center, and proof it again. To quote a sign in the classroom of Joe Owsley, Sun Valley High School (Aston, Pa.) math teacher, "The harder you work, the luckier you get."

The following sections take a closer look at punctuating and capitalizing references.

Punctuating your references

APA establishes a punctuation style for references. Create a personal list of APA punctuation relative to your research. Here's a look at APA punctuation rules specific to the reference list.

>> Use a comma to separate author initials from additional authors' names. Use an ampersand (&) with two authors: Lee, J. T., & Albright, M. A.

>> Use a serial comma with an ampersand for three or more authors: Anderson, C. A., Brown, W. W., & Davis, A. W.

>> Follow periods with one space.

>> If no date is available, use the abbreviation "n.d." (no date) with no space between "n." and "d."

>> Use a comma to separate initials from suffixes: Garcia, T. T., Jr., & Katz, S. T.

>> Enclose in parentheses additional book information that follows the title, and follow the parentheses with a period: (3rd ed., Vol. 2).

Table 12-1 lists specific abbreviations for references.

TABLE 12-1

Reference List Entry Abbreviations

Abbreviations	Explanations
ed.	edition
3rd ed.	third edition
n.d. (no space between letters)	no date
Ed. (Eds.)	editor (editors)
p. (pp.)	page (pages)
para. (paras.)	paragraph (paragraphs)
Vol. (Vols.)	volume (volumes)
Pt.	part
No.	number

Spell authors' last names exactly as they appear in published works: diGregorio, A'lloway, Maria-Cortez-Lopez, and d'Marco. Also spell publications exactly as they appear in published works: *SciENTIFIC*, *ReVISor*, *ReKlamations*, and *Re$alables*.

Capitalizing references

APA utilizes two capitalization styles for titles of works and headings within references:

>> **Title case** requires capitalization of major words (nouns, verbs, adjectives, adverbs, pronouns, and all words four letters or longer). Minor words that aren't capitalized include three-letter or fewer conjunctions, prepositions, and

articles. In title case, you always capitalize the first word of the title and subtitle, even if they're minor words: *The Great Escape: The Story of Educating Poverty.*

Here are some uses of title case:

- Titles of books, periodicals, and reports used in text, but not in reference lists
- Heading levels within text (see Chapter 14)
- Figure and table titles (see Chapter 13)

>> **Sentence case** requires lowercase for most words. Capitalize proper nouns, the first word of the title, and the first word after a colon, dash (em dash), or end mark of punctuation: *The great influenza: The story of educating poverty.* Sentence case is used in the reference list.

Here are some uses for sentence case:

- Titles of works in the reference list
- Table column headings
- Notes headings (see Chapter 13)

Playing by the Rules: Specifics for Formatting Periodicals

You have your go-to snacks, your go-to comfort foods, your go-to music — and in this section your go-to reference choice: periodicals and scholarly journals.

Periodicals are so common to academic research at all levels that your professors may question not seeing one. Here's a look at guidelines that are exclusively for periodical entries in reference lists:

>> Capitalize periodical titles in title case. Review the section, "Clarifying Elements: Reference Conventions and Abbreviations," earlier in this chapter.

>> Enter the periodical title exactly as it appears in the publication.

>> Italicize the title, followed by a non-italicized comma.

>> Italicize the volume number.

>> Enter the issue number (if available) in parentheses immediately following the volume number, without a space, and follow the issue number with a comma: *8*(4),

>> Follow the issue number with a space and the page range. Follow page ranges with a period: 56–84.

>> If volume numbers and issue numbers are unavailable, you can obviously exclude them from the entry.

>> End with a DOI or URL if available and applicable. Do not follow a DOI or URL with a period.

Refer to Chapter 11 for more on specific titles of journals and periodicals.

Here's a template of what a journal article in a reference list looks like:

[Author(s)]. [(Year)]. [Title of the article.] [*Name of the Periodical the Article Appears in Title Case*]. [*volume*(issue).] [page range] [DOI or URL]

Wilson, J. K., & Albright, W. M. (2020). Academic liabilities of elementary students in major cities with limited broadband. *Educational Technology in Major Cities*. *15*(5). 191–246. https://doi.org/4938

The following guidelines walk you through how to format this journal article:

>> Names of two authors are separated by an ampersand (&), and the ampersand is preceded by a comma. The date of publication follows the authors' names.

>> The title of the article is written in sentence case (not italicized) and followed by a period.

>> The volume number (15) is written in italics.

>> The issue number (5) in parentheses follows the volume number. No space separates the volume number and issue number. The issue number isn't italicized (nor are the parentheses surrounding the issue number).

>> The range of pages follows the volume number and issue number.

>> The entry ends with a DOI if available. If no DOI is available, end with the URL. Don't follow the DOI or URL with end punctuation.

Seeing Is Believing: Real-Life Reference Items

Here you assemble all the parts from this chapter and look at models of a variety of reference entries. In this section, you have models to duplicate. You have major categories of entries followed by annotations highlighting key features. The reference samples include all the likely models you'll need in order to write successful undergraduate research papers.

The terms *periodical* and *journal* are frequently used interchangeably, but they have some subtle differences. A *periodical* is a regularly published document that passed the test of time. A *journal*, frequently scholarly and academic, refers to a newspaper, magazine — or scholarly journal. Periodical refers to a more general publication, and journal refers to a more specific and usually more scholarly publication. If you want to sound more scholarly, use the term *scholarly journal*.

Books and reference works

Books and reference works are common to most undergraduate research. Here's a look at some reference samples.

Book

Here's a look at a book reference entry:

Carlos, J. A., & Delaney, S. G. (2019). *Literary practices of successful secondary students: A long-term approach.* National Literacy Commission. https://doi.net/8.8407/88880903-450

Keep the following in mind:

» The book title (Literary practices . . .) is written in sentence case and italicized.

» The two authors are separated by an ampersand, and a comma precedes the ampersand.

» The publisher (National Literacy. . .) is not italicized.

» No period follows the DOI.

Authored eBook (Kindle book or audiobook)

An eBook and audio book require the following reference entry style:

McClain, J. D. (2016). *Feeding your brain math skills* (J. Ritchie, Narr.) [Audiobook]. Clipper Cove Sounds. http://byt.er/1710B/

Authored book with editor

Here's a sample entry for an authored book with an editor:

Galloway, A. H. (2019). Thinking your way through college: A freshmen primer (E. Styx, Ed.). Island Way Publishing.

One volume of a multivolume work

Here's a look at a reference listing for a volume or multivolume:

Klein, R. B., Sidwell, Y. A., & Clarke, S. P. (2019). *Anthology of turn of the century literature in remote habitats* (3rd ed., Vol. 5). John Clarkson Publishing. https://doi.org/10.7509/9265473090013

Dictionary, thesaurus, or encyclopedia

Here's a sample entry for a reference book:

World Baseball Association (2009). *Baseball encyclopedia of world records*. Retrieved April 15, 2019, from https://baseballrecords.mbb.org/

Religious work

Take a look at a reference for a religious work:

Church of the sacred way Bible. (2011). Sacred Way Bible Online. https://www. sacredwaybibleonline.org/ (Original work published in 1806)

Edited book chapters and works in reference books

Here's a look at reference samples for edited book chapters, works in reference books, and a Wikipedia entry.

Edited book chapter

An edited book chapter is referenced as follows:

Sakers, L. P., & Carpenter, E. J. (2018). Writing in the contents: Math and science centered. In J. Mayberry & M. Lutrell (Eds.) *Writing across the curriculum in the twenty-first century: A close up look* (3rd ed., pp. 327–384). Writing Curriculum Association. https://doi.net/8.8407/8890903-450

Chapter in edited book with DOI

Here's a sample entry of a book chapter with a DOI:

Harrelson, W. T. & Roisetta, R. I. (2018). Behavioral psychology: Practices among special populations. In P. P. Louis & L. W. Parker (Eds.), *Cognitive behavior practices in search of treatment* (3rd ed., pp. 315–423). Cognitive Practice Society. https://doi.org/10.3402/1111987-002

Wikipedia entry

Here's a look at a Wikipedia entry:

List of states with most graduate degrees. (2020, February 1). In *Wikipedia.* https://ed.wikikis.org/w/indexiki?degrees=8640823

Periodical and journal articles

Here's a look at reference entries for periodicals and journal articles.

Journal article with DOI

Journal article entries with a DOI look like the following:

Rodriguez, R. A., & Levy, A. M. (2020). Developmental reading strategies for special populations: A conceptual approach. *Reading Review Journal, 8*(21), 83–129. https://doi.org/10.0000091-333

Keep the following in mind:

>> The comma before the ampersand separates the two authors' names.

>> The article title (Developmental . . .) is written in sentence case and is neither italicized nor enclosed in quotation marks.

>> The journal, the source (Reading Review . . .), is written in title case and italicized.

>> The volume number (8) is written in italics and the issue number (21) follows in parentheses, with no space between the volume number and the issue number.

>> The range of pages (83–129) is followed by a period.

Print magazine article

Here's an entry for a print magazine article:

James, K. (2019, November 15). Strategies for financial security on a limited budget. *Money Saving Magazine, 75*(10) 67–71, 98.

Keep the following in mind when referencing a print magazine article:

>> The article extends from pages 67–71 and continues on page 98.

>> The date is written with the year first, followed by the month and day.

Print newspaper article

Print newspaper article entries look like the following:

Parker, C. (2019, May 13). Home schooling socialization strategies. *Talk-in-Town*, E12.

Keep the following in mind when referencing a print newspaper article:

» *Talk-in-Town* is a delivered print newspaper.

» The article location in the newspaper is E12.

» The newspaper date is written as year, month, and day.

» The newspaper title is written in title case and italicized.

Journal article from secondary source

A journal article entry from a secondary source looks like the following:

Marks, A. (2017). American *Journal of Verification. 23*(8), 431–462. https://doi.org/10.2245/j9800134 (Reprinted from "The new intrusion in daily life: face-recognition software," 2007, *American Journal of Constitutional Rights, 23*(13), 324–386. https://doi.org/10.5432/f.1943.1884

Editorial

Here's an example for an editorial reference:

Pierez, A. (2019). When animals listen to other animals [Editorial]. *Journal of Comprehensive Veterinary Medicine 46*(9), 311–343. https://doi.org/10.2343/8756588697000

Film review in journal

Here's a look at a film review:

White, W., & Barbera, K. (2018). Seeing good in children when they see bad. *Psychology of Children Today. 2*(3), 110–115. https://doi.org/10.2210/fae0000405

Book review in newspaper

A book review in a newspaper looks like the following:

Williams, T. (2015, April 10). Contemporary jazz. *The Daily Tribune.* https://doi.org/20.3572/dtm0000865

Reports

This section provides samples of reference entries for various types of reports.

Group author

A group author entry looks like this:

National Writing Commission. (2017). *An assessment of writing in secondary schools in America in the past five years.* https://pssa.national/secondary/87540/463067/USA RHD 23ger.pdf?ed=0

Keep the following in mind:

» The group author (National Writing . . .) is capitalized and followed by a period.

» The report (*An assessment* . . .) is written in sentence case and should be italicized.

» A URL is listed because a DOI wasn't available.

» A period doesn't follow the URL.

Government report

Here's a look at a government report entry:

National Nutrition Institute. (2019). *Foods of the future: High value low maintenance food supplies* (NNI Publication No. 874-9530). Department of Services, National Nutrition Institute. https://www.nutrition.gov/publications-education.pdf

Report by task force

A task force report entry looks like this:

Environmental Solutions for Climate Change. (2019). *Fossil Fuel Problems Task Force report: Fossil fuel impacts.* Society for Climate Change. http://www.scc.com/documents/ESCC_fossil_report_087.pdf

Code of ethics

Here's a look at an entry for a code of ethics:

American Sporting Association. (2020). *2020 ASA code of ethics.* https://www.sporting.org/ethics-center

Audiovisual media and works

The following provides reference entries for various media and visual displays.

Film or video

Film or video entries look as follows:

Burkett, A. (Director). (2020). *Ensuring the right vote.* [Film]. Allied Artists.

Television series

Here's a sample of a television series entry:

Allen, U. (Writer & Producer). (2017–2020). *Weekend* [TV Series]. Premier
Productions; CBN.

TED Talks

A TED Talks entry looks as follows:

Rittenhouse, P. (2020, November). *The joy of talking with strangers* [Video]. TED
Conferences. https://www.ted.com/talks/the_joy_of_talking

Recorded webinar

Recorded webinar entries look like this:

Crist, R. R. (2020). *Evaluating life in small rural towns* [Webinar]. American Rural
Life Association. https://rural.org/users/small.elst/?834

YouTube or streaming video

Here's a look at an entry for a YouTube or streaming video:

Junto, A. (2020, February 22). *Surviving storms* [Video]. Marcus. https://marcus.
com/9d3kdj88

Podcast

Podcasts are referenced as follows:

Wade, A. W. (Host). (2018–present). *Technology for non-nerds* [Audio podcast].
NTN. https://www.ntn.org/series/89746/technology-nerds

Speech audio recording

List an audio speech recording as follows:

Overton, R. S., Sr. (1945, August 7). *A win for democracy* [Speech audio recording]. *Freedom Forecasts.* https://www.freedomforecasts.com/speech/archive/windemocracy

Artwork

Here's a sample of an artwork listing:

Schmidt, P. (1958). *European impressionism* [Painting]. Art Institute of South Florida, Tampa, FL., United States. https://www.art.edu/isf/08998/

Clip art or stock image

Follow this sample for listing clip art or a stock image:

NJCArt. (2021). Highway association visual image collection [Clip art]. Openclipart. https://highway.org/collection/9865555/assoc-image/76542

Infographic

If you use an infographic, enter it as follows:

Weber, F. T., & Brown, C. D. (2020). *Exploring old world molecules in modern times* [Infographic]. National Physics Society Annual Meeting. https://www.nationalphysicsnationalmeeting.com/2020/infographic

Map

List maps in your Reference list as follows:

Thomas, C. T., & Moore, R. S. (2005). *The population density map* [Map]. University of Central Livingston, Center for Population Analysis. https://population.analysis.org/population.density/map

Photograph

Here's a look at an entry for a photograph:

Kosegian, A. A. (1999). *Seascapes* [Photograph]. Ocean Images. https://www.oceanimages.com/ocean/images/765446-annual-1999.jpg

PowerPoint slides

Enter PowerPoint slides like this example:

Walker, F. K. (2020). *Strategies for source engagement and first year writing* [PowerPoint slides]. Blackboard Open Source. https://shr.blackboard.com

Online media

Here's a look at reference entries for online media.

Blog post

Here's a look at a blog post entry:

Fay, I. E., (2020, March 25). When siblings become rivals. *The Kitchen Korner Blog.* http://mercurymedia.org/blog/2018/10/when-siblings-become-rivals/

Tweet

List a tweet as such:

BCS Electronics [@BCSElectronics]. (2020, May 20). *Home owners are short circuiting home safety @popularelectronics* [Tweet]. Twitter. https://twitter.com/bcselectronics/short/circuiting/65447988664434

Facebook post

Facebook post entries look like the following:

Wright, D. (2018, May 1). *College football playoffs need expansion for non-power five schools.* [Image attached] [Status update]. Facebook. http://bit.Ly/7LQxNCA

Instagram photo or video

Use the following sample for an Instagram photo or video entry:

Florez, A. D. POCCA [@florezpocca] (2020, April 27). *Challenged election results statistically insignificant in northern states* [Photographs]. Instagram. https://www.instagram.com/p/LiLK/

Instagram highlight

If you're highlighting an Instagram, follow this model:

The Central Association of Anthropologists [@caa] (n.d.). *When an artifact isn't an artifact* [Highlight]. Instagram. Retrieved April 18, 2020, from https://bitly.com/88KJht/

Conferences and presentations

Here's a look at reference entries for conferences and presentations:

Shields, J. T., (2018, January 6–8). *Grit is learned in the home* [Conference session]. HSCC Annual Convention. Clearwater Beach, Fla., United States. https://doi.org/10.0000965-323

Webpages and websites

Here's a look at reference entries for webpages and websites.

Webpage on a website

List a webpage or website as follows:

Ruddick, J.K., Klein, S. J., & Suber, I.P. (2019). *Writing strategies for underachieving college freshmen.* https://nassp.teaching/strategies/4674/4930567/NSARH4323

Webpage on a website with a retrieval date

Here's a look at a listing for a webpage on a website with a retrieval date:

Dawson, K. T., & Sausman, L. J. (2019). *Climate trends in tropical forests.* International Climate Organization. Retrieved November 11, 2019, from https://www.international.gov/census/

Note: The retrieval date is included because the page contents change regularly.

Legal reference

For legal references, APA recognizes *The Bluebook: A Uniform System of Citation*, the standard in the legal field in all academic disciplines. Variations of legal references are more common to professional scholars than undergraduates. Although in-text citations closely follow APA guidelines, with the name of the legal document followed by the date (*Marbury v. Madison*, 1803), reference entries vary slightly. Professors accept legal reference elements that follow the sequence: title, source, and date. Court cases in reference lists are written in roman font and aren't italicized as required in citations.

Here's an example of what a classic case looks like:

Brown v. Board of Education, 347 U.S. 483 (1954). https://www.oyez.org/cases/1940-1955/347us483

Note: The volume number is 347 and the page number is 483.

Extending References: Annotated Bibliography

Annotating references is like adding healthy toppings to your salad. From the professor's perspective, requiring students to submit an annotation of sources adds critical thinking to their academic experience. Annotation requires higher-order skills such as synthesizing purposes of the sources, evaluating their application to the argument, and justifying their use to the research.

Strategies for reference annotations include the following:

>> **Summarizing and paraphrasing** (as well as highlighting) major topics

>> **Evaluating** the effectiveness of sources as supporting or refuting the argument

>> **Reflecting** on the overall value of the source

>> **Combining** these elements, beginning with a brief summary

Formatting the annotation requires double-space alignment, directly under the indentation of the reference entry. The alignment transitions the idea flow from the source to the annotation. The length ranges from three to five sentences to a longer paragraph. Don't copy and paste sentences from the abstract, because doing so is plagiarism. Ask your professor for annotation guidelines, and if none are offered, use the combination of strategies. A good time management strategy is to prepare for your annotation when you first begin summarizing sources, which includes highlights of major topics covered.

Here's a sample of what annotation looks like:

Brogan, J. K., Miles, J. L., & Iacone, A. J. (2021). *Community climate conditions for successful schools: A city approach* (2nd ed.). STJPress. https://doi.org/10.1248/0000056-084

The authors examine community conditions conducive to building a successful school environment. They focus on conditions such as encouraging reading and academics, supporting the arts, and maintaining perspective on athletics. The authors' long-term study supports the thesis that successful schools result from an environment of supportive academic strategies. The authors underestimate the challenge of implementing these strategies in nonsupportive communities.

4

Perfecting Presentation: Beginnings, Endings, and Other Writings

Chapter **13**

Preparing Appetizers and Desserts: Front and Back Materials

et the questions begin. *Front and back materials* represent the intersection of APA requirements and your professor's requirements — and you know who assigns the grade. Where specific professor guidelines end, your student initiative begins. You're unlikely to give yourself credit for the academic initiative and ingenuity that contributed to your being the successful college student you are today. But you're the captain who navigated your course to academic success.

Somewhere after middle school, you took responsibility and developed the skills to become an independent learner. Now that you're a college student, the point where APA requirements are either vague or nonexistent, you need to rely on your academic instincts to make good choices on inclusion of research parts. You also need to ask your professor a mouthful of questions.

Here's a list of questions to ask your professor about front and back materials:

>> Is a model of front and back materials available, or should I strictly follow APA guidelines and the online models?

>> Is a numbered table of contents required?

>> Are figures or tables required? May I use them? Are they required to be embedded?

>> Are appendixes required? May I use them?

TIP

The best time to ask initial assignment questions is the day assignments are introduced, when your professor allocates time and expects student questions. Before asking questions, read the assignment directions that include a description of the assignment, the due date, and how to submit it. Always avoid questions with a nonacademic tone, such as, "What does this assignment have to do with the course?" Also avoid prefacing a question with, "I'm confused." Instead, preface with, "Could you please clarify . . .?"

In this chapter I show you the periphery of the research assignment, the front and back sections that can improve your presentation and also improve your grade. I show you how to create an opening impression with a table of contents, abstract, and list of figures. Then I explain features to help you create a memorable lasting impression — appendix, glossary, footnotes, and endnotes. Professors' preferences for front and back materials with assignments vary as much as your online shopping choices.

Opening Impressions: Formatting Front Matter

What do Broadway and your professor have in common? They both love good openings. Unlike Broadway, front matter for your research papers is optional — unless your professor designates them as required. As a professor who has graded thousands of research projects, I can tell you that organizational features that clarify content influence grading. The following sections take a closer look at what constitutes front matter.

Previewing your paper: Table of contents

APA doesn't require a table of contents, but why not take advantage of an opportunity to clarify your presentation, show your professor how organized you are, and highlight your inclusion of assignment requirements? If your table of contents could speak, it would say, "I am a preview of the organization and content sequence within this research paper. My purpose is to make a good impression on my professor and begin the process of earning a good grade."

As a real-life example, how disoriented would you feel if this book lacked a table of contents to search for the location of "Front and Back Materials"? It would be like trying to find your parked car "somewhere in New York City." This *For Dummies* book shows the importance of a table of contents by containing two: the traditional one and a Contents at a Glance.

Begin your table of contents by identifying the major topics of your paper, followed by the headings, such as introduction, literature review, argument, discussion, conclusion, reference, and appendix.

Don't include an abstract or list of figures in the table of contents.

Keep these formatting guidelines in mind for your table of contents:

>> Center and bold "contents" (without quotation marks) at the top of a new page. Don't underline or italicize.

>> Use title case, capitalizing key words, and double space all lines.

>> Avoid the word "page" above page numbers. Readers know the number at the end of the dotted line is a page number.

>> Align page numbers flush right.

>> List only the page number where the content begins, not the range of pages that contain the content.

Some professors may require that you number content and include subheadings, as in Figure 13-1. *Note:* Endnotes and appendixes are optional sections and not required by APA.

If your professor follows strict APA guidelines, and requires numbering and subheadings, then your contents page should look like Figure 13-2.

Also use numbered contents if APA instruction is part of your course content.

Contents

Introduction 1
Literature Review 3
Argument 5
Discussion 7
Conclusion 11
Reference List 13
Endnotes 14
Appendix A: Figures and Tables 15
Appendix B: Topics for Further Study 16
Appendix C: Summary of Professional Resources 17

© John Wiley & Sons, Inc.

FIGURE 13-1: A sample table of contents that most professors will accept.

Contents

1.0 Introduction 1
  1.1 Statement of the Problem 2
  1.2 Background 2
2.0 Literature Review 3
3.0 Argument 5

© John Wiley & Sons, Inc.

FIGURE 13-2: Contents page with numbering and subheadings.

Listing figures and tables

Figures in an academic paper enhance text and add to the professionalism of your presentation. *Figures* represent a large category of visuals, including photographs, images, signs, clip art, drawings, diagrams, graphs, and charts. Contrary to the belief of many students, figures don't speak for themselves. They need context and the companionship of nearby sentences.

The role of figures depends on the course and topic. Figures enhance text for any topic, including education, business, art, and science. They infrequently appear in literature and other humanities topics. In a history paper, for example, figures include artifacts, maps, and historical photographs. Examples in business include bar graphs, comparison data, and mission statements.

The purpose of *tables* in research writing is to display large quantities of numerical data. Tables are rare in undergraduate research writing, unless you're reporting on extensive scientific data. Information on constructing tables is available online. When tables are used, they're referenced in the text, similar to figures. APA recommends including a list of tables in an appendix on the page immediately following the reference list. Many professors (and department guidelines) prefer tables and figures to be embedded in the text and not in an appendix. Ask your professor what they prefer.

Formatting figures

Four to six well-formatted images can improve your paper and your grade. But one misaligned figure can make your paper look as unprofessional as a misaligned resume. Many online images are adaptable to copying and pasting inside a text box, with a citation. As I discuss in Chapter 10, a parenthetical citation for images requires an author and date — and a page number for quotations.

Guidelines for utilizing figures include

>> Legible and limited text

>> Size and content adaptable to a text box

>> Colors that avoid clashing

REMEMBER

Figures require a number and title, and are written in title case. Bold the word "figure" and the number. Italicize the figure name. Here are some examples:

Figure 1: *Johnson's Hierarchy of Academic Skills*

Figure 2: *James' Steps for Team Designing*

Figure 3: *Photo of Civil War Sword*

Figure 4: *Map of Category 5 Hurricanes*

REMEMBER

Figures also require reference within the text. When figures are referenced within the text, don't bold the word "figure." Here are some examples:

Figure 1 compares the cost of college in the '80s with costs today.

Figure 2 identifies Albertson's steps for achieving financial independence.

Figure 3 shows a 1950s kitchen coffeemaker.

Occasionally, a figure requires a brief explanatory note, as in the following example:

Hurricane tracking in 1960 consisted of identifying the path travelled.

Placing the list of figures

APA's order of pages recommends placing the list of figures in front of the appendixes, or as the last page if no appendix is used. Your professor may prefer the list of figures immediately follow the table of contents. Ask your professor what they prefer. Begin your list of figures on a new page, as shown in Figure 13-3.

FIGURE 13-3:
A list of figures.

© *John Wiley & Sons, Inc.*

REMEMBER

This is why you need to ask your professor questions to clarify the following:

>> APA recommends placing figures and tables in an appendix, and it offers you the option of combining them in one appendix.

>> Many professors (and department guidelines) prefer that you embed figures and tables within the text where they have more relevancy, rather than placing them in an appendix.

>> If figures and tables are embedded, many professors prefer a list of figures and a list of tables, which are usually located after the table of contents.

Focusing on abstracts

Think of the *abstract* (usually associated with published articles) as the "about us" page of your research project. Unless your professor provides other guidelines, your abstract begins with the purpose of the research and highlights major topics in your report. The length is a paragraph or two, about 200 words at the under-graduate level. Generally, as an undergraduate, you don't reveal study results or disclose new information in your abstract.

Depending on the course or topic, professors usually require an abstract or executive summary. At the thesis level and above, abstracts include a summary of the problem, findings, conclusions, and recommendations. If you're writing a thesis or above, this book is a warm-up for the *Publication Manual of the American Psychological Association* (Seventh Edition), which describes a half-dozen variations of abstracts.

TIP

Write the abstract after completing the research report. It's written in the past tense and frequently contains the first-person plural pronoun "we." Formatting guidelines for the abstract include the following (Figure 13-4 shows an example):

>> Position the abstract on a new page following the title page.

>> Center and bold the word "Abstract" (no quotation marks) at the top of the page. Avoid quotation marks, italics, and underlining. Don't indent. Write paragraphs in block style.

Abstract

We investigated the causes of online bullying through social media, a phenomenon that has been increasing in recent years and that resulted in a number of deaths in the past year. Our study focused on the high-school age population because victims of that age group are frequently identified in print and online media sources. We analyzed psychological characteristics of perpetrators, such as childhood security, school discipline, and family birth positions. We limited our study to Facebook and Twitter since they are the venues most commonly used by the population studied. We correlated causes of bullying with academic achievement, participation in sports and activities, and average weekly hours online. We chose not to correlate bullying with online gaming because gamers introduce variables that could skew results. We limited our study to incidents that occurred between 2013 and 2018. We compared our findings with studies from leading experts in the field who identified classic characteristics of victims of bullying as well as perpetrators of bullying. Among our results, we concluded that more than 70% of perpetrators had a history of school discipline issues and that more than 65% of perpetrators had both a younger and older sibling.

FIGURE 13-4:
A sample abstract.

>> Double space.

>> Follow the chronological organization of the report.

Including an executive summary

An *executive summary*, serving a similar purpose to an abstract (which I discuss in the previous section), is a frequent requirement of government and business reports. In the workplace, the audience of the executive summary are decision makers who determine their interest in the topic. Executive summaries are frequently required in business courses in place of abstracts.

The real-world goal of the executive summary is to entice the decision maker to read the report. Executive summaries include multiple variations because they serve multiple purposes — unlike abstracts. Their business purposes, for example, include previewing business proposals, business plans, investment proposals, recommendation reports, sales pitches, and product introductions. Executive summaries in college business courses usually preview reports on topics such as introducing a new policy implementing a change of procedure, and analyzing a workplace issue.

Unlike abstracts, executive summaries frequently include graphic organizers such as headings, subheadings, and bullets, strategies that are common to business writing. Their length, a little longer than an abstract, ranges from three-quarters to a full page, and they frequently contain four or five paragraphs.

Here's a look at a typical organization of an executive summary (see Figure 13-5):

>> Begin with an anecdote that engages the reader with the business issue.

>> Transition into a statement of the problem.

>> Describe the urgency of solving the problem at this time.

>> Identify financial implications of the problem.

>> Offer solutions to solve the problem.

Executive Summary

The 2020 pandemic forced many businesses to reluctantly require employees to work remotely from home, a practice that employers feared because of loss of employee accountability. Employees welcomed working remotely because it eliminated work commutes and related expenses, as well as reducing their accountability to an immediate supervisor. But preferences were soon reversed when employers saw an increase in production and decrease in workplace expenses such as travel and office-related energy. Simultaneously, employees longed for socialization of their peers at work and subsequent after-hours gatherings. The purpose of our report is to propose a flexible remote and office work schedule that capitalizes on the synergy of employees working face-to-face, as well as allowing them the flexibility to realize the financial benefits of reduced commute expenses.

During the pandemic, remote working became a common and mandated practice of many companies, but without a thoughtful action plan. Employees welcomed the independence, and a number of studies validated an increase in employee productivity, and consequently, an increase in employer profits. Employers experienced another windfall when business travel almost stopped nationally, and savings resulted in nearly $5,000 per employee per month. Initially, employees welcomed working from home. Post-pandemic, employees' desire to return to the old normal affected their morale, and a number of studies reported "a decline in remote production by at least 12 percent." A flexible remote and office work schedule offers an opportunity to increase remote productivity and also increase office productivity.

Our plan proposes a four-week rotating employee schedule requiring employees to work two weeks remotely and two weeks in the office. The rotation allows teams of employees to work with alternate teams during a monthly rotation. Office capacity never exceeds 75 percent, within CDC guidelines for the first year of the introduction of the COVID vaccine.

Employees benefit from reduced commuter costs. Work production studies forecast a 10 percent increase in employee production, and companies also benefit from reduced energy costs. After one year, the plan will be evaluated by an independent consultant. The evaluation will also include the effectiveness of regular remote video communications with employees. The study will also compare productivity working at home with productivity working in the office.

FIGURE 13-5:
A sample executive summary for a business topic.

Closing Remarks: Formatting Back Matter

What's more important than a good first impression? A good last impression, especially when it's the first evaluation criterion that determines your grade. The back sections of a research project, which are optional with many professors, provide the final touches to wrap up organization and presentation before submitting your research. It's like a good ending to a good movie. What follows are your final options to strengthen your paper and your grade.

Wrapping up with appendixes

You may or may not have an appendix. And your professor may or may not require an appendix. *Appendixes* are an add-on — similar to the add-on attached to your small intestines — that provide an opportunity for supplemental content for your paper. Some professors require an appendix or two to enhance the academic experience of your research. APA recommends an appendix "only if it helps readers understand, [and] evaluate. . .the study or theoretical argument being made."

Here are some topics for appendixes:

>> Further development of a topic in your paper, such as a detailed description of suggested topics for further research

>> An interview summary with a person related to the research topic

>> A description of links for additional topic information

>> A survey or questionnaire used in your research

REMEMBER

When formatting appendixes, keep these guidelines in mind:

>> At the top of a new page, the last page of your research project, center and bold "Appendix A . . ." followed by the appendix title. Use title case. Don't italicize, underline, or use quotation marks.

>> Write paragraphs in the same indented format as the body of the paper.

>> For successive appendixes, label them Appendix B, C, and so forth.

>> Double-space text and don't exceed one page.

>> Verify that wording in the appendix accurately duplicates wording in the table of contents.

Figure 13-6 shows an example of an appendix that most professors will accept. Use this style appendix for bulleted lists of similar items.

Appendix A: Topics for Additional Research

A number of topics related to the focus of the research need further study. Research questions for further investigation include:

* What is the academic influence of remote-learning students who focus on reading rather than their assigned school-work? Do they show growth?

* Do siblings learn from each other? Does the concentrated sibling time result in academic growth for younger children?

* What is the long-term effect of lack of peer socialization? What is the process of children becoming re-acclimated to their peers? Do some children prefer the isolation? What criteria expedited the process on re-acclimation?

* How readily are children to return to their sports and other organized activities?

* Did the quality of remote learning vary among school districts? What factors were relevant to strong and weak instruction?

* What were common factors in the home that influenced the quality of instruction?

* What did schools learn about their quality of remote instruction?

FIGURE 13-6:
A sample
appendix.

An appendix requires reference in the text. Similar to figures, appendixes don't speak for themselves. Here's a sample of language in the text that references an appendix:

Appendix A details pandemic remote-learning topics that need further study.

Figure 13-7 shows another style of appendix.

Ending with a glossary

Another optional back section of a research paper is a *glossary*, or list of terms used in the research project. A glossary of terms is common in research projects in the behavioral and social sciences, such as sociology, psychology, biology, economics, and political science.

TIP

Position the glossary on a new page following the appendix. Bold and center "Glossary" at the top of the page (see Figure 13-8).

Appendix B: Family Interview

As a requirement of the assignment, I interviewed an anonymous family and asked them their experience during the 2020–2021 mandated remote learning for their three elementary-age children: "Alexia," age 5; "Juan," age 11; and "Perez," age 13.

The children's parents explained that Alexia was sad that she could not begin school, meet new friends, and take a major step toward growing up. She soon became discouraged with her first-grade class and complained that her teacher would never call on her, even though she raised her hand regularly. After two weeks, she became disinterested in school and preferred to play with her iPad instead. Any attempts by her parents to read to her were met with dissatisfaction. Alexia did enjoy cooking with her mom, an opportunity for her mom to teach her food science. After two weeks, Alexia gave "Zoom school" another try and was encouraged by news that she could soon return to regular school.

Juan thought Zoom school was cool and initially enjoyed the computer time. He liked doing math problems and watching science videos. He and his friends would play video games after school lessons. His parents said they would allow more gaming time because he paid attention to remote school. He missed seeing his friends, but playing video games made staying home less boring. His parents allowed him to play outside in the backyard, but he was not allowed to have friends over yet.

Perez had the greatest challenge staying at home, attending Zoom school, and only having video gaming contact with his friends. He had just become a teenager, and his friends were becoming an important part of his life. He was a good student and frequently read on his own.

The parents accepted the idea of remote school because COVID was spiking in their community and they "had to do something to control the spread." Both parents knew how fortunate they were to be able to work from home and be available to help Alexia with her Zoom school. But they also knew the importance of all their children socializing with their friends.

FIGURE 13-7: Alternate style appendix.

Term	Definition
Abstract art	Art that does not represent visual reality but uses shapes and colors to represent its reality.
Baroque	Art that represents passion, emotions, and inner feelings and communicates a sense of movement and energy.
Bricolage	Creation of artwork from readily available materials.
Caricature	A painting or drawing of a person or object that distorts and exaggerates for the purpose of satirizing the subject.
Collage	Art resulting from placement of paper, photographs, objects, and so forth, arranged on a flat surface.
Decalcomania	Art resulting from a blotting process of media squeezed between two surfaces to create a mirror image.
Fresco	A form of mural painting with water-based paint directly applied to wet plaster.
Land art	Art incorporated directly into the landscape using naturally available materials.
Patina	A distinct brown or green surface on a bronze sculpture.

FIGURE 13-8: A sample of glossary terms common to a research paper on the topic of art.

© John Wiley & Sons, Inc.

Including footnotes and endnotes

Footnotes and endnotes, also common to research in the behavioral and social sciences, offer a brief enhancement of information in the text of the report. You identify them with sequentially numbered superscripts.

REMEMBER

APA allows three locations for footnotes:

>> In a figure or table as an explanatory note

>> At the bottom of the page they are used (similar to Chicago Manual of Style)

>> On a separate page following References

REMEMBER

When notes are located at the bottom of the text page, they are called *footnotes*. When notes are located on a separate page, they are called *endnotes*.

APA endorses two types of footnotes: content and copyright. I explain them here in greater detail.

Footnotes based on content

The primary uses of content footnotes (refer to Figure 13-9 for an example) are as follows:

>> Brief development of a single idea that amplifies text

>> Brief development of further reference on a topic

The history of the island included many shipwrecks[1] that resulted from hurricanes, and was recorded in diaries by elders on the island[2]: "Frequently after storms, we walked through the jungle to the beach and witnessed ship debris washed ashore. We saw food stores, clothing, and large sections of wooden ships. We knew that over the next few days bodies would follow."

Endnotes

[1]See Kimmel (2018), Chapter 12, for detailed information of shipwrecks in 1913.

[2]From the chapter, "Hurricanes and Horrors," in *Diaries and the Depths*, by R. Scoville and W. Jennings (Fulton Publications, 2018), 222–252. Reprinted with permission.

FIGURE 13-9: The correct way to format.

© *John Wiley & Sons, Inc.*

REMEMBER

APA advises including footnotes only if "they strengthen the discussion." Use footnotes and endnotes sparingly and without citation because the note itself is the citation. Notes are meant to clarify and not to formally document.

REMEMBER

When content footnotes exceed two sentences, create an appendix.

TECHNICAL STUFF

As an alternative to footnotes, appendixes, and other supplemental materials, APA offers the option of providing online, downloadable files such as oversized figures, and audio and video files. APA explains that the purpose of these files is to "enrich readers' experience and understanding of the content." For example, a research project analyzing presidential inaugural speeches could provide links to recorded speeches.

Footnotes based on copyright

Copyright footnotes identify authorization to include in the text a 500-word or longer quotation or reference from another source.

Chapter **14**

Acing a First Impression: Formatting Title Page and Page Layout

College students love options, such as which college to accept, which gym to go to, which account to take money from, which car to drive, and which island to go to for spring break — don't you wish. But you don't want options for organizing research assignments.

APA reduced options for formatting and organizing research with its seventh edition by recognizing the difference between professional paper requirements and student paper requirements — like recognizing the difference between student debt and student financial stability. APA introduced student paper guidelines such as title page requirements, font selections, line spaces, margins, paragraph alignment, and heading levels.

In this chapter, I guide you through formatting the title page, creating research titles, organizing content pages, and reviewing seventh edition upgrades before submitting your final draft.

This chapter also addresses APA's seventh edition changes for title page formatting and page layout, such as the following:

>> A student title page model replaces the one-size-fits-all professional scholar title page of previous editions.

>> An affiliation is required with your name.

>> Font specifications are expanded for accommodation needs.

>> Running heads are deleted for student papers.

>> Heading levels are upgraded.

TECHNICAL STUFF

Prior to the seventh edition, APA's title page guidelines addressed requirements almost exclusively for professional scholars seeking publication. Consequently, college writing departments and professors designed APA requirements to meet their students' needs. For example, many professors designed in-house bare-bones title pages that required the title, student name, professor name, course name, and date. Formatting and layout were left to the student's judgment, which sometimes conflicted with the professor's judgment. With APA's introduction of a student model title page, many colleges are slow to transition to the new model — and many students experienced trepidation between two title pages. Most of those professor and department guidelines remain the standard today for your APA requirements. With APA's seventh edition, professor requirements will begin to transition to APA's new standard — like transitioning from dialup to wireless.

Naming Writes: Title Page and Titles

The title page of a research paper is like your job interview clothes that say, "This is important, and I want the outside to look good because the inside will impress you." The title page is the beginning of an introduction that builds a relationship with your reader and the professor who grades your research.

Because APA wants you to make a good first impression, they designed a new title page for you, the undergraduate student who's not yet a professional scholar and not yet writing for publication in a scholarly journal.

REMEMBER

Title page elements in this section represent APA's recommended design for research papers, the most formal papers you create as an undergraduate. Chapter 15 presents more details about title page designs for essays and similar shorter papers.

Recognizing title page elements

A professional–looking title page greets your professor with a smile. APA identifies the following elements of title page design (refer to Figure 14-1 for a sample template of title page elements):

» **Title:** A summary of the paper's focus and approach, approximately 12 to 16 words.

» **Author:** Your name (first name, middle initial, and last name) — the name that appears on your formal course registration.

» **Affiliation:** The name of the department that teaches your course and your school's name.

» **Course identification:** Your course name and number and section number.

[One-inch margins on all four sides]

[Page numbering flush right in upper right corner]

[Paper title three to four spaces from the top of page, bold and centered]

[Student name]

[Department name and school name]

[Course name]

[Professor's name]

[Due date]

[Remaining three-quarters of page blank below]

[End title page with hard page break]

FIGURE 14-1:
A title page
template.

© *John Wiley & Sons*

>> **Professor's name:** Your professor's name and title: Dr., Mrs., Ms., Miss, or Mr. — the name that appears on your course registration.

>> **Assignment due date:** The assignment due date, written in standard business format: July 17, 2020.

>> **Page numbering:** The number "1" located in the upper-right corner (it isn't a standard practice in publishing to number the title page and position the number in the upper-right corner).

Ask your professor the following questions about title page design:

>> Do your title page preferences include APA's seventh edition design or another design?

>> Is a model title page available?

An author note is a frequent requirement for professional authors who are obligated to disclose conflicts of interest and affiliations that may compromise content. If you have an association with your content, such as that you work for a company affiliated with your research, disclose that information in an author note. Position "Author note" centered and bold (without quotation marks) in the bottom half of the title page.

Most professors aren't obsessed with their academic titles. But you should be obsessed with accurate spelling of their titles and names. If you inaccurately identify your professor's name on the title page, you raise a red flag about the accuracy of the information in your research project. And if your research inaccuracies result in a "C," that grade won't be a misspelling.

Activate your word processor's automatic page numbering by clicking Insert, then selecting Page Numbers from the drop-down menu. In the dialog box that appears, select Top of Page, then select Right. Be sure to click the check box next to Show numbers on first page. Click OK.

A major title-page change in APA's seventh edition is that they've omitted the running head, an abbreviated version of your paper's title that appears on every page. A running head remains a requirement for professional scholars and writing for publication — if you're thinking about it. But the running head ran aground on student papers.

Formatting the title page includes the following requirements:

>> Insert an extra double space after the title line, and double-space all lines after that.

- » Use title case, which includes capitalizing all nouns, verbs, and all words that are four letters or longer.

- » Capitalize both parts of prefix-hyphenated words — for example, Pre-Administered.

- » Write names in standard sequence.

- » List all author names for team projects.

- » Avoid abbreviations and a period at the end of the title.

Figure 14-2 shows an example of a real-life title page.

1

First World Healthcare Features: Scaled for Third-World Nations

Arthur S. Coleman

Department of International Studies, Widener University

INS 2798-2: Comparative Finances

Dr. Sheldon Cromwell

February 22, 2021

[The remaining three-quarters of the page is blank.]

FIGURE 14-2:
A title page.

Strategizing for writing titles

Early in my teaching career — sometime between Nether Providence Middle School (Wallingford, PA) and Neumann University (Aston, PA) — a student submitted a paper to me and said, "I know you want a title, but I couldn't think of one." The words "couldn't think of one" reinforced the importance of requiring titles; they require thinking.

A research paper may not be judged by its cover, but it is judged by its title. After surveying the layout of the title page, professors focus on the first line they read, the title. They make the first judgment of your paper, such as "sounds interesting" or "another boring student research paper."

That means you want to write something that gets your professor's attention (and ideally keeps it). Guidelines for writing successful titles (and subtitles) include the following:

>> Focus on the purpose of the paper.

>> Predict the paper's approach to the topic (usually in the subtitle).

>> Identify the question the paper answers.

>> Create reader interest.

TIP

A successful title is one you would click if you were scrolling a page of titles on your topic. If you wouldn't click on it, then your title isn't good enough.

The process for creating a title includes asking yourself a few questions:

>> What is the question your paper answers?

>> What are key search terms that appear in your research?

>> What would you say to someone who asked you what your paper's about?

From your answers, delete unnecessary and overused words and revise your list of keywords. From your keywords, create a title that focuses on the purpose of your paper and a subtitle that predicts your paper's approach. Avoid titles with too many *too's*: too long, too vague, too descriptive, and too emotional. Also, avoid wordy expressions such as "A Complete Study of . . .," "An Investigation of . . .," and "A Complete Understanding of. . .."

Here are some examples of effective titles in various content areas:

>> **Finance:** Achieving Financial Stability: From Early Career Entrepreneurs

>> **Literature:** Shakespeare's Female Characters: Common Emotional Strengths

>> **College athletics:** College Athletes and COVID-19: Long-Term Effects on Athletic Performance

>> **Technology:** Educational Technologies of the Future: Delivering Them at Reasonable Costs

These example titles establish focus and create interest (Achieving Financial Stability). Subtitles, following the colon, identify the approach (From Early Career Entrepreneurs). Each title answers a research question such as, "What are the common emotional strengths of Shakespeare's female characters?"

REMEMBER

Begin your research with a working title, a general title that helps you maintain focus until the paper's completion. Create your final title when you know the content better.

Packaging Appearance: Formatting and Organization

Formatting research titles and organizing content represent real-life standardization of APA requirements — and increase readability for professors' grading. Lack of consistent organization is like reading each page written in a different language. APA's consistency begins with the title page and continues with the format and organization of content pages. Check out the following sections for more nitty gritty about formatting and organization.

REMEMBER

Ask your professor the following questions about page formatting and layout:

>> Do your page layout preferences include any exceptions to APA guidelines?

>> Are APA's five levels of headings required?

>> Is a model of your preferences for bulleted lists available?

Page formatting: Consistency is key

Using page formatting is like avoiding walking into objects in a dark room: you know the layout. Consistent page formatting helps you navigate the page from top to bottom without running into any layout obstacles.

REMEMBER

When formatting an APA page of text, keep in mind the following guidelines:

>> Create a one-inch margin on all four sides (a Microsoft Word default).

>> Use Times New Roman, a friendly font for many eyes, at 12-point font size.

>> Double-space lines and headings.

>> Align paragraphs flush left and indent new paragraphs with a tab (or five spaces).

>> Strive for a project word length between 2,500 and 3,000 words.

The main body of the paper begins on a new page after the title page (and following the abstract or executive summary if required). APA requires that the title be repeated on the first line of the first page following the title page. Figure 14-3 shows what page 2 looks like.

2

High Tech Swimsuits: Swimmer or Technology Advantage

   The remaining text of the paper begins on this line with each new paragraph indented and double spaced for the remainder of the page. Use your imagination for one-inch margins on four sides of this sample page. Also notice one space after periods at the end of the sentence in this paragraph, another formatting change in APA's seventh edition.

FIGURE 14-3:
Page 2 in an APA paper.

APA's seventh-edition upgrades offer font options for students with accommodation needs. Optional fonts include Calibri 11, Arial 11, Lucida Sans Unicode 10, and Georgia 11. Times New Roman 12-point font is standard for most college papers.

TECHNICAL STUFF

A *serif* is a small line or a flare of short strokes attached to the ends and corners of a letter. Look at this capital "A." Note the small lines at the baseline on each side of the "A." Each stem ends in a serif. Some serifs challenge readability for some people, especially when they're reading from a distance. Fonts or typefaces without serifs, *san* (without) *serif*, accommodate a variety of readers, and so APA thoughtfully recommends the previously listed fonts.

REMEMBER

"I can't open your file." Is anything more stressful to you than receiving this email response from your professor after submitting your assignment? You can avoid this unnecessary stress by conforming to the program. Microsoft Word may be the most popular word processing program used in college. Pages and Google Docs are also popular, but check with your professor. Almost all professors' computers are compatible with Microsoft Word, and many professors respond to assignments with Word Markup, which isn't compatible with Pages and Google Docs. Microsoft Word, standard to the PC, is easily adaptable to Apple and other platforms, and free versions are available online.

Page organization: Sequence is essential

Page and content organization are the supply of information that flows to the reader and requires logic, sequence, and pace. The body of content is organized into a beginning, middle, and ending — a strategy adaptable to introducing an argument, developing it, and applying it to a thesis. See Chapters 5 and 7 for structural organization and developing an argument.

Some advanced college papers include headings such as statement of the problem, methods, results, and discussion. These headings adapt within the organization of the beginning, middle, and ending. For example, results and discussion are adaptable to the ending of a piece of writing.

APA recommends a sequence of content pages that looks like the following:

>> Title page

>> Abstract or executive summary

>> Text body of paper

>> References

>> Endnotes

>> Tables and figures

>> Appendixes

APA identifies labels for some of these content pages as *section labels*, which are positioned at the top of a new page, bold, capitalized, and centered. Section labels include abstract, references, endnotes, tables, figures, and appendices. Because section labels require a new page, you need to insert a hard page break at the end of the page that finishes the previous section.

As a regular reminder, APA's sequence of content and formatting is superseded by your professor's requirements. Also, specialized papers for some courses and advanced certifications will require variations of APA requirements.

Using five levels of headings

Another APA primary organizational strategy is the use of five levels of headings to differentiate levels of information. Figure 14-4 is a template of what the headings look like and how they coordinate with text.

Level 1	**Centered, Bold, Title Case Heading** New paragraphs begin here, indented and double spaced from the heading.
Level 2	**Flush Left, Bold, Title Case Heading** New paragraphs begin here, indented and double spaced from the heading.
Level 3	***Flush Left, Bold Italic, Title Case Heading*** New paragraphs begin here, indented and double spaced from the heading.
Level 4	**Indented, Bold, Title Case, End Punctuation.** Text begins on the same line immediately after the period and continues to develop the paragraph.
Level 5	***Indented, Bold Italic, Title Case, End Punctuation.*** Text begins on the same line immediately after the period and continues to develop the paragraph.

FIGURE 14-4:
A template for headings.

© John Wiley & Sons, Inc.

REMEMBER

Similar to an outline, headings require two or more subheadings. A heading may have no subheadings, but not one subheading. Headings and subheadings for a topic, such as "National Healthcare Benefits a Nation," look like the following:

Level 1   Saves Long-Term Healthcare Costs

Level 2   Children Benefit Earlier in Life

Level 2   Adults Experience Fewer Chronic Illnesses

Utilizing bulleted lists

APA offers bulleted lists as a content organizational strategy, a technique for writing sentences with large quantities of similar information. Bulleted lists are used throughout this book, including numerous lists in this chapter. Lists (bulleted, lettered, and numbered) increase readability by visually highlighting the beginning of each point. Here's an example of a bulleted list on the topic of advantages of bulleted lists:

» Show similar multiple ideas in concise sentence format.

» Increase readability by highlighting ideas.

>> Visually guide the reader to the beginning of each new idea.

>> Increase readability by beginning each new idea with similar grammatical constructions.

>> Utilize white space on the page to focus on major points.

CAPITALIZING BULLETED LISTS

Capitalization for bulleted items follows standard capitalization rules: If bulleted items are sentences, begin each item with a capital letter, as in the following examples:

>> Set oven temperature at 450 degrees.

>> Mix flour with sugar and salt.

>> Combine wet ingredients with dry ingredients.

If bulleted items are phrases, not sentences, begin each item with a lowercase letter (unless the first word is a proper noun), as in the following list of strategies that contribute to academic success:

>> managing time

>> balancing course work and social life

>> dedicating time for reading and writing.

Because these academic strategies aren't individual sentences, they aren't capitalized or punctuated at the end of each item. But the end of the last strategy (dedicating . . .) is the end of the sentence and requires end punctuation. End-punctuation omission at the end of a list of nonsentence items is a common neglect of college writers.

If you've been an observant reader throughout this book, you've noticed the *For Dummies* style includes capitalization of list items that aren't sentences. Also note in the previous list that each academic-strategy item begins with the same grammatical construction, a gerund (managing, balancing, and dedicating). See Chapter 6 for more information on parallel structure.

PUNCTUATING BULLETED LISTS

APA offers the option of end-item punctuation for lists of phrases. Here's what ending punctuation with commas looks like:

» managing time,

» balancing course work and social life,

» dedicating time for reading and writing.

A variation of comma end-item punctuation is semicolon end-item punctuation, when items contain a series of commas. Here's what semicolons at the end of lines look like:

» managing time, work, and play;

» balancing course work, social life, and home life;

» dedicating time for reading and writing.

REMEMBER

This end-list punctuation style isn't preferred among popular publishers and isn't used in this book. A good punctuation guideline is similar to one for consuming calories: Fewer is healthier.

Using numbered lists

Numbered lists, unlike bulleted lists, represent sequential steps in a process. Here's an example of numbered steps to complete a research project:

1. Identify a research topic that interests you.

2. Research background information to help focus the topic.

3. Formulate a research question and argument.

4. Research sources to develop the argument.

5. Evaluate the argument.

6. Summarize and cite sources.

7. Create a reference list.

8. Draft a first copy.

9. Elicit feedback and revise drafts at three levels.

10. Edit and submit.

Listing terms and definitions

Another variation of lists is the term–and–definition format, which looks like this.

easy listening: mood-generating music without vocals or a focus on pop and rock hits

classical: an orchestral musical style that developed between 1750 and 1825 in reaction to the restrictions of baroque

grunge: music developed from rock and punk, popular in the '90s

APA doesn't capitalize terms. The term definition ends with a period only when a sentence follows the definition. Here's what that looks like:

grunge: music developed from rock and punk, popular in the '90s. You won't find too many professors who listen to grunge music in their offices.

Chapter 15

Understanding First Year Writing: APA Essays and Reaction Papers

Research papers are like fine dining; essays and reaction papers are like fast food. Both experiences are necessary for the health and development of college students.

Your research paper provides an extensive academic exercise resulting in new findings in a field of your choice. As a professional scholar-in-training, you contribute new insight to the academic community. Within the parameters of APA guidelines, you excavate knowledge using digging tools comparable to those of a civil engineer. Transitioning from research papers, essays, and reaction papers requires laser focus, precision pacing, and APA adaptions.

APA developed guidelines for professional scholars to submit their scientific research for publication, but essays, reaction papers, and similar message-focused projects require less extensive guidelines and formatting. APA abdicated responsibility for shorter papers, and professors and university departments accepted that responsibility for standardizing submission requirements.

In this chapter, I align the APA writing style and guidelines with essays and reaction papers. I provide default formatting for the title page and page design when APA or your professor doesn't provide them.

REMEMBER

As a regular reminder, your professor's assignment guidelines supersede both APA's guidelines and the guidelines that I offer you in this book.

Conquering College Comp: Essay Basics

Writing a research paper is like running a marathon in the dark; you face many obstacles and frequently must reorient your path. The essay is like a sprint in the park; you can get sidetracked frequently and stray off topic, but your success depends on finding your way to the finish line.

The essay, college's first gatekeeper assignment, fast tracks the writing demands of the research paper — like transitioning from driving a semi to riding a skateboard.

Schools that adopt unabridged APA guidelines for serious research also adopt a lighter version for essay writing. General adherence to APA guidelines includes writing style, plagiarism policies, citations, and references (when required), as well as margins, line spacing, and fonts — guidelines for almost all academic writing.

Think of the college essay as a mini-version of the research paper — requiring good writing skills with the same laser focus, but fewer sources and less development. Your APA challenge will be developing a format that fulfills your professor's requirements.

Differentiating essays from research writing

The essay, recognized by many researchers as the single most reliable measurement of college literacy, demonstrates your ability to think, organize thoughts, and express yourself clearly and succinctly. It's the Snapchat of your academic toolbox.

Many first-year college writing programs require a portfolio of three to four essays that meet department goals and are developed with feedback and revised drafts. Essays introduce to students the writing experiences necessary for college success.

APA guidelines were designed for research writing and adapted for smaller writing projects, including research papers. Table 15-1 shows how research writing differs from essay writing.

TABLE 15-1 **Research Writing versus Essay Writing**

	Research Writing	Essay Writing
Purpose	Argue new findings, supported by synthesis of experts' findings	Argue author's opinion, integrated with experts' opinions
Length	2,500 to 3,000 words	650 to 700 words
Approach	Expert-centered, dependent on support of a variety of experts' opinions	Author-centered, dependent on author's interaction with experts' opinions
Audience	Professor as representative of research community	Professor as representative of academic community
Paragraphs	Longer and more developed	Shorter and more focused
Tone	Serious with research language	Varies with splashes of playful language
Sources	Primary and secondary	Occasional primary with secondary and popular

Chapter 5 developed the principles of academic writing: audience, purpose, focus, approach, transitions, flow, tone, and use of respectful language. Audience and purpose vary with assignments, and first-year writing experiences offer as many variations as your morning campus coffee.

Identifying the fundamentals of writing an essay

The next few sections guide you through the fundamentals of writing an essay, beginning with the often-overlooked process of selecting a topic with high reader value and potential high-grade value for you. I also guide you through writing a thesis, developing support, and establishing tone. This section also explains the importance of writing beyond the traditional five-paragraph essay structure.

Write your essay using the basics of good academic writing, as described in Chapter 5 (which covers active verbs and specific nouns) and Chapter 9. Revise as you write and after you write. Review Chapter 8 for a three-level approach to revising.

Topic

The most important essay decision that determines the success of your essay is deciding on your topic. Within the options of your essay assignment, choose a topic you're passionate about, or at least a topic you are interested in. Your essay will be less challenging if you avoid abstract and ethical topics such as "Goodness Always Overcomes Evil." Values are an important part of life, but they are a challenge to support in essays. Also avoid topics that lack opposition such as "Good Health is the Secret to a Good Life." Would anyone argue for poor health?

TIP

You, the writer, accept responsibility to offer readers a message of value for the time they invest in your essay. If you're bored with the topic as the writer, imagine the boredom your readers will experience.

When you choose an essay topic, ask the following:

» Am I offering the reader something new and interesting?

» What value does this topic have for readers, such as my professor?

» What information is available to support my topic?

» Who opposes my topic and why do they oppose it?

Thesis

The most important sentence you write as a student is your *thesis statement,* your promise to the reader that determines the purpose and direction of your essay. (By comparison, the most important sentence of a professional writer is the first sentence, the sentence that determines whether or not an editor will buy a piece of writing.) You can create an essay's thesis statement by completing this sentence: "The purpose of the essay is to argue that. . .". Here's what a thesis statement looks like:

> During the 2020 pandemic, K–12 schools struggled with remote learning and discovered many faults and liabilities. The purpose of this essay is to argue that successful strategies for remote learning increased standardized test scores in a number of school districts in 2021.

Support

The difference between a high school essay and a college essay is found in the support for the thesis. Many high school teachers accept opinion. Some high school teachers are just happy that students submitted the essay. College professors hold you more accountable because they teach fewer students than do high school teachers. They expect that essay support includes studies, expert opinions, and data. College support also includes your engagement with sources, as in the examples in Chapter 11. Two major differences between high school essays and college essays are in how well you engage with sources and how well you create a "conversation" among your sources and yourself as the author of the essay.

Tone

Because essays communicate a variety of subtle messages, unlike the research paper, tone is more relevant to essays. *Tone*, your attitude that accompanies your message, helps you express sarcasm, humor, sympathy, righteousness, satire, and so forth. See Chapter 5 for more detail on tone.

Transitions

Transitions are basic to almost all forms of writing. The fast pace of essays, sprinting from opening to exit, requires numerous bridges for a smooth ride. Flip to Chapter 5 for more information on transitions.

BEYOND THE FIVE-PARAGRAPH ESSAY

You grew up with the five-paragraph essay. It taught you the basic structure of an essay — a beginning, three middle paragraphs, and an ending. But just as the training wheels eventually came off your two-wheeler, expanding on the five-paragraph model became a necessity for navigating the world of college academics. The restrictive "three supporting reasons" of your former life does not meet the needs of complex college writing. Support for thesis statements today requires more than the traditional three paragraphs, and also a combination of long and short paragraphs. The five-paragraph essay belongs in a museum next to artifacts such as the typewriter and tractor-fed printer.

Focusing on Essay Structure and Formatting

Congratulations on the A's you earned for your high school essays; your professors are not impressed. They expect more, as does APA, which established standards for academic writing style and documentation.

Essays and research papers share similar foundations of a beginning, middle, and ending, but some essay elements vary. Here's a look at the essay's major parts and their purposes.

>> **Introduction:** A title that predicts the essay's contents, a first sentence that engages the reader, an opening that encourages reading, and a transition from the opening to the body.

>> **Body:** Middle paragraphs that develop the thesis, supporting it with examples, data, and experts' opinions integrated with the author's opinion (source engagement).

>> **Ending:** Reflection and a final reader message, such as "what if" and "so what," and referencing the opening.

TIP

Your professor expects much more than a summary. The last paragraph is the last piece of information your professor reads before beginning the grading process.

KEEPING YOUR ESSAY MOVING

Essays have fewer moving parts than research papers. They lack the research paper's abstract, table of contents, figures and tables, and appendices. But successful essays do require a strong focus, condensed development, and intense engagement — in addition to memorable reader value. Here are some essay approach strategies for achieving those objectives:

- Analyze assignment requirements and identify wording of major tasks, such as *argue, trace, prioritize, explain,* and *compare.*

- Read background information on the topic.

- Research sources for thesis support and author engagement.

- Outline content for the beginning, middle, and ending.

- Identify citations and corresponding references.

Your professor may require a reference list for some essays. Always ask. Review sources and reference lists in Chapters 11 and 12.

Writing a memorable essay title

Titles are as important to essays as names are to courses. Would you read a book that had an uninteresting title, order an entrée with an unappetizing name, or go to a movie with an unappealing title? Obviously, no, and neither would your professor have much enthusiasm in reading your essay with an uninteresting title — also your first step toward ensuring an uninteresting grade.

When you begin an essay assignment (or any other writing assignment), identify a working title, using it as a general reference to the topic that provides some focus until you identify your formal essay. Professional writers finalize titles at the end of their projects when they know the content they're titling.

Begin your essay with a title that identifies the topic and previews the argument's focus. Essay titles are less formal and more playful than research titles. Here are some title techniques and examples:

>> **Repetition:** Repeat sounds that attract reader attention. Perfect Apartment Pets; Tips for Transitioning into College Technology; Major College Admissions, Major Admission Problems

>> **Rhymes and opposites:** Engage with language memorable to readers. Small Colleges with Big Debt

>> **Puns:** Play with language that appeals to readers. Service Projects That Make Dollars and Sense

>> **Literary references:** Refer to classic literature familiar to your readers. The Best of College Athletics, The Worst of College Athletics; The Walter Mitty of Madison Avenue; To Fee or Not to Fee

Avoid titles that promise too much and reveal lack of focus: Three Dozen Steps for a Fantastic College Experience.

Starting your essay with a bang

The most important sentence that may influence your grade is the first sentence of your essay. Your investment in the extra time can produce high yields. Follow the title with a first sentence that engages the reader. First-sentence and opening strategies for essays include the following:

- **Expert quotations:** Connect readers with words of experts. "Insanity is doing the same thing over and over and expecting different results," allegedly said Albert Einstein.

- **Unusual information:** Surprise readers with little known information. The Nation's Report Card, The National Assessment of Educational Progress (NAEP), reveals a startling fact about students who score high in all subject areas: They write more in school than students who score poorly.

- **Series of questions:** Challenge readers with questions on the topic, such as: When do we stop college tuitions that approach a hundred thousand dollars a year? When do we stop student loans that exceed monthly luxury car payments? When do we stop the insanity of the cost of higher education?

- **Emotional appeal:** Appeal to readers' sentiments, such as: Next to loving and caring about their children, parents' most important responsibility is to provide them with the best education available. Fulfilling your child's educational needs requires your active participation. Making homework sessions a regular part of your nightly routine is an excellent way to do this. Your child's educational tomorrow is based on the accumulation of help with each night's homework assignments today.

- **Summary:** Preview the topic with one sentence, such as: Is all work and no play synonymous with college success? Not according to a ten-year study by a team of Harvard researchers who analyzed academic habits of a successful college experience.

- **Anecdotes:** Describe a personal experience that previews the topic, such as: When I started freelance writing in the late eighties, I frequently asked editors to recommend the best book for future writers. The book unanimously suggested, and the book that remains the foundation of my teaching and writing, is Strunk and White's *The Elements of Style*.

WARNING

Don't begin an essay (or any other college paper) with a standard dictionary definition.

TIP

Don't underestimate the importance of an engaging title and opening. Research on scoring essays shows that strong essay openings encourage scorers to think, "This essay is going to be a strong piece of writing, and I'm going to find the evidence to support the good grade I think it deserves."

RISKY WRITING REINFORCES READER INTEREST

Essay readers expect information. Unlike research readers, they also expect entertainment and an occasional surprise. Here are some examples of rhythmical language techniques that provide entertainment and surprise:

- **Adjective noun patterns:** Many college students experience the frustration of a *wet pet.*

- **Verbs in successive clauses:** The candidate *backed* by one party was *attacked* by the other party.

- **Compound nouns:** Ocean resorts offer *sun* and *fun.*

- **Verb noun rhymes:** Pennsylvania drivers *fear deer* every fall. Stop *texts*; stop *wrecks.*

- **Compound action words:** Successful people know when to *stop* worrying and *start* producing.

Giving the body what it needs: Figurative language

Figurative language that occasionally elicits a reader's smile adds reader interest while developing the body of the essay. Here are some examples:

>> **Personification:** Attributing human qualities to inanimate objects. Alaskan spruce trees look tired in the summer.

>> **Similes:** Comparing the familiar with the unfamiliar. Walking on a cold bathroom floor is like ice-skating barefooted.

>> **Metonymy:** Words that express a broader idea. English author Edward Bulwer-Lytton said, "The *pen* is mightier than the *sword.*"

>> **Chiasmus:** A verb reversal commonly used in speech. Joe Logue, my high school coach, always said, "When the *going gets tough*, the *tough get going.*"

John F. Kennedy said, "Ask not what *your country can do* for you, *ask what you can do for your country.*"

>> **Hyperbole:** Extreme exaggeration. My printer *drinks gallons* of ink.

Avoiding crash endings

Everything that begins has an end — think about that. Here are some techniques for ending essays.

>> **Lead-reference:** Clarifies or amplifies the opening and unites the beginning and ending

>> **Memorable sentence:** Leaves the reader with an inspirational message

>> **Transition:** Amplifies the message from the previous paragraph

>> **So what:** Provides the big-picture implication

>> **Prediction:** Expresses what could happen as a result of this message

Formatting your essay

Essay structure lacks the complexity of research structure because research support depends on data, whereas essay support depends on explanation. Consequently, APA provides fewer formatting guidelines for essays, and formatting becomes the primary responsibility of the professor. With your professor's guidelines taking precedence, here are some standard formatting guidelines for essays:

>> Length between 650 to 700 words

>> Margins one inch on all four sides

>> Double spaced text and headings

>> Times New Roman font, 12-point size

>> No running head

>> Page numbers in the upper-right corner

>> A title page with the title placed in the middle of the page. If a separate title page is required, use the research paper title page design in Chapter 14.

An acceptable design for a title page includes the following:

>> In the upper-left corner, single space your name, the course name, the assignment name, the professor's name, and the due date.

>> Begin the title about one-third down the page. Type the title in title case (Chapter 14), center, and bold. Don't underline or italicize.

>> Begin text double spaced below the title. Indent new paragraphs.

If your professor doesn't provide guidelines for an essay title page, refer to Figure 15-1.

Isiah Buteford
English 103
Essay #2
Professor Olsen
May 1, 2021

Third World Housing: First World Location

   Begin the first paragraph indented here and continue double spaced to the bottom of the page. Format one inch margins on all four sides. Word's default formatting page includes one inch margins. Locate page numbering in the upper right corner. Many professors prefer contact information located single-spaced in the upper left corner.

FIGURE 15-1: Example of essay title page.

© *John Wiley & Sons, Inc.*

Formatting your essay citations

Many college writing departments adopt an informal citation format exclusively for essays, which is an adaption of APA citation style. Ask your professor if your school provides a model for informal essay citations. Research papers require APA's formal citation style.

Essays don't require scholarly peer-reviewed sources of research papers, but one or two primary sources help support your paper. (You can review primary and secondary sources in Chapter 10.) Essays can thrive with a primary source and combinations of secondary and popular sources. Popular sources are written for general audiences and usually lack peer review and citations. They include publications such as *Forbes, The Atlantic, U.S. News and World Report, National Geographic,* and *The Economist.* Other popular sources include *TED Talks* and *Office for National Statistics.*

Successful college essays can be written with four to five sources, but check with your professor for requirements. Essays also require source engagement. Although research writing requires source engagement to support the research argument, essay source engagement requires integrating the author's (your) essay argument with experts' research. Here's an example of essay engagement:

> Brown's (2015) "Managing Student-Athletes' Stress" argues that "the combination of athletics, grades, and social life" positions student-athletes in the "at risk level" on Clarkson's mental health scale (pp. 99–100). Robertson (2017) recommended "psychology maintenance" as part of athletes' regular training routine (p. 79). As an athlete at a Division III school, I am not aware of the athletic pressure I envisioned at Division I scholarship schools, where athletic pressure and academic performance cause high stress on athletes.

Implementing Essay Variations: Common College Essays

College writing programs are designed to introduce you to the writing experiences you'll need to succeed in college. You'll be required to write a variety of essay structures (called *essay styles* or *modes*). Each of the essay styles that follow represent an independent essay or a strategy used in other essays. For example, comparison and contrast can be an essay in itself, as well as a technique in an expository or persuasive essay. These essay genres are representative of essays required in almost all college writing programs. The explanation of each essay genre is followed by a description of what that type of essay looks like.

Narrative

Narrative writing is a style of essay writing that tells a story, usually chronological, exemplifying a single theme. Narratives can be a self-sustaining essay or part of another essay. Characteristics of narrative essays include plot, setting, characterization, dialogue, and conflict. Novels and most fiction are examples of a narrative. When you tell someone about your weekend, you are usually telling a narrative.

REMEMBER

Narratives are frequently written in the first person, and first-year writing programs usually include a narrative requirement because of its application to other types of writing. Here are a few examples:

>> Children who grow up too fast

>> Lessons learned at the beach

>> Is crying allowed at college?

>> Expensive life lessons

An example of a narrative essay is a story about a visit to the September 11 memorial, 15 years after the attack on the World Trade Center. Written in the first person, the essay opens with a description of the assassination of John F. Kennedy in 1963 and the death of teacher Christa McAuliffe aboard the *Challenger* spacecraft in 1986. The essay chronicles the events of September 11 and a description of the memorial reflection pool with names of victims etched in the bronze perimeter of the pool. The essay tells the story of victims' photographs in the memorial and artifacts from the attack, such as a pair of blood-stained pink high heels, a ripped airplane window, and a 19-foot fragment of a transmission tower. The theme is revealed at the end, when the author describes current differences between Americans and recalls the compassion and serenity Americans shared with each other in the days after the attacks.

In addition to narration, the essay uses comparison to show differences between September 11 and other American tragedies. Cause and effect (see the next section) is used to show the effects of the attacks on the lives of American people. Persuasion (refer to the section, "Persuasion," later in this chapter) is used to convince readers of the importance of showing compassion. Author engagement includes sources related to the United Airlines Flight 93 crash in Somerset County, Pennsylvania, psychological effects on people following September 11, and television news accounts of September 11.

Cause and effect

Cause and effect essays identify relationships between events and the results of those events. They also include consequences, analysis, and implications of the events. Cause and effect essays explain how and why events happen. Here are examples of cause-and-effect topics:

>> Why saving is fundamental to financial security

>> How exercise improves academics

>> Benefits of fitness centers on college campuses

An example of cause and effect is an essay comparing taxation in major cities across the country. The essay opens by referencing newspaper headlines proclaiming tax increases in a number of major cities. Residents are quoted explaining the effects of increased taxes on their lives, such as reducing their spending power for housing, food, and transportation. The essay explains the city's point of view by saying the tax increase is a result of rising costs of many city services and healthcare and other benefits for city employees. The essay ends by offering a compromise solution of reducing tax increases and reducing city spending. Author engagement includes sources related to taxes and services common to major cities.

Comparison and contrast

Comparison and contrast essays show similarities and differences between events, objects, beliefs, people, and so forth. The information provides decision-making criteria. Examples of comparison-and-contrast topics include the following:

- » Big cities and big corruption
- » Life adaptations in Alaska and Hawaii
- » Differences among economic systems

An example of comparison and contrast is an essay comparing and contrasting career salaries of people who finish high school, college, and graduate school. The essay opens with research comparing the average salary of each, and statistics showing how over a lifetime, college graduates earn almost two million dollars more than high school graduates, and graduate school graduates earn almost five million dollars more than high school graduates. The three levels of graduates are compared and contrasted according to health, savings, and quality of life. Many statistical comparisons are made throughout the essay. The essay ends with an argument for increased levels of education.

REMEMBER

In addition to comparison and contrast strategies, the essay uses narration to tell the stories of different-level graduates, cause and effect to show results of various levels of education, and persuasion to convince readers of the importance of more levels of education. Author engagement includes sources related to education levels, and comparisons of health and income.

Expository

Expository essays provide an explanation of a process and how things work. They emphasize *how* rather than *why*. Take a look at these examples:

>> How children train parents

>> Animals that domesticate humans

An example of an expository essay is an explanation of the process of baking banana nut bread, including an explanation of the chemical process in baking, and the effect of baking on reducing stress. The essay begins with a narrative explaining the increase in home baking in recent years and the popularity of baking banana nut bread. The baking process is explained, which includes heating the oven to 350 degrees, mixing dry ingredients, observing the chemical effect of baking soda on the bread, and combining dry and wet ingredients. The essay explains the importance of mixing a half-teaspoon of flour with the nuts, which prevents the nuts from settling to the bottom of the batter during baking. The essay ends with a description of the comfort value of foods as a stress reducer and a reference to a study showing that people who bake are often happier than people who don't bake.

REMEMBER

In addition to expository techniques, the essay uses narration (refer to the section, "Narrative," earlier in this chapter) to tell the story of people who bake, cause and effect (see the section, "Cause and effect," earlier in this chapter) to show the effect of the chemical process in baking, and a comparison of happiness levels between bakers and non-bakers. The essay also uses persuasion (see the next section) to convince readers to occasionally bake to reduce stress. Author engagement includes sources related to causes of stress, and strategies for reducing stress.

Persuasive

Persuasive essays convince the reader to take action on issues such as environmental protections, river management, and Internet accessibility. Take a look at a couple of persuasive topics:

>> Should military service be mandatory?

>> Is the Electoral College headed for failure?

An example of a persuasive style is an essay convincing readers of the benefits of stronger support for K–12 education, especially public education. The essay begins with the snowball effect of more people working at higher-paying jobs, resulting in more buying power, more tax money collected, and fewer people needing public assistance. The essay makes a convincing argument that increased levels of education result in increased earning power. The essay also convinces readers of the economic benefit of taxpayer-supported, tuition-free two-year colleges. The essay's supporting evidence includes anecdotes of first-generation college graduates who influenced younger siblings to attend college.

In addition to persuasive strategies, the essay uses comparison and contrast (refer to the section, "Comparison and contrast," earlier in this chapter) to show income variations among people with different education levels, cause and effect (refer to the section, "Cause and effect," earlier in this chapter) to show the results of more education, and narration (refer to the section, "Narrative," earlier in this chapter) to tell stories of first-generation college graduates who influence younger siblings. Author engagement includes sources related to how education is funded across the globe.

Descriptive

Descriptive essays describe people, places, objects, and experiences using the senses of sight, hearing, touch, taste, and smell. They're infrequently assigned as standalone essays in college because they are supported primarily by opinion. But describing experiences plays a major role in other forms of essay writing. The key to successful descriptive writing is the creative use of sensory description, as in, "The food tasted free." Similar to all essay structures, a descriptive essay contains a beginning, middle, and ending — and focuses on a central theme.

An example of a descriptive essay is a description of my favorite beach location. The essay begins with a brief narrative of my arrival that includes driving to the beach shortly after sunrise and parking my turquoise convertible under the shade of palm trees and within the sound of waves lapping at the shoreline. I describe the short walk through the white, sugary sand to the water's edge, where I'll homestead. I park my chair under the shade of my three-piece, green-and-white-striped beach umbrella and prepare for three hours of reading and writing. Author engagement includes sources related to the sound of water reducing stress.

Reading and Responding: Reaction Paper Basics

Reaction papers, also known as *response papers,* are the younger siblings of research papers and the cousins of essays. Reaction papers like to hang around with the college kids. Reading and responding by analyzing is similar to analyzing sources for your research papers.

For your academic enjoyment, many professors require reaction papers as their go-to assignment. From the professor's perspective, they're easy to design and apply to almost every academic experience. They're popular in content courses such as history, economics, psychology, and political science. They're frequently assigned orally, which challenges you to be ready with your questions about assignment details. If you earn B's on your research papers and essays, you should earn A's on your reaction papers, because they lack the formulaic structure of research papers and essays. Like swimming in the ocean, you have many directions to go with reaction papers, but you should avoid rip currents and areas where you can lose control of your direction.

Reaction papers are also a test of your reading skills, especially between-the-lines critical-thinking skills such as evaluating, prioritizing, applying, contrasting, questioning, authenticating, and synthesizing.

APA's stamp on reaction papers includes writing in an academic style, citing sources, and listing sources on a reference page. APA lacks specifics for title page design and formatting, but you can easily apply principles from research formatting. In these sections, I guide you along the way. If citations and references are not part of your requirement, using them accurately will impress your professor and improve your grade.

Here are some questions to ask your professor about essays and response papers:

>> Do you have a preferred title page design?

>> Is APA's page formatting style acceptable?

>> How many and what type of sources are required?

>> Is a reference list required?

>> Are formal citations required?

Writing a successful reaction paper

A successful reaction paper requires application of your two most important college skills, reading and writing.

Reading and reacting generally requires you to read one or a few articles and to respond with your supported reactions. If you are assigned two or more authors, you are expected to respond to a synthesis of concerns. You may also be asked to respond to a lecture, book, video, PowerPoint presentation, current event, website, or social media post. Your writing purpose is to engage with the author. You do not need to follow the chronological order of the readings.

TECHNICAL STUFF

Some professors lie awake at night thinking of academic experiences to respond to — a class, a person in the news, a holiday, a podcast episode, a commercial, an election, a speaker, and so forth. Professors lose sleep thinking of experiences for students to react to.

You can respond to reading by agreeing, disagreeing, questioning, or confirming. Your response can be generated by anger, surprise, belief, or doubt. Write your response guided by the principles of good academic writing, especially audience and purpose. You can review these principles in Chapter 5.

Other writing guidelines specific to reaction papers include

>> Write in the first person *I*. Avoid the first-person plural *we*, and avoid third-person references such as *the writer, the author,* and *the researcher*. See Chapter 6 for more information on *person* (point of view).

>> Regularly use the phrases "such as" and "for example" to support your reactions.

>> Connect reactions to the course for which the paper was assigned, other courses, your life, society, books, the arts, current events, and your independent reading.

>> Prioritize reactions you want to respond to.

>> Support your reactions with partial quotations.

REMEMBER

Of course, you don't want to write an unsuccessful reaction paper. But if you receive an unsuccessful grade, it could be attributed to any of the following:

>> Summarizing rather than analyzing

>> Submitting a paper that's too short

>> Lacking support for reactions

>> Lacking citations and reference list, if required

>> Formatting a reference list without hanging indentations

TIP

If you want to overachieve, cite an outside source or two to additionally support a reaction. Include your citation in the reference list.

Analyze; don't summarize. Analysis includes who and what the experience affects. Here's an example of analyzing and connecting a reading to a college experience:

Shatner's (2020) principle of "creating a safe and supportive academic climate" is demonstrated in our class (pp. 84–85). Professor Callahan encourages us to express our opinion on course topics, especially when the opinion is unpopular. For example, I recently expressed an opinion that our college lacks equal support of men's and women's athletic teams. I said this as a female athlete in a class with numerous male athletes. Because of the respectful classroom environment created by Professor Callahan and his encouragement to create unpopular discourse, I felt confident to express my opinion. I felt comfortable knowing Shatner's principles were part of my classroom experience.

Your writing response is preceded by your reading. Review Chapter 9 for strategies such as applying, questioning, evaluating, speculating, articulating, and synthesizing. Also read as a believer and doubter.

Organizing a reaction paper

Reaction paper organization includes the following structure.

Introduction

Identify the elements of the source(s) you're reacting to (author, source, publisher, and publication date), followed by a topic summary of the source's major points.

TIP

You can exceed your professor's expectations by creatively titling your reaction paper and beginning with an engaging first sentence prior to identifying your source. Here's an example:

To Fee or Not to Fee

Not all fees are created equal. Jenkins' article, "The Cost of Feeing High School Activities" (*Academic Times*, August 19, 2021), proposes handsomely charging students for participation in sports and other activities. The twist to his plan is that . . .

Thesis

The *thesis* identifies the purpose of the paper and a promise to the reader of what will develop. Formulate a position that summarizes the responses you are reacting to.

Here are a few examples:

> First World countries have a moral obligation to share medical knowledge with Third World countries.

People want their freedom; they also want their safety. Where do these two desires intersect?

Support for public education is not a shared responsibility throughout the country; it should be.

Body

The *body* develops the thesis with references to evidence, conclusion, ideas, and description. Develop reaction points in separate paragraphs, supported with summary, paraphrase, quotations, and citations. Your grade depends on how well you support your reactions.

Ending

The *ending* represents your final thoughts on your reaction, the last message to the reader. Ending strategies include reflecting on the topic with a prediction, so what, or big-picture meaning.

Reference list

Insert a hard page break at the end of the last line of text. Center "References" in bold (not in quotations). See Chapter 12 for reference list guidelines. Be sure to include the source(s) you're reacting to in the reference list.

From APA writing skills that I discuss in Chapter 5, prioritize the following skills when writing reaction papers: audience, purpose, tone, focus, and transitions.

Formatting a reaction paper

Here's a look at APA formatting guidelines (some are similar to the research paper) that apply to reaction papers — assuming your professor didn't provide any:

- >> Length about 3–4 pages, with about 800 words (a little longer than an essay)
- >> Margins one inch on all four sides
- >> Double-spaced text and headings
- >> Times New Roman font, 12-point size
- >> No running heads
- >> Page numbers in the upper-right corner, similar to research papers
- >> Heading levels, if applicable, similar to heading level guidelines in Chapter 14

An acceptable design for a title page (see Figure 15-2) includes the following:

>> In the upper-left corner, single space your name, the course name, the assignment name, the professor's name, and the due date.

>> Begin the title about one-third of the way down the page. Write the title in title case (Chapter 14), center and bold. Don't underline or italicize.

>> Begin text double spaced below the title. Indent new paragraphs.

1

Samantha Lawson
Economics 404
Reaction Paper #4
Professor Joseph Nava
April 20, 2021

Supply and Demand of Fossil Fuels in the Twentieth Century

    Begin the first paragraph indented here and continued double spaced to the bottom of this page. You can influence your grade with an engaging title and opening sentence.

FIGURE 15-2:
An example of an acceptable title page for reaction papers.

REMEMBER

Your professor's first indicator of an unsuccessful paper is one that neglects to meet the length requirement. You may be a proficient, economical writer, but an assignment that is a page under length will raise suspicion and scrutiny. Many professors believe that papers that don't meet length requirements are inferior papers.

Chapter **16**

Mastering Advanced Writing: APA Review of Literature

t's time for a taste from the menu of professional scholars — reviewing the literature, known pretentiously as "the literature." Consistent with the inconsistent language of scholarship, a review of literature isn't a review; it's a synthesis of literature, a much more intimidating assignment.

A review of literature, sometimes referred to as a literature review, is like a research paper on steroids. A professional review requires a full semester's work of collecting research, analyzing and synthesizing it, and writing a document that includes an introduction, body, and conclusion — with an essay sandwiched in.

Literature reviews are frequently assigned to undergraduates as stand-alone assignments related to a specific topic in an academic field. For example, you may be assigned to review literature on topics such as bullying in the workplace, online learning successes in elementary schools, or the logistics of vaccine dissemination.

In this chapter, I offer an overview of a professional literature review and follow up with the undergraduate version for professional scholars-in-training like you. I also demonstrate with models of key sections of the review. And, as always, APA comes along for the ride. Note that one of the side effects of this chapter is that you'll see dozens of ideas for future research topics.

Reviewing Literature: Searches and Steps

If you're a graduate student who is required to write a literature review for a master's thesis or doctoral dissertation, put a cover on this *For Dummies* book and buy the APA *Publication Manual of the American Psychological Association, Seventh Edition*. A literature review requires APA's professional, scholarly approach. At the same time, you can use *this* book as a guide for improving your academic writing style and for referencing the basics of APA citations and formatting.

Also focus on Part 2, which offers you classroom-tested strategies for developing an effective academic writing style, accompanied by conventions and revising strategies.

At the graduate level, a literature review is a major part of a document submitted for an advanced degree, or a scholarly article submitted for publication. The review at that level is part of a formal document that includes an abstract, a description of the research question, a methods description, an analysis of previous investigations, and a plan for moving the research forward. The undergraduate review of literature is usually required as a separate assignment that analyzes scholarship in a field of study.

A stand-alone literature review is sometimes required for undergraduate students who are enrolled in combined undergraduate and advanced degree programs. A review is also assigned as a research exercise for special interest topics across majors. For example, a biology major may review literature on a topic such as obstructions in the human digestive system, and a political science major may review literature on a topic such as unexpected consequences of Title IX.

A separate review focuses on the introduction and conclusion sections of the professional review, with reduced reference to synthesis and interpretation of sources. Your professor determines the depth of the body of the review. The organizational strategy of a separate assignment is usually chronological, whereas a professional review is organized thematically, theoretically, or by methods of research.

The following sections guide you through the process of beginning your search and focusing your topic. Follow my advice for analyzing literature review models, and you'll have a better understanding of the big picture of a literature review. The thesis statement models help you develop your own. Also, explore the steps I provide for the search process.

Educational research identifies getting started as the most difficult part of any assignment, especially an overwhelming project such as a literature review. But you have a team to start with that includes your advisor or the professor who assigned the review.

Starting the search

Assume you're an upper-level undergraduate, and you have the good fortune of being assigned a literature review. Your immediate questions are, "What the heck is it?" "What's the purpose?" "How do I do it?" and "Where do I start?" Here I explore some answers to help you understand why. I show you how to review literature in the upcoming sections that include "Focusing on the topic and "Sequencing the process."

WHY UNDERGRADUATES REVIEW LITERATURE

Scholars study scholarship. One of the most intense exercises for exploring scholarship is analyzing a literature review — an academic activity second only to writing a doctoral dissertation and designing an original research project. A literature review gives you experience with research, researchers, and research projects.

Reviewing requires focus and intensity. You've completed research projects in the past, but you haven't been required to analyze and synthesize a body of 15 to 20 scholarly articles common to a focused research question. Your past research offers a foundation of topics to select from for further study. Consider topics that interest you and curiosities that yearn to be satisfied.

A review requires you to analyze each article individually and then the body of all the articles. A crown jewel of a review of research is locating a landmark or seminal study that influences research direction. Research is like scuba diving; reviewing literature is like scuba diving while exploring the *Titanic*.

Your review represents a contribution to current research, and your synthesis of sources identifies not only trends, similarities, and consistencies, but also gaps, irregularities, and inconsistencies that need further study. Reviewing literature builds your expertise on a topic in your field and positions you for future research.

Your good fortune is an opportunity to dig a mile deep into research on a topic related to your field. Undergraduates explore topics such as the following:

>> Communication styles that contribute to miscommunication

>> The psychology of disagreement in the classroom

>> Social media's influence on high school athletes

>> What screen time doesn't tell us about screen addiction

>> What the Dow Jones tells us about financial stability

At the thesis, master's, and dissertation levels, purposes of a literature review include the following:

>> To show your understanding of an overview of research during a specified time frame, usually within the last five years

>> To investigate theories and knowledge on the topic

>> To find your niche among other researchers on the topic and move the topic forward

>> To identify gaps, inconsistencies, shortcomings, and controversy in the field of study

>> To identify topics for future research

REMEMBER

With a stand-alone assignment, your purpose is to analyze current research and demonstrate your knowledge of issues related to the topic. The difference between graduate-degree reviews and undergraduate reviews is that your review doesn't require collection of original data, as needed by a dissertation. Lucky you.

ANALYZING LITERATURE REVIEW MODELS

One of the best ways to improve how you write your literature review is to study and look at other reviews. You can find dozens of literature review models by searching Google Scholar and your university database. Search for models related to your field; annotated models provide additional instructional information. Locating APA style models also benefits you. Formatting exclusive to APA includes the resource list in the back, titled "References" or "Annotated Bibliography," and hanging indentations at the beginning of each reference entry.

After you find a few models, keep the following tips in mind as you inspect them. Identify the following types of information:

- Any language identifying the statement of the problem in the introduction, the thesis statement, synthesis of issues in the literature analysis, and inconsistencies in the literature

- Language patterns in major sections: introduction, body, and conclusion

- APA formatting for title page design, page formatting, heading levels, and running heads

- The number of citations in each major section and the number of entries in reference sections, to get an indication of the range of sources used

- Whether citations and references offer potential research resources

Also study models for writing style. Estimate average words per sentence, sentences per paragraph, and paragraphs per section.

Undergraduate reviews of literature are frequently required for honors' theses, senior projects, and combined undergraduate and graduate degree programs. If you aren't enrolled in a graduate-level path, choose a topic based on the assumption that you'll be enrolled.

TIP

When a review is part of a larger degree-granting document, it's positioned after the introduction section and before the methods section.

Focusing on the topic

Begin focusing on your topic with some preliminary research prior to scheduling an appointment with your advisor. Search "topics for literature reviews (in your field of study)." Reference these searches when you meet. Professors are impressed with students who show initiative before a conference.

TIP

Another topic-brainstorming strategy includes meeting with a small study group to discuss topics, approaches, and ideas.

Begin your review by discussing your topic with your advisor and formulating a working thesis statement. Also study online review models for samples of completed projects.

When you meet with your advisor, review department guidelines and discuss your topic interests and your advisor's interests. A match of interests with your advisor can be an asset, but lack of compatibility isn't necessarily a liability. Begin with a broad approach to topics such as social media, literature, film study, communication, government, history, technology, environmental issues, business, science, education, psychology, and sociology.

Narrow broad topics to focused interests, such as narrowing social media to issues related to education, privacy, the First Amendment, addiction, availability, and access. Narrow your time frame to study the topic, usually within five years.

Formulate your topic into a question, such as, "How do social media patterns correlate with use by four generations: Generation Z, millennials, Generation X, and boomers?" Topics are developed into thesis statements such as, "Each generation's use of social media has developed differently."

Table 16-1 lists some topics developed into thesis statements.

TABLE 16-1   **Topic Ideas and Theses**

Topics	Thesis Statements
Effects of home cooking experiences on elementary science grades	Children's early experience with cooking in the home contributes to their understanding of science and improves their science grades.
Hemingway's influence on today's best-selling writers	Ernest Hemingway's direct writing style and emphasis on nouns and verbs appears in the work of today's best-selling writers.
Effects of siblings' birth order on career success	Birth positions of siblings show common trends and influence career choices.
College writing and academic success	Success in writing first-year essays predicts college and career success.

TIP

In addition to your main focus question, list additional questions that your major question will answer. Here are some examples:

>> How does technology familiarization correlate with social media use?

>> How significant is the first social media experience?

>> Does level of education correlate with social media use?

>> Does social media fulfill humans' need for interdependence?

Validate your topic selection by answering questions such as the following:

>> Does the topic have relevancy and currency to the academic community?

>> Is a body of research on the topic available?

>> Is the topic compatible within the study of similar topics?

>> Do you (the author) have a personal investment in the topic?

Your topic and focus are a trial balloon at this point (called a *working topic*) and may be refined as your research and analysis progress.

Sequencing the process in four steps

I have a four-step process that guarantees you a successful review of literature. After you select your working topic, follow these steps:

Step 1: Search for literature

Identify key search terms such as Generation Z, millennials, Generation X, boomers, human development stages, Facebook, Twitter, Snapchat, and Instagram.

In addition to your university database, other search sites for a review of literature include

>> **Google Scholar:** Contains a wide variety of disciplines for scholarly literature, most of which are peer-reviewed.

>> **JSTOR:** Contains a wide variety of scholarly journals, nearly all peer reviewed.

>> **EBSCO:** Offers an extensive database of academic resources, most of which are peer reviewed.

Search for sources that most directly address your research question. Always include sources identified as landmark, pivotal, or seminal. A graduate-level review includes between 17 and 20 sources. A stand-alone undergraduate review includes between 15 and 18 sources.

REMEMBER

An asset to your literature review is including a *landmark article*, referred to as a *pivotal*, *core*, or *seminal* work. Landmark articles change thinking on a topic and are frequently cited in research. An example of a landmark study is the connection between reading and writing. Writing improves reading and reading improves writing.

TECHNICAL STUFF

Use Boolean operators to refine your search.

>> **AND:** All search terms connected with AND appear in search results.

>> **OR:** Search terms connected with OR produce one of the two options.

>> **NOT:** None of the search terms connected with NOT appear in search results.

>> **NEAR:** Search terms that appear within the designated number of words appear in search results.

SEARCH TIPS FOR A REVIEW OF LITERATURE

Begin your literature review search using key words identified from your topic and the-sis statement. As you search, refine key words and apply Boolean operators, which include the words *and, or, not,* and *near.* Start by searching familiar academic databases from your university library. Library databases will access more content than online databases. Extend your search to content-specific databases and general, scholarly databases. If you need to broaden your results, search reference lists. If you need to narrow your search, limit database parameters and apply Boolean limitations. Search within the year limitations of your topic.

Evaluate your sources as I explain in Chapter 11. You're searching exclusively for peer-reviewed scholarly articles. Popular sources don't make the grade for a review of literature.

REMEMBER

Research papers are supported with a combination of primary, secondary, and popular sources. Reviews of literature require exclusively peer-reviewed scholarly articles.

Step 2: Read and analyze the literature

Read each piece of research and identify specifics such as the following:

>> Author credentials, affiliations, and approach to the topic

>> Problem or question addressed

>> Major argument and evidence that support the problem

>> Key concepts to the argument and their definitions

>> Contributions to the topic at issue

>> Strengths and limitations

>> How the researcher's position aligns with similar researchers

Also identify summaries, paraphrases, and quotations that may appear in your review.

Step 3: Categorize patterns in the literature

Identify patterns common to all articles. Here are examples of patterns:

>> Recurring themes such as social media proficiency began later in life.

>> Boomers' use of Facebook exceeded that of Generation X.

>> Facebook use was common to all generations.

>> Twitter use declined among all generations.

>> Pivotal studies didn't appear in the search.

TIP

During the early readings of your sources, begin notations for annotated references, to expedite citations and source engagement.

Step 4: Write the review

If you're an outline person, list topics addressed in the review prior to writing. They include the following:

» Identification of the topic

» Description of the importance of the topic

» Limitations of the topic

» Highlights of the literature

» Arguments, analysis, and synthesis of the findings

» Recommendations for moving the research forward

TIP

As an example of graduate-level research, the APA *Publication Manual of the American Psychological Association, Seventh Edition*, details professional requirements for literature review that include "historical antecedents," "qualitative goals," and "mixed methods."

ADAPTING THE APA WRITING STYLE TO REVIEW LITERATURE

The APA writing style adapts to a variety of writing strategies including reviewing literature. Audience and purpose shape writing more than any other writing strategy. Here's a look at how audience and purpose, along with other influences of academic writing, affect how the APA writing style adapts to writing a review of literature:

- **Audience:** Think of your audience as your professor, a member of the academic research community. Your audience represents serious researchers focused on addressing research questions.

- **Purpose:** The purpose of your research is to review literature, analyze and evaluate sources relevant to your topic, and determine their position among other sources.

- **Tone:** Research writing requires a serious academic tone that shows respect for the content and for the reader. Save your sense of humor for essay writing, not for reviewing literature.

- **Focus:** The writing focus is centered on answering the research question within the framework of the literature you're reviewing.

- **Transitions:** The primary transitions in research are the headings and subheadings that direct information from topic to topic. Create your transition headings with action verbs and specific nouns, and apply parallel structure.

Studying Samples: Introduction, Body, and Conclusion

As part of the process of achieving success as a student, you learned the value of studying models. As a professor, I learned the value of using models to help college students because so many students asked for a model every time an assignment was introduced. To use the wording of a famous commercial, good student models are *priceless*.

Similar to the structure of almost all academic writing, a literature review must be organized into a beginning (introduction), middle (body), and ending (conclusion). The following sections focus more on that organization.

Starting with the thesis: The introduction

The introduction includes a description of the research question and its purpose. It ends with the thesis statement.

The introduction model in Figure 16-1 begins with a statement emphasizing the importance of the topic and progresses to background on the topic, including research from Winegarner and Sheetz and Brookover. The second paragraph introduces social media habits of the four generational populations (Generation Z, millennials, Generation X, and boomers) and their uses of technological devices to access social media. The second paragraph ends by explaining how the term *social media* is applied in the review. The third paragraph ("This review . . .") further explains the purpose of the review, and the paragraph ends with the thesis statement: "The influence of social media . . ."

REMEMBER

Figure 16-1 follows APA page formatting that includes running heads (SOCIAL MEDIA AND FOUR GENERATIONS), page numbering located in the upper-right corner, one-inch margins on all four sides (use your imagination on the margins), indented paragraphs, and double-spaced text. *Note:* APA requires that research be reported in the past tense. More information on formatting appears in the section, "Laying Out Pages and the Title Page of the APA Literature Review," later in this chapter.

Developing the thesis: The body

The body of a literature review houses the engine of the review, and it's a three-part engine, which the following three sections examine.

Introduction

Social media has become part of the fabric of society and for many people it represents their most common form of personal interaction today. Winegarner and Sheetz found that most people communicate more by social media than by email and telephone combined (2019). Social media posts are so common that lack of social media contact represents personal rejection to some people and compromises their mental stability (Brookover, 2019, p. 203).

Each of these generations approaches technology and social media from different perspectives and backgrounds, with Generation Z and millennials having more "intuitive technology" than Generation X and boomers (Haskill, 2018, p. 48). For example, Generation Z and millennials were more likely to post on Facebook with smart watches, compared with boomers who were more likely to post on Facebook from their home computers (Harvin, 2018, p. 68). Akins (2019) reported that Generation Z owned twice as many smart devices as Generation X and boomers, and they accumulated twice as many minutes of weekly screen time as Generation X and boomers combined. For the purpose of the study, the definition of social media exceeds "personal communication" and includes meanings such as product reviews and e-commerce (p. 243).

This review of literature examines social media trends among those four generational populations and their interaction with Facebook, Twitter, Instagram, and Snapchat. The timeframe studied ranges between 2014 and 2018. This research advances study of social media trends across generations and the influences common to these trends. For example, it correlates education and use of social media as well as geographical trends. This information has implications for additional study in the fields of psychology, sociology, education, business, and technology. The influence of social media support correlates with four stages of generational development: Generation Z, millennials, Generation X, and boomers.

FIGURE 16-1: An example introduction of a literature review.

© John Wiley & Sons, Inc.

Highlighting sources and identifying patterns

The body of the paper develops the thesis by analyzing ideas in the sources. Part 1 of the body model identifies sources and patterns of all the literature (refer to Figure 16-2).

Social media has been energized by the human instinct to aggregate. Cave space was destined to evolve into Myspace. Gladville (2019) explained it like this: "Humans' desire to communicate electronically evolved from a need to communicate musically and vocally" (p. 7). The 2020 Kline Research Report on social media showed that 60% of adults worldwide used social media in 2019, compared with only 35% in 2005, the year after Facebook debuted (p. 187). In less than a generation, Facebook and other social media evolved into a major personal communication tool, as well as a major marketing tool and part of the lives of billons of people.

In the United States today, 70% of adults use social media: 65% regularly use YouTube, 70% Instagram, and 75% Snapchat. Only 50% of adults used Twitter in 2019 (Tasker, 2019, p. 245). Worldwide, social media was used by half the global population (Wilson, 2019). Global social media use crossed generational lines. Internationally, Facebook lacked the popularity that Generation Z and Generation X experienced in the United States. In Scandinavian countries, Snapchat was the most popular social media platform used by millennials, and doubled that use in the United States.

YouTube use by boomers increased in the United States in 2018, while Twitter continues to trend downward among Generation Z. Larson (2018) attributes the declining use of Twitter to "the generation that has too many toys to choose from" (p. 256). Generation X were the most prolific users of social media, and boomers the least frequent users.

FIGURE 16-2: Part 1 of the body section highlighting sources and identifying patterns.

© John Wiley & Sons, Inc.

For example, the author references Gladville's quotation ("Humans' desire to communicate electronically . . .") that provides historical perspective of humans' need to communicate. The first paragraph also offers statistical data that supports different generations' use of Facebook.

The second paragraph ("In the United States . . .") further explains statistical use of social media internationally. The last paragraph ("YouTube use by . . .") continues with data supporting generational uses of social media.

Engaging the source

The strength of the body of your paper is your discussion of sources, such as identifying your agreement, disagreement, or position on the source. Figure 16-3 shows the body of a literature review with source engagement. The first paragraph exemplifies multiple source engagement.

In most previously referenced studies, boomers were found to be the most infrequent users of all social media, consistent with the finding that generations owning the fewest technology devices used the least social media (Lee, 2019, p. 325). Somewhat inconsistent with Lee, Penwell (2020) found high ownership of smart watches among boomers, which Zandel (2019) attributed to "a desire for convenient access to medical devices" (p. 284). Zandel was referring to a smart watch's capability to measure heartbeats and record an EKG. The Gulf Coast Research Report found that while millennials owned the highest number of technology devices, their access to social media was 20% less than that of Generation Z (2018).

Marks (2019) analyzed social media use and education, and found that Generation X was the highest-educated generation, but not the largest consumers of technology among generational populations (p. 293). Lemon (2019) reported no significant correlation between years of achieved education and use of technology, a surprise finding to many of today's educators. Brewster (2018) endorsed Lemon's finding that "technology knowledge and social media activity does not necessarily correlate" (p. 325).

Purposes of engaging social media varied among generational populations. Ballinger (2020) reported that Generation Z and millennials "logged on a number of times daily to see what's happening" (p. 309). Generation X used social media primarily for "reviewing product information" (Will, 2020, p. 245). Boomers showed a variety of purposes for logging on, the primary purpose being "checking up on old friends" (Laube, 2019, p. 84).

FIGURE 16-3: Part 2 of the body section showing source engagement.

The paragraph begins with Lee agreeing with previously referenced sources ("In most previously referenced studies. . .") that "generations owning the fewest technology devices" are the "most infrequent users of all social media." In the second sentence, Penwell challenges Lee and reports that Zandell found "high ownership of smart watches among boomers" (as medical devices), and explains that boomers own technology devices, but don't necessarily use them to connect to social media.

In the last sentence of the first paragraph, the Gulf Coast Research Report also disagreed with previous studies arguing that "millennials owned the highest number of technology devices," but their social media access declined.

In the second paragraph, Marks challenged the correlation of high levels of education and high levels of technology use, saying that "Generation X was the highest-educated generation" in the study, but not "the largest consumers of technology." Source engagement continues with Lemon disagreeing with previous studies. The paragraph ends with Brewster supporting Lemon.

The first two paragraphs exemplify engagement among multiple sources that agree and disagree. The multiple engagement also showed inconsistencies in the review of literature.

Synthesizing sources

Figure 16-4 shows an example of the last part of the body section. In this case, it synthesizes the findings of Covich, Simmons, Kimmell, and Cavis. The four researchers integrated popularity of social media, financial success of Facebook and Twitter, financial growth of Generation X, and the extended definition of social media. The second and third paragraphs support that integration with research by Phillips, Reilly, and Levy.

Common threads strengthen the argument that social media shared common roots across four generations. Covich (2019) reported that social media is used by almost two-thirds of the world's population, and Simmons (2018) traced increased financial success of Facebook and Twitter from 2016 to 2018. Following the money trail, Kimmell (2018) reported five percent financial growth among the Generation X population in e-commerce and speculated growth in social marketing among Generation Z. Kimmell raised the issue that the definition of social media use extends to "personal communication" (p. 89).

Additional findings by Cavis (2020) supported the increased use of social marketing across all four generations, with Facebook showing the largest increase and Twitter showing the smallest increase (p. 432). Phillips (2020) added that Twitter showed increased use among boomers but did not distinguish between dedicated social media growth and dedicated political commentary growth. Phillips conducted his study during the 2020 U.S. presidential election year.

Snapchat, while popular among Generation Z, lacked the popularity of Facebook among boomers (Reilly, 2020). Reilly added, "Some populations lack the patience to post on Snapchat" (2020, p. 125). Levy agreed with Reilly's assessment of Snapchat, but questioned Kimmell's assertion that social media's popularity as a marketing tool overshadowed its use as a personal contact tool (2020).

FIGURE 16-4: Part 3 of the body section showing synthesis of sources.

Ending with significant findings: The conclusion

The conclusion summarizes major findings in the review and explains their importance. The summary also includes recommendations for new research.

The conclusion example in Figure 16-5 opens with a summary paragraph restating the importance of the topic ("Social media is used by billions . . .") and the goal of the review ("compare and contrast four social media venues . . .").

Social media is used by billions, almost two-thirds the world's population. For many of those billions, social media represents their exclusive contact with other people. The goal of this review of literature was to compare and contrast four social media venues (Facebook, Snapchat, Instagram, and Twitter) among four different generational populations (Generation Z, millennials, Generation X, and boomers).

The reviewed literature suggests that Facebook was the most popular social media site across all four generations and that it has remained the social media of choice among Generation X since its inception in 2004 (Crossman, 2020). Snapchat, which lacks the worldwide presence of Facebook, continues to increase in popularity among Generation Z (Bellview, 2019). Taylor (2019) reported that Twitter's popularity as a "safe haven to communicate with friends" has emerged into a "forum for political activity" (p. 289).

The literature also revealed that generations vary in their reasons for visiting social media sites. Cunningham reported that Generation X uses social media primarily for its "business potential to reach millions instantly" (p. 234). Boomers found comfort [with Facebook], "checking out Facebook to see who's still hanging around" (Grossman, p. 243).

Psychologically, the literature revealed that all four generational groups occasionally find comfort knowing that "someone I know is always online somewhere" and that "when I don't want to be bothered by anyone, I just shut down my computer" (Longman, 2019, p. 231).

FIGURE 16-5:
An example of a conclusion.

The second, third, and fourth paragraphs summarize findings: "generations vary in their reasons for visiting social media sites . . ." and "all four generational groups occasionally find comfort . . ."

The conclusion section also contains the recommendation section (see Figure 16-6), which lists topics recommended for additional research. These recommendations represent the author's effort to move the research topic forward.

The review of literature suggested the need to explore new research affiliated with social media and four generational populations of users. Foremost, psychological implications of the review needed answers to questions such as, "Does social media discourage personal contact affecting humans' interdependence?" and "Does lack of personal contact have varying consequences across generations?"

The correlation of social media use with other variables also needed exploration, answering questions such as, "Does social media correlate across generational lines with educational levels and geographical locations?" and "Does social media correlate across generational populations with economic patterns?"

And finally, does use of social media correlate with regular exercise and active lifestyles, raising questions such as, "Does time allocated for social media detract from time for exercising and living an active lifestyle?"

© John Wiley & Sons, Inc.

FIGURE 16-6: An example of recommendations for new research and its importance.

Determining other major sections

Within the organizational structure of the review of literature, APA designates the following major sections, some of which are identified as optional for undergraduates:

>> **Title page:** A literature review requires the professional-document title page with a running head. A sample title page appears later, in the section, "Laying Out Pages and the Title Page of the APA Literature Review."

>> **Abstract:** An abstract, a short highlight of the review (see Figure 16-7), is optional for an undergraduate review, but is frequently required for a graduate review.

>> **Methods:** A methods section, and explanation of how the story was conducted, isn't required for an undergraduate literature review because no original research is required for a separate literature review.

>> **References:** The reference section in a review of literature duplicates the reference section in a research paper. The references in a review of literature include all reviewed articles, in addition to references from sources cited (review Chapter 12).

>> **Appendixes:** Appendixes offer an opportunity to add related content beyond what's developed in the paper, such as relevant historical documents. Review Chapter 13 for additional uses of appendixes.

Abstract

Four different generations (Generation Z, millennials, Generation X, and boomers) approach social media from different background experiences. Those experiences result in different adaptions and comfort levels when using Facebook, Twitter, Instagram, and Snapchat. The study analyzes changing patterns of social media used among the four generational groups. It looks at influences educationally, psychologically, socially, and geographically. It traces each group's initial heavy use of Facebook and declining use of Instagram and Snapchat. The goal of the study is to analyze trends among the four generations for the purpose of understanding each generation's relationship with social media.

FIGURE 16-7:
An example abstract.

© *John Wiley & Sons, Inc.*

>> **Tables and figures:** If applicable, you can supplement your topic with tables and figures. Tables are common to scientific topics, and figures are common to many topics in the behavioral sciences (see Chapter 13).

>> **Conclusion:** This includes a summary of the findings, the importance of those findings, and recommendations for further research on related topics.

Laying Out Pages and the Title Page of the APA Literature Review

When APA formatting guidelines aren't provided, adapt APA general principles (based on student research paper design) to your writing project. Apply APA styles to title pages and page layout.

APA page layout for the review of literature follows guidelines for the research paper — with the exception that no running heads are required for the student paper. Here's a list of page formatting standards for almost all APA writing projects:

- » One-inch margins on all four sides
- » Page numbering in the top-right corner
- » Double spacing between lines and headings
- » Running head optional (ask your professor)
- » Times New Roman font, 12-point size
- » Hard page breaks prior to headings such as abstract, introduction, reference, and appendices

Your professor may require APA's professional scholarly title page version, which includes a running head. Figure 16-8 shows a title page for a literature review that a junior or senior may be required to use.

HEMINGWAY'S BEST-SELLER INFLUENCE   1

Hemingway's Influence on Today's Best-Selling Writers

Donavan E. Carsen

Department of English Studies, Valley Brook University

LIT 387 Literature Study

Dr. Corletta Swanson

October 20, 2020

FIGURE 16-8:
An example of a graduate-level title page for a literature review.

Meanwhile, Figure 16-9 is a sample title page for a stand-alone, less complex undergraduate literature review.

1

Hemingway's Influence on Today's Best-Selling Writers

Donavan E. Carsen

Department of English Studies, Valley Brook University

LIT 387 Literature Study

Dr. Corletta Swanson

October 20, 2020

© John Wiley & Sons, Inc.

FIGURE 16-9: A sample title page for a stand-alone review.

Chapter **17**

Perfecting Specialized Writings: APA Reports

You've been reading reports since your first report card in kindergarten. That first academic report was a treasure that someone in your family may still possess today. Reports are the ATMs of the writing genre: They perform a variety of services at a high level of efficiency.

You've been writing reports since your first book report as an elementary school student. Those early reports included an introduction, body, and conclusion — similar to the structure of reports you're writing today. The content of your first report was information, also similar to reports you're writing today. Writing and reading reports represents a skill you'll carry with you throughout your academic life, your career, and your personal life.

In this chapter I guide you through creating and organizing more than a dozen reports and adapting APA's writing style and formatting to those reports. I also model language representative of various sections of reports. The purpose of this chapter is to focus on information, information, and information. Report writing represents the last APA-specialized writing genre in this book. Finish strong, and I hope you earn yourself a good report in your course.

APA Report Writing: Creating and Organizing

Reports are like cereal; they come in a variety of packages, appearances, and content, but they're still breakfast. Reports contain a variety of structural elements. No two are alike, but all are focused on information. They're built on the foundation of writing research papers, essays, and reviews of literature. They require research, narrative explanation, and laser focus on answering questions.

REMEMBER

Some professors, especially in content areas, use the terms "report" and "essay" interchangeably, but these terms represent two ends of the genre spectrum. Be sure to clarify what your professor is asking for. Reports are common in business, science, technical courses, and in the workplace. Essays are common in literacy courses.

At this point in your life, you've read more reports than you've written: academic reports, health reports, credit reports, government reports, product reviews, employee evaluations, but hopefully not too many police reports. Report writing represents one of the most practical and valued writing genres today. Among modern businesses, institutions, and organizations, reports represent a valued intellectual property. They solve problems, establish policy, determine budgets, evaluate programs, manage spending, update projects, disseminate information, determine feasibility, recommend action, investigate incidents, and upgrade processes.

Think of report-writing as career-building skills and money-making skills, one of the best investments you can make in your future. The next few sections guide you through the why and how of report writing.

Eyeing the purpose and benefits of reports

A report is a focused package of information for a specific audience, organized into manageable sections. Table 17-1 breaks down the types of questions that different reports answer.

More than most types of writing, reports offer benefits for both the writer and the reader, because the writer is usually a member of the audience that benefits from the report. Reports are designed to systematically lead readers through information and present content in an easily retrievable format.

TABLE 17-1   **Determining the Type of Report**

Question the Report Answers	Type of Report
How am I doing at work?	Employee evaluation report
Can I make a large purchase?	Credit report
Was that accident my fault?	Police report
What was accomplished last month?	Monthly report
What's the condition of my teeth?	Dental report
Is the product I plan to buy reliable?	Product review
What's happening in the world?	News report
How am I doing in school this semester?	Academic progress report

Benefits of reports include the following:

>> Establish record-keeping and outcomes of major issues.

>> Record a history of successes and failures.

>> Communicate the development of projects.

>> Determine future actions needed for improvement.

>> Identify expectations.

Examining report characteristics

Writing reports is a requirement of academic life — from elementary-school book reports to workplace sales reports. They appear in a variety of sizes and formats; the following sections examine the characteristics of reports.

TECHNICAL STUFF

As you can see in the section, "APA Report Writing: Specializing and Personalizing," later in this chapter, research reports differ from research papers as lightning bolts differ from lightning rods.

REMEMBER

Unless your professor specifies otherwise, assigned academic reports are written formally and analytically for *internal audiences* — readers within the organization — and *vertical audiences* — readers up and down the organizational structure. Ask questions to clarify your audience.

Report length

One of your early report decisions is determining your report's length. Can you develop your workplace topic with eight or nine pages and limited optional features, or does the significance require more pages of development with additional supporting information?

Long reports extend to ten or more pages, and sometimes as many as 30 or more pages. The extended length requires organizational options such as a table of contents, executive summary, transmittal memo, and APA's five-level heading strategies (see Chapter 14).

They may also require a glossary, appendices, tables and figures, and links to audio and video clips. Longer reports are written in a formal tone and are commonly assigned in business courses. College short reports generally run from six to eight pages.

Formal or informal

Academic and organizational reports are structured formally and written in a formal tone. An informal tone is acceptable for reports within a small group or team. If you're unsure of which tone to use, prefer formal.

Internal or external

Internal reports are disseminated within an organization, and *external reports* are disseminated outside the organization. These two specialized audiences require distinctive tone, language, formality, and content. Misidentifying audiences can be as costly as giving the wrong person your credit card information.

Vertical or horizontal

Vertical reports are disseminated throughout the hierarchy of an organization. The writer's supervisor and supervisor's supervisor read vertical reports. *Horizontal reports* are disseminated throughout a department or across similar departments.

Informational or analytical

Informational reports communicate data with or without analysis. They include monthly reports, update reports, budget reports, and new information reports. *Analytical reports* add meaning to data for the purpose of supporting a position or recommending a plan of action. Analytical reports include recommendation reports, proposal reports, sales and marketing reports, and research reports.

WHY WRITE REPORTS

You may never write an essay after you graduate from college, but in most careers, report writing is as common as receiving a paycheck. Writing reports in college resembles what you'll do in the workplace. Reports in the workplace influence budgeting, policy, staffing, performance, and work conditions. Writing reports represents the staff development of an organization or institution. Organizations that write reports demonstrate an openness to solve problems and capitalize on their successes. Reports written by employees show an organization's respect for its workforce.

Writing Reports in Six Easy-to-Follow Steps

Psychologists and economists have recently begun to study choices, more specifically, how too many choices are a problem that can paralyze selection. Too many choices of information when developing a report represent a problem with report writing, but choice overload is reduced by answering key questions before you begin. Most answers to these questions come from the person requesting the report.

Here's a look at key questions to determine the focus and extent of a report:

>> Who asked for the report and what is the organizational level of that person?

>> What event initiated the need for the report?

>> How will the report be used?

>> What question should the report answer?

>> Who is the audience and what is the purpose?

>> Is the report internal or external?

>> Does the report require a recommendation?

>> Are any tables and figures needed to understand the report?

Answers to these questions will shape your report's structure, audience, purpose, focus, and tone — in addition to identifying optional sections. For example, if the report is vertical and disseminated up the hierarchy, it will be written formally and include an executive summary, table of contents, and transmittal memo.

After you establish the preliminary focus of your report, follow the steps in the following sections to complete the report.

ADAPTING THE APA WRITING STYLE TO REPORT WRITING

APA's academic writing style adapts to research papers (see Chapters 10, 11, and 12), essays (see Chapter 15), and reviews of literature (see Chapter 16). Here's how APA's writing style adapts to report writing.

- **Focus:** The topic focus shapes the report's structure and length. Reports require that focus be limited to one workable topic. Too narrow a topic, such as home-office color schemes, produces limited significant information. Too broad a topic, such as productive home offices, produces too much information. A focused topic produces a focused report, such as creating a distraction-free home office environment.

- **Purpose:** The report's purpose shapes the focus and structure of the writing. If the purpose of a report focuses on a project's progress, the report evaluates what has been completed and the probability of completing the project before deadline.

- **Audience:** Unlike many other audiences, readers of reports (especially internal reports) have a vested interest in the information in those reports (for example, content directly affecting the future of the organization they're a member of). Therefore, audience shapes what is said, why it's said, and how it's said. Successful reports address their audience directly and openly. For example, if the focus of a report is to explain a reduction in the workforce, the report needs to identify who, when, and to some extent why. Reports written to the wrong audience are as useless as a left-handed fork.

- **Tone:** Tone of reports is generally serious and formal, similar to research papers and reviews of literature. However, reports written to a small team may include informal language. Reports lack tone variations common to essays.

- **Transitions:** The structure of reports establishes the flow of content throughout headings and subheadings, which require organization such as general to specific, less important to more important, or sequential or logical.

Step 1: Plan and focus

Begin reports (and all writing assignments) by analyzing the assignment, brainstorming, and reading background information on the topic. Read for key terms, relevancy, and extent of the topic. Who and what is affected by the topic? What are the economic implications? Anticipate the information needed to answer the report's major question.

Step 2: Search for information

Using key terms from the assignment and background reading, search your library databases, focusing on content-specific sources (see Chapter 11). Concentrate on secondary and popular sources (see Chapters 10 and 11).

Step 3: Analyze the information

Some reports require analysis without taking a position. Most reports require an analysis of information to make a recommendation that an organization can act on. If a report supports an argument or position, it requires an analysis. Analysis frequently requires refuting the opposition, similar to research paper writing. Review Chapters 5 and 11 for more information.

Step 4: Organize major and optional sections

Answering the report's key questions prior to Step 1 determines the major and optional sections. For example, long reports, vertical reports, and analytical reports require a table of contents and an executive summary to help the organizational leader locate key information. A report with extensive statistical data and technical terms requires tables and a glossary. A report disseminated externally or throughout the organization additionally requires a transmittal memo (See the section, "Organizing Your Report: Other Essential Sections," earlier in this chapter.)

Step 5: Write the report

Before drafting the report, categorize the content into major sections: introduction, body, and conclusion. Begin drafting with a copy of the focused question in front of you.

Categorize content by asking questions such as these:

>> What content is background? (introduction)

>> What content contributes to the results and findings? (body)

>> What content covers implications? (body or conclusion)

>> What content is interesting, but supplemental? (appendix)

>> What content is off topic? (delete)

REMEMBER

Many writers begin projects by starting with the body of information because they don't know the information they're introducing. This approach requires writing in the sequence of the middle, ending, and introduction. If you can't write in this sequence, focus on revising the initial draft of your introduction. See Chapter 8 for revising strategies.

Here are some tips for writing reports:

>> Write clearly and directly, with an average of approximately 25 words per sentence. Generally, avoid more than one dependent thought per sentence.

>> Write primarily in the third person (review Chapter 6). Generally, avoid the second person. Avoid the first person, except for references to the collective *we*, for reports written by a team where you would use "I".

>> Refer to research in the past tense, as recommended by APA.

>> Use the active voice.

>> Emphasize active verbs and specific nouns.

>> Explain with the words "such as" and "for example."

TIPS FOR WRITING TEAM REPORTS

Unlike college, everyone in the work world accepts responsibility for team reports — paycheck motivation is higher than grade motivation. Ideal team composition includes members with diverse backgrounds. Studies have identified the ideal team composition as three females and two males.

The challenge of team writing is in orchestrating a collection of individually written sections and ideas into a symphony of sound as though it were written with one voice.

Here's a look at some guidelines for successful team writing:

• Select a project manager, someone with initiative and leadership, like you.

• Initially meet to analyze the task, answer key questions, brainstorm, narrow the topic, identify the question the report asks, and allocate work.

• Schedule deadline meetings for completion of assigned parts and review of writing. Post completed work in an online sharing file.

• Schedule a meeting to review compilation of completed parts.

• Schedule a meeting for revising strategies, as I discuss in Chapter 8.

- » Use unbiased and respectful language (see Chapter 5).

- » Write in a confident tone, avoiding language such as "hopefully" and "I think."

- » Write with formal language and avoid contractions. You aren't writing a *For Dummies* book.

Step 6: Revise

Revise at three levels: structural; sentence and paragraph; and word. Review the revising strategies in Chapter 8, especially model-revised sentences at the end of the chapter. If you're an overachiever, add personal models of revised sentences to the list.

Adapting APA Formatting to Reports

Successful writing projects begin with accurate formatting, especially the title page. APA doesn't offer a model title page for reports, so be sure to ask your professor for specific title page requirements. Most business reports include the phrases "prepared for" and "prepared by." Write the title in title case (refer to Chapter 7). Figure 17-1 shows a sample of a report title page that most professors will accept. Use your imagination for one-inch margins on all four sides.

REMEMBER

The report title identifies the focus of the report, and a subtitle narrows that focus.

The APA page layout for report writing follows standard guidelines for research writing. Here's a list of page formatting guidelines for report writing:

- » One-inch margins on all four sides

- » Page numbering in the top-right corner

REMEMBER

Even though APA requires running heads on title pages for professional scholarly publications, running heads and page numbering on title pages aren't commonly used on report title pages. Ask your professor about the use of running heads and page numbering on the title page.

- » Double spacing between lines and headings

- » Flush-left text with five-space paragraph indentations

- » Times New Roman font, at 12-point size

Causes of Employee Dissatisfaction in the Retail Industry:
An Analysis of Large World Retailers

Prepared for

Dr. Jonas Carlton
Southwest State University

Prepared by

Alisha Babson
John Davis
Eric Grayson
Jill Hillsboro
Rico Lamas

May 1, 2021

FIGURE 17-1: An example of a report title page.

REPORT WRITING — ENHANCE YOUR CAREER OPPORTUNITIES

Effective writing is a valued skill in the workplace, and many business leaders continue to identify writing as a deficient skill among college graduates. Report writing offers an opportunity to enhance your career prospects. Develop your academic report-writing skills by taking leadership of team report projects and team writing projects in general. Reports you create individually and as part of a team provide you with writing samples to accompany your portfolio of work experiences. In the workplace and during internships, volunteer to write reports. Listen for topics under discussion in your workplace environment, such as improving team structures, work-from-home production, communication apps for tablets, and successful employee incentives. Follow this chapter's guidelines for report writing. If a volunteer report doesn't result in a job opportunity, it may result in a recommendation. Write your way to career success.

>> Five levels of headings (refer to Chapter 14)

>> Hard page breaks prior to section headings such as executive summary, acknowledgments, table of contents, introduction, references, and appendices

Studying Report Samples: Introduction, Body, and Conclusion

Reports are among the most varied structured writing projects in both business and academic environments. However, reports, like variety among skyscrapers, lack support without a strong foundation.

The organization of reports is designed to present complex information in a simplified format, because some readers are focused on first identifying a specific piece of information. Reports are also designed to display specific pieces of information quickly.

Similar to the structure of almost all academic writing, reports require organization in a beginning (introduction), middle (body), and ending (conclusion). Here's a look at how that breaks down in writing a report.

Introduction

The introduction (see Figure 17-2) begins the report with an interesting opening, followed by background on the topic. The introduction identifies the topic, its importance, and implication. If applicable, the introduction includes methods, time frame, and limits of the report. The introduction ends with the purpose statement that references the question the report answers.

Body

The body of reports contains the essence of the information. What happened? How did it happen? Why did it happen? It's also the section of the report that most influences your grade. The body of the report (refer to Figure 17-3 for an example) includes the evidence or findings of the report and identification of those results. Subheadings frequently used in the body include findings and results. See Chapter 14 for formatting APA levels of headings in the body.

The value of a college degree today proves its worth economically, socially, and culturally. Studies by Thompson and Wright have reported that college graduates over a lifetime earn almost two million dollars more than high school graduates (2020, p. 56). Studies by Brooke and Shields also show additional benefits, including a stronger economy, reduced unemployment, and higher contributions to the tax base (2020, p. 62).

In the United States, approximately one-third of adults have earned a four-year college degree. But more significantly, more than half of students who begin college do not earn their degree within four years. This report analyzes a pilot program designed to increase the college graduate rate by decreasing the time required (and associated costs) to earn a four-year degree. This report examines a one-year pilot program that studied one hundred college freshmen enrolled in a program that awarded them with up to 30 credits (approximately one year of college) for life experiences such as military service, highly proficient literacy backgrounds, entrepreneurial experiences, volunteering experiences, and worldwide travel.

Students in the program are compared academically with other freshmen in areas such as GPA, scores on writing assignments, books read, and class attendance. The report also examines economic impact of the plan as a result of one year's reduction in tuition. The purpose of the report is to analyze the pilot study and make recommendations based on that analysis.

FIGURE 17-2:
Model language from a report introduction.

From the hundred students in the pilot study, three students dropped out of college for reasons related to "family health issues." This dropout rate was 50 percent less than the dropout rate of their peers in the freshmen class. Results of the study also revealed that 80 percent of the one hundred students in the pilot program earned a GPA of 3.3 or higher, with 10 percent earning a perfect 4.0. The average GPA, and the percent of students who earned a perfect GPA, exceeded the rate of their remaining freshmen class.

Additional results revealed that 70 percent of students in the pilot study scored higher in writing assignments. Higher writing scores also correlated with data that showed students in the study independently read 50 percent more books than the freshmen class average. The highest increase in independent book reading was performed by students who were admitted into the program for an "extensive literacy background."

In summary, students in the pilot study performed better than their peers in GPA, writing scores, reading, and classroom attendance.

FIGURE 17-3:
Model language from the body of a report.

Conclusion

The conclusion evaluates the report's answer to the focusing question and justifies the action to be taken. Subheadings frequently used in the conclusion (see Figure 17-4 for an example of a report conclusion) include recommendations and a discussion and analysis of the results. An analysis of the results includes identifying trends, uncertainties, and questions.

FIGURE 17-4:
Model language from the conclusion of a report.

> As a result of the students in the pilot group outperforming their peers in all academic areas, the taskforce recommends implementing credit for the life experience program into the university's admission process beginning next fall, while continuing to record data by extending the pilot study of the initial one hundred students.
>
> The taskforce also recommends examining criteria for awarding credits for the purpose of extending the definition of "life experiences," such as awarding credits for proficiencies in performing arts and graphic arts. At this time, life experiences in athletics are not under consideration for admission to the program. The taskforce also recommends reaching out to the students who dropped out of college, and providing additional support for first-generation college students in the pilot group.

Organizing Your Report: Other Essential Sections

Within the organizational structure of reports, APA designates the following sections as options for report organization.

Acknowledgments

Acknowledgements recognize people who were instrumental in creating the report, but not usually team members who wrote the report. This section includes the person who asked for the report, as well as your immediate supervisor. Never miss an opportunity to acknowledge your immediate supervisor.

Glossary

A *glossary* (or definition of terms) should be included in technical reports, with approximately six or more terms that the audience is unfamiliar with. A glossary increases readability of reports by listing terms in a common section. For an example of a glossary in research writing, see Chapter 13.

Executive summary

An executive summary (see Figure 17-5), common to business documents, differs depending on its purpose. (See an example of a model executive summary in Chapter 13.) Executive summaries range between 200 and 250 words. An executive summary is prepared for the busy executive who lacks time to read the full report. It identifies the importance of the report and highlights results without analyzing information.

This report completed by a university taskforce analyzes a pilot program awarding up to 30 college credits for life experiences such as military service, entrepreneurial experience, literacy background, worldwide travel, and volunteering initiatives. The pilot group of one hundred students between the ages of twenty and thirty were studied academically after their first year of college and compared with other freshmen in their class.

The report revealed that 80 percent of students in the program earned a GPA of 3.3 or higher, 70 percent averaged a B-grade or higher in writing assignments, and 90 percent attended at least 93 percent of their classes. Two students dropped out of the program for "family health issues" and planned to eventually return to school. Compared with other freshmen in their class, students in the pilot program earned higher GPAs, achieved higher writing scores, and had better attendance rates.

The taskforce recommended implementing the work experience program as part of the admission process the following fall, extending criteria for awarding life experience credits, and studying a program for reaccepting students who dropped out of the program for non-academic reasons.

The program provides a strategy for improving graduation rates and attracting additional students to offset tuition reduction caused by three years of college attendance rather than the traditional four or five years.

FIGURE 17-5:
An example of an executive summary.

Transmittal memo

Transmittal memos (*memos* is more commonly used as the plural form, rather than the formal *memorandum*) describe the document that is being transmitted from the memo writer to the document reader. Reports and other business documents are commonly passed on to the reader with a transmittal memo. Receiving a document without a transmittal memo is like receiving a package in the mail with no explanation. The one-page or shorter memo (see Figure 17-6 for a sample) contains three or four paragraphs and is organized in three parts as follows:

>> An opening that builds a relationship between the writer and reader

>> A body that identifies the problem, explains its significance, and offers a solution

>> A closing that builds goodwill toward the organization receiving the memo

TECHNICAL STUFF

Although APA doesn't address memo formatting, a couple of memo formatting styles are acceptable in the business community. One standard format used in the transmittal memo shown here includes flush-left, single-spaced block paragraphs with an extra line between the paragraphs. No paragraph indentation is included.

Table of contents

Although designated as an optional section, a table of contents in a report, especially a report exceeding four or five pages, improves organizational structure and the capability to easily retrieve information. See Chapter 13 for models of tables of contents. You can't complete the table of contents until you finalize the report and identify page numbers. Verify that table of content headings are structured to be parallel and that wording duplicates headings in the report.

Methodology

If applicable as an optional section, a methodology section contains a description of materials and procedures used to obtain data. A detailed description of methodology permits other researchers to duplicate the study.

Dr. Thomas Stanton
President
Southwest State University
University City, AZ 85000
December 2, 2020

Dear Dr. Stanton:

The Life Experience Taskforce thanks you for the opportunity to evaluate the first-year pilot program that awards up to 30 college credits for life experiences. Taskforce members value the opportunity to work with you on this ground-breaking effort.

Our attached report and recommendations provide opportunities for more adults to achieve their academic dreams and provide better lives for their families. Our report showed that students in the pilot program outperformed their freshmen peers academically in the areas of GPA, writing performances, reading, and classroom attendance.

Our taskforce recommendations include awarding life experience credits as part of Southwest State's admission policy, as well as expanding life experiences for admission credits. We also recommend continuing the pilot program another year to gather additional data on what makes these pilot students successful compared with their peers.

We thank you, Dr. Stanton, for your commitment to opening admission for additional qualified students and providing them with opportunities to achieve their academic dream and share in the academic enrichments of our outstanding university.

© John Wiley & Sons, Inc.

FIGURE 17-6:
An example of a transmittal memo.

Recommendations

Recommendations can be an optional section of a report or a dedicated report itself, such as recommendations for successful low-cost employee incentives. Figure 17-7 shows a sample of a recommendation in the conclusion of a report.

Based on the findings in this report, the taskforce recommends the following:

1. Increase life experiences eligible for receiving credits toward graduation, especially experiences related to performing and visual arts.

2. Continue the pilot study another year, making similar comparisons with peers.

3. Within the pilot group, study first-generation college students as a subset for additional data.

4. Study the economics of a three-year college program and its effect on the university budget.

5. Explore additional options for fast-tracking the college experience at our university, while ensuring there is no compromise in academic integrity.

6. Perform an in-depth analysis of the pilot group and peer comparisons, looking for evidence predictive of college success.

7. Increase the taskforce budget by 10 percent in the next academic year for the purpose of exploring additional research.

These recommendations align with the values and objectives of our university and represent groundbreaking thought towards offering our university's opportunities to a worthy population of students.

FIGURE 17-7: Model language from the recommendations of a report.

© John Wiley & Sons, Inc.

Appendixes

APA accommodates audio and video clips as in-text hyperlinks or supplemental content in an appendix. See Chapter 13 for more uses of appendixes.

Discussion

Discussion can be a separate subheading in the conclusion, or the conclusion can include discussion without a subheading. Regardless of the labeling, a discussion begins with a brief explanation of the results, followed by an analysis of the results, especially an economic analysis. An analysis includes who was affected and how they were affected. It also includes how well the report answered the focused question and identifies topics needing further research.

APA Report Writing: Specializing and Personalizing

Report specializations vary as much as professors' quirkiness. A unifying factor of variations of reports is APA formatting consistencies, which include title page, page appearance, heading case, levels of headings, major sections, and optional sections. The following sections describe numerous kinds of reports.

Business reports

Reports are to business what bats are to baseball; without them, you have no game. Report purposes in business include establishing policy, updating projects, justifying procedures, and evaluating performance. Business reports also measure an organization's effectiveness in achieving goals. As academic assignments, business reports frequently focus on a problem or case study. Many companies create specific guidelines and formatting for business documents, which supersede APA guidelines. APA writing style guidelines apply to business writing.

Education reports

In the field of education, the purposes of reports include proposing new programs, changing policy, justifying spending, and establishing curriculum. Education reports also include a variety of proposal reports for topics such as courses, programs, requirements, staffing, and budgeting. Education institutional reports generally follow APA guidelines.

Science reports

Science reports, sometimes called *lab reports* in the academic setting, generally follow a standardized format that includes report sections such as purpose, methods, materials, results, and conclusions. Science reports are as common to science students as white lab coats and a microscope. Another classification of science reports includes reports on science topics, such as recommendations for clean energy sources on a campus. Academic science reports (not lab reports) generally follow APA guidelines.

Periodic reports

Managers and project leaders are frequently required to submit performance and project reports weekly, monthly, quarterly, and annually. Periodic reports usually include a list of accomplishments during the designated timeframe and a brief reflection on those accomplishments. Periodic reports in the workplace generally follow company guidelines, which may or may not include APA principles.

Sales and marketing reports

Sales and marketing reports include the status of marketing and sales strategies, which often comprise analysis of data. They're usually written for internal audiences and contain confidential data such as profits, losses, and projections. Tables and figures are common to these reports. Sales and marketing reports generally follow company guidelines.

Proposal reports

Business proposals are persuasive reports designed to convince an investor to financially support a product, service, or other business opportunity. The proposal provides the details the investor needs to commit to the investment. The heart of the proposal is the research that provides an accurate statistical analysis of the opportunity. The writer of the report has an obligation (sometimes legal) to present accurate data. Proposals, which are complex financial documents, rank among the most important reports that businesses write. Proposal reports are unique business documents and generally follow company guidelines.

Feasibility studies

Feasibility studies assess a project's conditions that contribute to success, such as economical, geographical, environmental, and political. They identify obstacles that can cause a project to fail. Feasibility studies are completed prior to a commitment of time and resources.

Optional sections of feasibility studies usually include oversized tables and figures, and appendixes for supplemental information. Examples of topics include feasibility of a three-year college degree program, feasibility of earning a degree without debt, and feasibility of no-cost public transportation in major cities. Feasibility reports generally follow company guidelines.

Recommendation reports

A recommendation report, common to any discipline and almost any topic, analyzes information and offers recommendations accordingly. These topics include recommendations for reducing knee injuries among high school athletes, recommendations for avoiding student loans, and recommendations for navigating course requirements for graduation. For a model of recommendation language, flip to Figure 17-7 earlier in this chapter. Recommendation reports generally follow APA guidelines.

Technical reports

Technical reports explain technical information, for example, when recommending the installation of a building's ventilation system. The audience usually has less technical knowledge than the writer, which requires that the writer simplify technical information for the reader. A glossary is commonly included. Technical report content crosses academic disciplines and generally follow company guidelines.

Academic reports

College juniors and seniors are required to write numerous reports in content courses such as economics, finance, psychology, government, history, education, art, and health. An academic report can be as focused as a four-page report analyzing the causes of college dropouts or as extensive as a master's thesis or doctoral dissertation. Academic reports follow APA guidelines.

Project progress reports

Organizations track projects and associated progress with reports that generally include project accomplishments to date and goals to be completed. Evaluations and obstacles are also included in progress reports. Think of a project progress report as what you've been doing at work — or what you haven't yet accomplished at work.

A project completion report offers an opportunity to highlight the accomplishments of completed projects. These reports are much more detailed than update reports, and they contain almost all optional sections of reports. Project completion reports are disseminated up the company hierarchy, requiring your awareness of secondary audiences — your supervisor's supervisor and the person who hired you. Project progress reports are commonly required for college team projects, and they generally follow company guidelines.

Field reports

Field reports include an analysis of an observation or event. Field reports are common to course study in education, health and sciences, history, political science, psychology, medicine, and law. Events are analyzed within the context of classroom content. The length of field reports generally ranges between three and four pages, and the structure resembles that of a reaction paper (see Chapter 15).

A field report generally excludes optional sections such as executive summary, table of contents, glossary, figures and tables, and appendixes. Citations and references are frequently required and strengthen a field report. If citations and references are not required, professors are impressed to see your knowledge of academic protocol by formally identifying sources. Field reports as academic documents follow APA guidelines.

Research reports

Research reports represent a broad category of reports and provide detailed research data to support the value of a product or service. Research reports are written to validate product credibility. In addition to the major structural sections required in a report, they also include methodology, results, and discussion. Research reports generally follow company guidelines.

5

The Parts of Ten

Check out ten points for proficient academic writing that include referencing sources that exceed professors' expectations, developing a writer's work ethic, and focusing on specific nouns and action verbs.

Identify ten source engagement strategies that you shouldn't outsource include forming a peer review group, adding optional parts, and selecting a local topic with global application.

Try these ten time-tested tips to improve research papers, such as identifying power language, applying critical thinking, and mastering a variety of signal phrases.

Chapter **18**

Ten Priorities for Proficient Academic Writing

You've been writing since you first wrote your name as a kindergartener or first grader as your teacher towered over you and proudly proclaimed, "Nice job." As you progressed in school, writing became more challenging — words, clauses, sentences, paragraphs, and essays. And now, as you master the APA writing style, you also face the challenges of APA citations and reference lists.

As your academic career moves forward and you gain confidence in your writing, you should accept new writing challenges and ask what you can do to improve your writing. This chapter offers advice for improving your writing by listing priorities for strengthening skills, utilizing resources, and improving organization.

Analyze Assignments

Your best resources for fulfilling assignment requirements are the assignment itself and the author of the assignment, your professor. Your first reading of the assignment should identify the task you're required to complete. Look for key words like *argue, trace, prioritize, evaluate, synthesize, compare,* and *contrast.* Each word requires you to address a different writing purpose.

Also read the background information provided with the assignment to gain a sense of what is required for the completed assignment. For example, reading the background about an act of heroism offers a clue that heroism is a theme in the paper, and so similar readings about heroism may be a resource.

Finally, identify assignment details such as the preliminary draft due dates, final due date, submission formats, approaches, options, required resources, supplementary submissions, and point values. If a preliminary draft is due, your professor isn't expecting it to be "rough," an assumption that could result in a rough grade. If the assignment contains a rubric, align your efforts with point values. For example, if high-point values are designated for source engagement, prioritize time with source engagement.

Focus on Audience and Purpose

Concentrate on audience and purpose, each of which shapes the development of text. *Audience* dictates whom you're writing to; *purpose* dictates your message. Without a focused audience and purpose, your message will be spam. Chapter 5 develops many principles of good academic writing: audience, purpose, tone, approach, focus, and transitions.

REMEMBER

Some assignments require you to write to a fictional people as your primary audience, such as community leaders, college administrators, or the CEO of a major organization. In such instances, use language that speaks directly to them. Remember you're additionally writing to the person who awards your grade, your professor as a member of the academic community. Think of your audience, your professor, as a person who values high-level thinking, a person who values "why" more than "what," and a person who expects evidence supporting everything you say. Your professor doesn't want to hear your unsupported opinion.

REMEMBER

Purpose also shapes writing. Most writing instructors will agree that an inherent purpose in almost all writing is persuasion, convincing the audience to believe your message. More explicit writing purposes are determined by the task in the assignment: justify, evaluate, and so forth. Similar to your professor being designated as a secondary audience, a secondary purpose of every writing assignment is convincing your professor that you deserve a good grade.

Begin Assignments with Background Reading

The step that immediately follows assignment analysis is researching background information on the topic. Get yourself acclimated with the language of the topic, issues, implications, events, experts, locations, timeframes, and so forth. Take notes identifying highlights as you read. Identify supporting information for source engagement.

Read for answers to questions such as, "Who are the experts in the field?" "What publications do they write for?" "What issues are current and ongoing?" "What are the implications of the topic economically, culturally, and politically?" Information answering these questions provides launching points for determining assignment approaches. Information answering these questions could also provide sources for documentation. Preliminary reading will also provide information that generally follows the introduction in many writing assignments.

Plan Projects

You've heard the expression that not having a plan is a plan for failure. Study the experiences of people who failed to plan and then failed. Plan writing projects like you would plan your own college graduation party. Overestimate the time required for major tasks and assume time conflicts with other courses. Begin planning the day the project is assigned and reviewed in class, while the information is fresh in your mind.

TIP

Schedule the most important challenges first: developing a focused topic, researching, and gathering evidence. Schedule peer review time and revising time. Keep a to-do list that includes questions to ask your professor. Record assignment-related dates in your electronic calendar. If you don't have an electronic calendar, make the transition; you're the Snapchat generation, after all. Schedule dates in your plan to have your assignments completed for reviews.

Determine goal-accomplishment deadlines for major and minor projects. College deadlines are carved in stone. Professors discover early in their careers the long-lasting implications of the slightest change in any deadline. If you feel like you over-plan, you have it right. If you under-plan, resources are available on your campus to help you with planning and time management.

Focus on Specific Nouns and Action Verbs

Two primary parts of speech that need emphasis for successful writing are nouns and verbs. Nouns are the people, places, events, and ideas that are relevant, and verbs are the actions that are completed. Compose your sentences by first identifying the person, event, or idea you are making a statement about, and then following that topic with an action verb. Nouns and verbs are detailed in Chapter 6.

TIP

Observe your literary world through nouns and verbs. In addition to reading, observe nouns and verbs on signs and messages. They're two parts of speech that can make a difference in your writing. Specific nouns plus active verbs equal good writing.

Reference Sources Beyond Professors' Expectations

Most college assignments include references to required readings, sources you are expected to engage with. These required sources include formal citations in essay projects such as research papers and informal citations in projects such as essays and response papers. In addition to fulfilling these requirements, include additional primary sources to develop your argument. You can exceed your professor's expectations by referencing sources such as your textbook, class discussions, interviews with experts, current events, popular books, and life in general. Also consider referencing primary sources such as artifacts, diary entries, period clothing, and photographs. Chapter 10 offers everything you need to know about how to cite, and Chapter 11 explains sources to cite.

Establishing a goal to exceed expectations is not only a good rule for writing, but also a good rule for living. Reach for the moon, and if you miss, you'll land among the stars.

Write Tight and Revise

Revising is the key process to successful writing — more important than initially composing. View revising as a recurring process that takes place until the writing is submitted. Revise between the thought process and the keystroke process. For example, the thought process in your mind may be "got," as in, "Bonnie got an A." But when the word travels to the fingers, it changes to "earn" as in, "Bonnie earned an A." Avoid your personal pattern of vague verbs, general nouns, cliches, and unnecessary words. Recognize and revise lengthy word patterns.

REMEMBER

Revising is like playing the piano: The more you practice, the better you get. Think revising as you read, and as you see signs on a highway. How would you improved clarity, precision, and economy? As your revising skills improve, revise papers you wrote a year ago and identify improvements. When you recognize differences between editing and revising, you're learning revising. For example, revising requires changing organizational structure, paragraphs, sentences, and words. Inexperienced writers associate revising with editing spelling, grammar, and punctuation. See Chapter 8 for more about how famous writers approach revising.

Read and Read Some More

Reading correlates with academic success. You practice one and you develop the other. Reading (and writing) requires thinking, and whenever you're thinking, you're making yourself smarter. Chapter 9 offers a list of books that self-educated super-achievers read. Chapter 16 discusses a landmark study that validated the interdependence of reading and writing — like a two-for-one sale.

Develop the habit of reading while waiting, even though you may miss a few texts. Sometimes this involves making a decision between increasing your "likes" and increasing your brain power. You have choices.

In addition to reading information, you should read as a writer by answering questions such as the following:

>> How would I have structured the writing differently?

>> How could the message be improved?

>> How could the title, first sentence, and introduction be improved?

>> What wording would I revise to be tighter?

>> What sentences would I write more clearly?

>> What nouns and verbs would I improve?

>> What is the message in one sentence?

>> What evidence supports that message?

>> What's the most memorable sentence in the piece of writing?

Finally, reading is the most important academic skill you can pass on to family members, just as it was passed on to you. Demonstrate your appreciation of reading by talking about books and giving books and book certificates as gifts.

Write, Write, and Write

If you want to be good dancer, dance; if you want to be a good baker, bake; and if you want to be a good writer, write. Writing is also a career-building skill. When business leaders were asked to identify the one skill that college graduates lacked, they responded that it was writing. Writing can help you land a job and advance *in* a job. When you apply for a job, you should submit samples of your college writing.

When you serve an internship, volunteer or initiate topic-related reports. For example, if a company is discussing flexible work hours or introducing a new technology, offer to write a report on the topic.

Similar to reading, writing increases brain power. In addition to writing to fulfil course requirements, you can also utilize writing as a tool to learn. For example, you can summarize notes after a class, list similarities among topics in different courses, reflect on career thoughts, and journal about content in a course.

Some enterprising college writers transform words into dollars by writing for blogs, websites, podcasts, and YouTube channels. Writing interesting content attracts subscribers, subscribers attract advertising, and advertising generates income.

Online resources also provide opportunities to learn about writing. Your writing will reach another level of proficiency when you can identify your favorite writing podcast, YouTube channel, and TED talk. Happy writing and happy reading.

Develop a Writer's Work Ethic

Writing is a challenging skill. It's also a commitment that takes effort and concentration. You can't write a successful essay and also multitask by texting, talking on the phone, and playing video games. The brain doesn't work that way. Writing requires a one-track mind that is focused on writing. If you try to write an essay while multitasking on your phone, your essay will read as if you wrote it while multitasking on your phone.

REMEMBER

If you want to be successful at college writing, commit to the time and effort required to write. Writing a successful essay requires a commitment of hours over a couple of weeks' time. Writing a successful research paper requires more hours' commitment over more time.

Writing isn't a commitment that requires you to find time; you can't find time because time never gets lost. Successful essay writing requires you to plan to use the time available to you, 24 hours each day. Here's a secret to writing successfully in college: Planning and committing time to write separates good college writers from not-so-good college writers.

Chapter **19**

Ten Strategies for Creative Source Engagement

Source engagement is the show-me-the-money part of academic writing, the difference between writing that impresses and writing that implodes. More than any other part of your writing, good sources and good engagement generate good writing grades. They also reflect a major difference between high school writing and college writing, and the best college writers master source engagement effectively.

REMEMBER

Sources add value. They're the evidence that validates the meaning behind the words. Ideas without sources are like printers without ink.

Source engagement requires a smooth transition from source citation, to source analysis, to source engagement. When it works, it's like participating in a triathlon and smoothly transitioning from swimming, to cycling, to running. This chapter dives deeply into ten creative strategies that can help you transition successfully.

Look for Power Language within Sources

When you analyze sources, capitalize on language that provides opportunities for strong engagement and that provides directions to help you advance the academic conversation and your argument. For example, if a source suggests that green energy is good for the environment, advance your argument with language such as this: "Endorsement of green energy also provides employment in the fields of retail, technology, construction, maintenance, and research and development. These jobs contribute to local economies and help fund local, state, and national taxes."

Another source may suggest that national wireless networks reduce small business costs. You can advance the argument with language such as "support of small businesses also benefits education, and improved education improves the economy."

TIP

Search your sources for language that represents broad applications — words like *support, refute, agree,* and *disagree.* Broad language has wider implications than limited endorsements such as *somewhat agrees.* Broad endorsements offer broad applications. Look for language that expresses strength, passion, anger, and compliance. When you find it, engage with it.

Think Critically to Analyze Sources

All sources aren't created equal. Some sources contain a vein of gold, while others are only a chunk of coal. Here's a tale of two sources:

> The first source explains a college admission process that includes evaluating a candidate with 95th-percentile high school grades, exceptional standardized test scores, a proficient admission essay, and participation in activities, primarily clubs.

> The second source explains a college admission process that includes evaluating a candidate with 85th-percentile high school grades, exceptional standardized test scores, a proficient admission essay, and participation in activities, primarily community service and leadership.

Essay language engaging these sources looks like this:

> Source 1: "The better candidate earned top grades and displayed time management skills and socialization skills by participating in club activities while maintaining excellent grades."

Source 2: "The better candidate, even though their academic scores were ten points lower, displayed people-centered activities and leadership representative of a well-rounded candidate who prioritizes helping people."

Source engagement language that includes the author looks like this:

"From my perspective, both candidates demonstrate scholarship, time management, and participation in activities. Both candidates should be strongly considered for admission."

Utilize Professors as a Source

Some of the most obvious sources to engage with are the ones you see in every class: professors. Professors are sources of expert knowledge; in fact, the media frequently call on them to comment on current events.

Professors regularly teach courses with topics that reflect their expertise. Search professors and their courses at your school, and you'll see your list of topic expertise. Most colleges have faculty with expertise on topics such as social media, business law, pop culture, language and literacy, online sales, business management, health and exercise, and sports management.

TIP

Contact a professor in a field related to your writing topic and request to meet for no longer than 15 minutes. Explain that you're a student working on a research project and want to reference their expertise in your paper. Most professors are readily willing to extend themselves to help students. They chose their profession to help students. Show respect for the professor's time by preparing three or four questions that elicit the information you're looking for. Form questions that require a *why* or *how* response. Briefly explain your paper and ask your questions.

Keep these additional tips in mind:

>> Don't extend your 15 minutes.

>> As soon as you leave, expand your notes, clarifying what you learned.

>> Cite the professor in your paper and follow up with a thank-you.

>> When you reference the professor as a source, look for opportunities to advance your argument.

Extend Conversations

A characteristic of successful source engagement is what researchers identify as "extending the conversation." You can extend source relationships to areas such as everyday life, campus life, community, economics, politics, current events, literature, social media, and technology.

For example, a source that supports intercollegiate e-gaming competitions extends the source engagement with the following conversations:

» Competition with campus broadband

» How e-gaming competes with other majors

» E-gaming viewed as another sport competing against academics

» E-gaming viewed as video gaming

» Attracting students who think e-gaming is a non-academic major

The e-gaming conversation extends to additional implications. These can include encouraging video gaming among high school and college students, increasing screen time, conflicting with homework and leisure reading, questioning the academic value of an e-gaming facility, questioning the academic value of an e-gaming major, and attracting students who think e-gaming is a non-academic major.

Each extended connection provides engagement options to agree, disagree, support, refute, and question.

Master a Variety of Signal Phrases

Signal phrases are your turn signals that indicate the direction of your source engagement. Knowledge of a variety of phrases gives you, the writer, the option of turning 90 degrees right, 80, 70, or 60 degrees. Signal phrases also provide you with the language to turn 180 degrees in the opposite direction. Signal phrases also start and stop a speaker.

REMEMBER

Mastering a folder full of signal phrases is like having a fully charged phone: You have the power for a full day of communicating. Chapter 11 details the use of signal phrases. Signal phrases also provide a range of tone for representing sources in context. Note the variances of tone here:

>> Bradberry *confirmed* the results of the lab study.

>> Bradberry *was fairly confident in* the results of the lab study.

>> Bradberry *certified* the results of the lab study.

Use Source Engagement with Every Applicable College Paper

Recall the sandbox lesson you learned as a child to share your toys. Source engagement isn't a one-course tool. It's a skill that you share across all courses. Every time you write a paper in a nonlanguage course, you can apply the skills that you learned in your language courses. Source engagement is a skill that has legs.

In a business course, for example, engagement applies to support for a topic such as advocating employee profit sharing: "Fish (2019) said, 'Profit sharing increased employee responsibility toward each other' (p. 47)."

Here are additional examples across the curriculum:

>> Hover (2019) argues, "Learning is not a spectator sport" (p. 34).

>> Watson (2018) said that success can be defined as "average intelligence and above-average work habits" (p. 44).

Your writing professors are impressed when you effectively use source engagement. Professors in content courses seldom see effective use of sources, rarely see source engagement, and are happy to reward source engagement with good grades.

Engage Exclusively with Classic Sources

Classic authors are experts of many pages. They speak volumes. Engage them in a "conversation" and let them talk like a circle of students celebrating a spring day on the campus quad.

TIP

Identify three or four classic authors that you're familiar with from previous readings, research, and courses. Integrate themes and messages. Compare and contrast their credentials, causes, and experiences. Analyze assets and liabilities. Engage in the conversation. Here is an example:

> "Dickens' *Tale of Two Cities* argues that social inequities and class conflict are reflected by the selfishness of the upper class. Jane Austen's *Pride and Prejudice* shows social inequities through the romance of Elizabeth and Mr. Darcy, who represent the top one percent and one-tenth of one percent of wealthy English society.

Social inequity is a common theme among classic writers and continues to appear in literature today.

Engage with Anecdotes

One of the largest sources of support and engagement for writing is *anecdotes*, or personal experiences. Any living person has experiences that can inspire their writing. The engagement focus isn't on the writing of the anecdote, but on applying the anecdote to a broader message.

Conversation with the anecdote can be extended to other anecdotes. Here's an example:

> Jason, an eighth-grade student who comes from a home that values helping others, organized a food drive for unemployed neighbors. With his teenage friends, he organized a plan to collect food for his neighbors. His plan received attention on Twitter, and he soon received donations to sustain his food pantry. Jason credited his mother with inspiring him to help others.

This anecdote about Jason supports a theme of helping others. The conversation could be extended if additional anecdotes were added, describing the experiences of other teenagers who were motivated by Jason to initiate community service projects of their own. Additional engagement could include an anecdote describing a local business leader sharing expertise with Jason and his friends on creating nonprofits.

Learn from Sources

Source engagement is a gift that continues to give. Researching sources for engagement offers an opportunity to discover experts' theories and opinions that apply to topics beyond the project you are working on. For example, while researching for sources, I recently discovered a researcher's theory that writing places a demand on the working memory, the brain location that stores on-demand information used in the writing process.

When the working memory reaches the half-tank level, writing will be compromised. The number of ideas located in the working memory corresponds with ideas that are available to incorporate into the writing. The researcher discovered that conflicting demands on the working memory — such as younger students struggling to form letters or older students allocating working memory to recall grammar and punctuation rules — reduced working memory that was available to apply to writing fluency.

Turn to Primary Sources

Primary sources are the reliable evidence of support and source engagement. Chapter 11 identifies examples of primary sources: eyewitness accounts, original studies, artwork, photos, diaries, and artifacts. In the following example paragraph, the interaction and engagement of primary sources describe a two-century-old lifestyle:

> The diary entry of a town elder explained that "procurement of food" was the "business of the day." What could not be grown was bartered for with people from nearby towns. Early photographs showed a "raised stage" in the town square where people from neighboring towns brought their food and goods for barter. A nearby museum displays an artifact of a food container that was excavated from the town square site. The museum also contains original artwork showing a town square theme that could be described today as a farmers' market.

Chapter **20**

Ten Tips for High-Scoring Research Papers

Y ou're a focused person who has a healthy obsession with earning good grades. You're reading this chapter to discover tips for earning high grades on your research paper. Your initiative and determination represent the mind-set required to improve your research writing.

If you apply the energy, determination, and focus, I'll supply the strategies that I have found worked in my classrooms. After applying a few strategies, review your paper and identify where you need to improve it. You can also use the tips that follow as a checklist of strategies to apply as you work on your paper.

These tips represent decades of grading college research papers and identifying characteristics of high-scoring papers. They represent proven strategies that improve research writing and include sources of feedback and organizational tips to improve your paper. Read them, evaluate them, and apply as many as you can.

Form a Study Group

Any three of you are smarter than any one of you. Small study groups increase your ability to write successful papers. Form a small study group that meets regularly to review parts of papers that you're working on.

A study group can also motivate you to meet deadlines. You can develop a plan with deadlines for completing and reviewing major sections, such as the title page, introduction, citations, and so forth. In addition to getting feedback from your professor, you can also benefit from getting feedback from each other, and from sharing models of papers with each other.

One approach to organizing your group includes members alternating five-minute presentations on research topics such as formatting, references, citing, source engagement, developing an argument, APA writing, spelling, punctuation, and title page design. Another approach includes group members requesting topics they prefer to have reviewed. Allocate time for questions at the beginning or end of each session. See Chapter 9 for additional specifics on forming a successful study group.

Peer Up

Another strategy is peering up with conscientious classmates. Peer pairing offers similar benefits to a study group, and finding a responsible peer may be easier than finding two or three. A peer pair may also be more convenient because you can work asynchronously by email.

TIP

Plan your peer partnership by explaining your purpose to one or two classmates: to provide mutual feedback on specific parts of your research project. If two people agree, organize a round-robin rotation. Organize your feedback, focusing on a number of specific aspects of the paper. Feedback can consist of one page comprising a half page for each of two prompts: "I like how you . . ." and "Have you also thought about . . .?" Agree on a deadline for returning feedback.

Coordinate feedback topics by following the sequence of completing the paper. Here are some topic examples: topic selection, argument development, source engagement, citations, title page, and reference list.

Include a Few Optional Parts

Showing initiative and exceeding expectations impresses professors. A strategy for exceeding expectations is to submit optional front and back parts that aren't required in the assignment. Optional parts improve your content organization and presentation. For example, a table of contents provides a visual display of topics and a directional guide to locating sections.

An optional part that can guide you with citations and reference items is an annotated bibliography. A description of your sources improves the accuracy of citations and the extent of source engagement. An annotated bibliography may be optional, but it's an organizational strategy that can help clarify your use of sources.

A one-page appendix offers an opportunity to develop in-depth content that is too extensive for the body of the paper, or to explore a tangential topic such as the background of an expert used as a source. The inclusion of figures or tables can enhance the explanation of content. Chapter 13 explains procedures for optional front and back sections of research papers. For example, if your research includes an interview with an expert, you can detail the interview in an appendix.

Schedule Reviews with Your Writing Center

Your writing center is your second-best resource to receive feedback on your writing; your professor is first. Unlike your professor, your writing center is more available, and you can visit as often as you want. If you plan well and complete sections of your paper before the deadline, you can have almost all parts of your paper reviewed.

College writing centers, most of which belong to a national affiliation of college writing centers, are staffed with trained tutors who are conveniently available to help you with your writing. You can easily find a tutor trained in your content area, APA formatting and citations, and academic writing style. You can schedule weekly visits for the weeks prior to your submission deadline. Some writing centers offer an online review where you can email your paper and receive specific feedback.

A plan for coordinating your weekly visits includes discussing your topic selection and thesis statement, the development of your argument, uses of your sources, and the reference page. Complete your paper before the deadline, and you'll have time to discuss sections such as the title page, abstract, table of contents, and appendices. You'll also have time to address improvements. After each writing center session, list questions that you want to ask in the following sessions.

Perfect Your Reference List

Your *reference list* is your primary show-and-tell of the quality of your research. It says, "I am a serious scholar, and I value the rules of scholarship displaying my research." A model reference includes a ratio of primary, secondary, and popular sources appropriate for the topic. A model list also includes appropriate primary sources such as artifacts, diary entries, and photographs.

REMEMBER

A model reference list also includes impeccable formatting, beginning with a hanging indentation, the first visual sign of an APA scholarly reference list. Verify that the word "Reference" is bold and centered at the top of a new page, and verify differences between "reference" and "annotated bibliography."

Another point of detail for reference formatting is punctuation. Review punctuation such as that for the following name elements in reference items: Smith, A. B., & Jones, R. S. Create your models for reference items that are common to the types of sources you are using. Refer to Chapter 12 for more about formatting your reference list.

Select a Local Topic with a Global Application

Professors read hundreds of research papers early in their careers and thousands of papers later in their careers. At any point in that time, all professors look forward to reading interesting topics with interesting approaches.

In addition to choosing an interesting topic, approach it with a local and global application. For example, papers that argue national use of solar power, eliminating food waste, and converting refuse into renewable energy, can also argue these topics for campus and community use.

Approach local application of these topics by analyzing need, projecting feasibility, and creating an action plan. Analyze implications economically, socially, and politically. Suggest a plan for implementation. Research local experts who would contribute to your topic. Also design a survey to assess community interest in the topic, and include the survey as a primary source in your paper.

Contact an Expert for an Interview

An interview provides you with an opportunity to support your evidence using a primary source. You can exceed your professor's expectations by soliciting local experts who can contribute to your paper. Ask family and friends if they know experts who are available in the field of your topic. Email businesses, organizations, and institutions. Identify your university and the topic you're researching for expertise; send two to three questions. Carefully focus your questions, as in the following examples: "What have you found successful or unsuccessful about employee incentives?" "What is the best advice you can offer for a successful career in management?"

Provide contact information. Request a phone call but accept an email. Ask for ten minutes of the expert's time. An opportunity to talk or visit provides professional networking for eventual jobs and recommendations. Cultivate contacts and follow up with a thank you.

Create Checklists

Many college students thrive on checklists or to-do lists to organize their everyday life. If you're a checklist person, utilize checklists to organize your research writing. Create checklists for topics such as due dates, paper parts, citations and references, writing style, source engagement, reference punctuation, plagiarism, revising, review of literature, reports, table of contents, and capitalization.

REMEMBER

Organizing your checklist items provides a review of major points to address. For example, checklist items for formatting include page numbering, heading levels, hard page breaks, margins, one space following periods, and so forth. If a peer uses checklists, exchange checklists. Checking completed items provides a sense of accomplishment and moves you toward earning an exceptional grade.

Attend to Details

Good grades result from attention to detail, especially the detail required for research papers. Attending to details reduces errors such as the following: incorrect hanging indentations in references; not formatting the word *References* in bold and centered at the top of the page; underlining or italicizing the title and major heading; lacking or incorrectly formatting citations; single-spacing text; misaligning margins; incorrectly placing page numbers; lacking required resources; lacking hard page breaks; and omitting dates in citations.

Attending to details also includes addressing minor issues that can accumulate and affect grades. Here are examples of minor issues that need addressing: incorrect spacing following a period at the end of a sentence; omitting a comma preceding an ampersand in a reference item; and not including an available Digital Object Identifier (DOI). Details needing attention also include punctuation, spelling, and other language conventions. You can check out language conventions in Chapter 6.

A final detail that needs attention includes proofreading a few days prior to your deadline. You can review proofreading strategies in Chapter 8. After proofing, email your paper to yourself to ensure there is no loss of formatting. If you're required to submit a hard copy, ensure that pages are in sequence. Not only is the devil in the details, but so are the grades.

Utilize the Professor's Office Hours

Writing resources abound, and they're all within your budget, free. Your best resources are the ones you can interact with and ask questions of. Your best resource to improve your writing is the one right in front of you every day in your class: your professor. Professors' office hours are the most under-utilized resources on campus. You receive one-on-one instruction on any writing concern, and you can ask questions. You have the added benefit of showing your professor your commitment to improving your writing. You also receive improvement recommendations from the person awarding the grades. It's almost like professors grading themselves.

TIP

Keep these tips in mind:

>> Prepare for the conference with your professor by emailing two weeks in advance and asking for a meeting to review your writing project. Ask for a time at the beginning of office hours, because this will allow you more time.

>> Prepare two or three questions to begin your conference, such as, "Could you look at how I develop my argument?" and "Could you look at my source engagement?" Don't ask questions about APA because you can get those questions answered at the writing center.

>> Immediately after leaving your professor's office, find a quiet location and make notations of what your professor said and suggestions they made. That time is the golden 30 minutes when information is fresh in your working memory.

>> Send a thank you and reference a specific improvement you learned from the conference.

Index

base-formation compounds, 121
bias-free language, 10, 86–90
  age and disability references, 87–88
  APA seventh edition, 34–35
  gender and sexual orientation references, 88–90
  overview, 86–87
  racial and ethnic references, 87
  socioeconomic references, 90
Big Data Baseball (Sawchik), 162
biretta, 54
Blink (Gladwell), 162
block quotations, 174–175
blog posts, 224
Bloom, Benjamin, 49
The Bluebook, 225
Blume, Judy, 128
Bodeen, S.A., 128
body of writing, 276
  literature reviews, 289–293
  reports, 309–310
  revising, 137
bold headings, 31, 205
Book Review Index, 189
books
  chapters, 211
  reading, 76, 151–167
    academic success and, 327–328
    active, 156
    beginning assignments with, 325
    characteristics of, 152–153
    strategies, 154–162
    study-group learning, 166–167
  reviews, referencing, 220
  samples of references, 217–219
Boolean operators, 286
brackets, 113–114
brain
  imaging studies, 154
  working memory, 337
Brizendine, Louann, 162
bulleted lists, 252–254
  capitalization, 253

punctuation, 254
Business Ethics Quarterly, 188
business reports, 316
byline, 29

C

capitalization
  bulleted lists, 253
  overview, 122–125
  proper nouns, 123
  in references, 214–215
  titles and headings, 124–125
career opportunities
  proficient writing and, 328
  report writing, 308
cause and effect
  essays, 269–270
  transitions, 83
CCI/II (College Composition I and II), 18
Cell, 188
chapters, book, 218
charts, 185
chats, online, 183
cheat sheet, for this book, 4
cheating, 60
CheckForPlagiarism software, 66
checklists, 343
chemistry, 12
chiasmus, 265
Chicago Manual of Style (CMoS), 6, 12
Christensen, Clayton, 160
citing and citations, 10, 171–189
  APA seventh edition, 32–34
  avoiding plagiarism, 65
  coordinating, 178–184
    academic authorities, 183
    author-date format, 179–180
    authors with same surname, 182
    legal references, 183–184
    missing or anonymous authors, 181
    numerous authors, 181–182